Immigration and
America's Cities

Immigration and America's Cities

A Handbook on Evolving Services

Edited by
JOAQUIN JAY GONZALEZ III *and*
ROGER L. KEMP

McFarland & Company, Inc., Publishers
Jefferson, North Carolina

ALSO OF INTEREST AND FROM McFARLAND: *Urban Transportation Innovations Worldwide: A Handbook of Best Practices Outside the United States,* edited by Roger L. Kemp and Carl J. Stephani (2015); *Global Models of Urban Planning: Best Practices Outside the United States,* edited by Roger L. Kemp and Carl J. Stephani (2014); *Town and Gown Relations: A Handbook of Best Practices,* Roger L. Kemp (2013); *The Municipal Budget Crunch: A Handbook for Professionals,* edited by Roger L. Kemp (2012); *Cities Going Green: A Handbook of Best Practices,* edited by Roger L. Kemp and Carl J. Stephani (2011); *Cities and Adult Businesses: A Handbook for Regulatory Planning,* edited by Roger L. Kemp (2010); *Documents of American Democracy: A Collection of Essential Works,* edited by Roger L. Kemp (2010); *Cities and Sports Stadiums: A Planning Handbook,* edited by Roger L. Kemp (2009); *Cities and Water: A Handbook for Planning,* edited by Roger L. Kemp (2009); *Cities and Growth: A Policy Handbook,* edited by Roger L. Kemp (2008); *Museums, Libraries and Urban Vitality: A Handbook,* edited by Roger L. Kemp and Marcia Trotta (2008)

LIBRARY OF CONGRESS CATALOGUING-IN-PUBLICATION DATA

Names: Gonzalez, Joaquin Jay, editor. | Kemp, Roger L., editor.
Title: Immigration and America's cities : a handbook on evolving
    services / edited by Joaquin Jay Gonzalez III and Roger L. Kemp.
Description: Jefferson, North Carolina : McFarland & Company, Inc.,
    Publishers, 2016 | Includes bibliographical references and index.
Identifiers: LCCN 2016000168 | ISBN 9780786496334 (softcover :
    acid free paper) ∞
Subjects: LCSH: Immigrants—Services for—United States. |
    Municipal services—United States. | United States—
    Emigration and immigration—Social aspects.
Classification: LCC HV4010 .I44 2016 | DDC 362.89/9120973—dc23
LC record available at http://lccn.loc.gov/2016000168

BRITISH LIBRARY CATALOGUING DATA ARE AVAILABLE

ISBN (print) 978-0-7864-9633-4
ISBN (ebook) 978-1-4766-2379-5

Front cover images © 2016 iStock

Printed in the United States of America

McFarland & Company, Inc., Publishers
  Box 611, Jefferson, North Carolina 28640
  www.mcfarlandpub.com

To Michelle, Coral, and Elise
—Joaquin Jay Gonzalez III

———⟨∞⟩———

To my granddaughter, Anika
—Roger L. Kemp

Acknowledgments

We are grateful for the financial support of the Mayor George Christopher Professorship and the Russell T. Sharpe Professorship at Golden Gate University. We appreciate the encouragement from Dean Paul Fouts and our wonderful colleagues at the GGU Edward S. Ageno School of Business, the Department of Public Administration, and the EMPA Program. Thank you Bibbero Trust and Adrianna Boursalian.

Our heartfelt "Thanks!" goes to the contributors listed at the back of the book and the organizations and publishers below for granting permission to reprint the material in this volume. Most waived or reduced fees as an expression of their solidarity with America and its immigrant communities.

American Planning Association
Atlanta Journal-Constitution
Center for Popular Democracy
Clark Consulting and Training
Educational Leadership
Governing
International Association of Chiefs
  of Police
International City/County
  Management Association
Internet Journal of Healthcare
  Administration
ispub.com
Kaiser Health News
Los Angeles Times
Maryland Municipal League
Migration Policy Institute
Municipal Action Guild
Municipal Maryland
NACo County News

National Association of Counties
  Research Foundation
National Conference of State
  Legislatures
National League of Cities
New York Times
Planning
PM Magazine
Police Chief
Population Reference Bureau
REFORMA
San Francisco Chronicle
State Legislatures
Texas Library Journal
Today's Research on Aging
Tucson Weekly
Urban Land Institute
U.S. Conference of Mayors
USA Today
Washington Post

Table of Contents

Preface

Generations ago, droves of immigrant populations came to the U.S. from Europe and Africa. Now they are arriving mainly from Latin America and Asia. Most are authorized, but there is a large number who are not.

While the Congress, federal, and most state governments, have done little to directly confront pressing immigration and immigrant issues, except for U.S. border areas and ports of entry, public officials and community-based organizations in cities, towns, counties, and other local jurisdictions, have been busily delivering commonsense and pragmatic services to accommodate and incorporate these new members of American society.

As professors who witnessed changes unfold during our tenure in public service, we felt that it was our responsibility to compile the lessons from the trends, practices, and experiences to help concerned citizens and public officials in municipalities who are in search of possibilities, inspiration, or concrete examples.

Trends and Issues

Part I delves into the intersections between immigration as a national issue and a local concern. Our chosen pieces discuss the social, political, economic, and demographic realities of immigration in the United States to understand the how and why cities crafted immigrant services even though immigration is under federal law.

They elaborate on the complexity of building a nation by and for immigrants, including the issues that divided citizens, communities, and Congress. Starting with an eye-opening *USA Today* piece which discusses the relative size and magnitude of the current wave of immigrants and how they are changing America's diversity. This is followed by equally stirring *Gov-

erning, LA Times, Tucson Weekly, NACo County News, Washington Post, and National League of Cities write-ups on the real-time trends facing citizens and cities. The section ends with a Population Reference Bureau research team report on the issues of elderly immigrants.

Practices and Experiences

Faced with growing numbers and Washington gridlock, many cities have had no choice but to act on their own. Thus, the collection of practices and experiences we gathered for this main section of the book shows no national one size fits all fix for America's cities. Mayors, local councils, citizen committees, and city departments developed homegrown programs and services. There are patterns of similarities but most are different depending on each of their contexts and capacities.

We grouped together best practices and good experiences on creating immigrant policies and services under the section headings: safe havens and open doors, language accessibility, identification card and driver's licensing, employment, business and investment, English language learners, education and literacy, library services, civic engagement and voting, policing and public safety, legal assistance, as well as seniors and health care.

These practices and experiences reflect the thoughts and actions of Republicans, Democrats, U.S. Conference of Mayors, National League of Cities, National Association of Counties, International Association of Chiefs of Police, and Maryland Municipal League members. Moreover, this section includes reporting from influential publications like the *San Francisco Chronicle,* the *Washington Post, PM Magazine,* the *Los Angeles Times,* the *Atlanta Journal-Constitution,* and *Kaiser Health News.* It also explores the views and analyses of the Center for Popular Democracy, International City/County Management Association, REFORMA, Migration Policy Institute, and the Urban Land Institute. We also include a chapter on the essentials of courting the Filipino American immigrant vote. We hope that you are able to find helpful lessons.

The Future

We conclude the volume with some thoughtful pieces on the future directions of immigration and America's cities. The first article amplifies a mayor's friendly call for new municipal citizens who will "help to re-grow and reinvigorate the neighborhoods in which they put down roots." More cities will echo this call moving forward according to the succeeding piece. These two *Governing* pieces are followed by an article discussing healthcare as the biggest possible breakthrough for states and the federal government to make a contribution to immigrant services. We end this future section with an annotated compilation by the Immigrant Policy Project of the National Conference of State Legislatures examining the present and future fiscal and economic impacts of immigrants to selected U.S. states and the New England region.

Appendices

Our appendices yield lessons too. Besides articles on trends, issues, practices, experiences, and the future, we append a sequence of public documents, listings, and other resources which we felt citizens, advocates, and decision makers would find useful. These include resolutions and calls to action of the U.S. Conference of Mayors, National League of Cities, and the National Association of Counties. Also, appended are President Barack Obama's executive action speech and San Francisco Mayor Edwin Lee's executive directive. Finally, we provide a listing of sanctuary cities, a how to guide for developing a language access plan, a list of federal benefits available to unauthorized immigrants, and a national immigration resource directory.

Part I

Trends and Issues

1. Second Immigration Wave Lifts Diversity to Record High

Greg Toppo and *Paul Overberg*

SOUTH ORANGE, N.J.—From a distance, the small group of Haitian immigrants at the public library looks like a prayer meeting or political gathering. Dressed colorfully but comfortably, the women speak in heavily accented English and sit every day for hours around a small wooden table studying to be nurses.

The library sits at the heart of one of the most diverse counties in the USA. More than 50 languages are spoken in the public schools, and this is what more and more communities across America will look like soon—very soon.

Racial and ethnic diversity is spreading far beyond the coasts and into surprising places across the USA, rapidly changing how Americans live, learn, work and worship together—and even who our neighbors are.

Cities and towns far removed from traditional urban gateways such as New York, Miami, Chicago and San Francisco are rapidly becoming some of the most diverse places in America, an analysis of demographic data by *USA Today* shows.

Small metro areas such as Lumberton, N.C., and Yakima, Wash., and even remote towns and counties—such as Finney County, Kan., or Buena Vista County, Iowa—have seen a stunning surge in immigrants, making those places far more diverse.

The USA is experiencing a "great wave" of immigration—call it a "second great wave." The first, which stretched from the 1880s to the 1920s, coin-

Originally published as Greg Toppo and Paul Overberg, "Second Immigration Wave Lifts Diversity to Record High: Collision of Cultures, Languages, and Politics Poses Perils and Promises," *USA Today*, October 21, 2014. Reprinted with permission of the publisher.

cided with the opening of Ellis Island and the social and political transformation of the nation.

The people in this second wave, arriving roughly since 1970, are more likely to be middle-class and, because of improved transportation and technology, can assimilate more quickly.

The result: For the first time, the next person you meet in this country—at work, in the library, at a coffee shop or a movie ticket line—will probably be of a different race or ethnic group than you.

USA Today used Census data to calculate the chance that two random people are different by race or ethnicity and came up with a Diversity Index to place every county on a scale of 0 to 100. The nationwide *USA Today* Diversity Index hit 55 in 2010, up sharply from 20 in 1960 and 40 as recently as 1990. In South Orange, the index is 59.

This is just the beginning. Barring catastrophe or a door-slam on immigration, the Diversity Index is on track to top 70 by 2060, according to a *USA Today* analysis of population projections by ProximityOne of Alexandria, Virginia. That means there will be less than a 1-in-3 chance that the next person you meet will share your race or ethnicity, whatever it is: white, black, American Indian, Asian, Native Hawaiian or Hispanic.

As people from varying cultures and races come together or collide, local governments and other institutions deal with a host of new issues, from conflicts over spending and diverse hiring to violence in the streets and language barriers.

This month, health workers in Dallas going door-to-door at the 300-unit apartment complex that housed the first U.S. patient with Ebola had to translate leaflets about the disease into eight languages. Among the tenants, the complex's owner said, were many refugees being resettled.

Students witness the changing face of the country firsthand: Public schools began the 2014-15 school year with an unprecedented profile: For the first time, non–Hispanic white students are in the minority, according to Education Department projections.

Almost half of the Americans, 49 percent, polled by *USA Today* say the country will be "better off" as communities diversify, racing toward a point where no racial or ethnic group has a majority; 25 percent say the country would be "worse off."

The fastest change is happening in regions such as the upper Midwest, where there was almost no diversity 30 years ago. Minnesota's Diversity Index rose from 7 in 1980 to 31 in 2010. Diversity has sprouted in many places because of local factors. In Finney County, Kan., the Diversity Index rocketed from 46 to 60 from 1990 to 2010. Two big meatpacking plants that employ more than 2,500 drew immigrants. The county is 47 percent Hispanic. The same pattern has made Buena Vista County, Iowa, pop. 20,000, the most diverse in the state. Its Diversity Index soared from 6 in 1990 to 49 in 2010. In Monroe County, Pa., in the Pocono Mountains, the Diversity Index jumped from 9 in 1990 to 48 in 2010 as minorities from Queens and Brooklyn, N.Y., came looking for a home they could afford to own.

Just 3 percent of counties had a Diversity Index that topped 50 in 1990, but today, 14 percent do. At the top end of the scale, hyper-diverse counties whose index tops 67 have nearly doubled since 2000, from 33 to 60. They, too, are spreading. They're located in 17 states, up from 10 states in 2000.

An inner-ring suburb of Newark, South Orange has consciously struggled for decades to maintain its racial, ethnic and economic diversity, even as rising housing prices have squeezed moderate- and low-income families out of neighboring suburbs. Here, the index was just 8 in 1970. It soared to 57 in 2000 and 59 in 2010.

Extremely multiracial, multicultural Gwinnett County, Ga., with a Diversity Index score of 71, offers lessons on where the nation will be in 2060. Jeff Reid, WXIA-TV, Atlanta.

Like Newark, it's part of Essex County, where the index has hit 72, up from 69 in 2000. Librarians increasingly find themselves not just checking out books but providing space for groups of immigrants—as well as for a growing corps of volunteers who tutor newcomers in English and run conversation groups. Nearly a third of the library's patrons speak a language other than English at home, and among the most requested products is an online language tutoring program, library Director Melissa Kopecky says.

"I've always said that the public library is the living room of the community," says Keisha Miller, who runs the library's teen programs. "This is where you come—you have conversations, you meet people, you see your neighbors, you make new friends, you see old friends." Miller, 32, attended school here as well. She's the daughter of immigrants from Trinidad and Jamaica.

For decades, much of South Orange's diversity has been driven by effective "fair housing" laws that opened up affordable housing beyond Newark city limits. Activists have also pushed to keep these suburban neighborhoods diverse, working with Realtors to persuade them to show prospective families a broader swath of houses for sale. In many cases, activists have taken newcomers on a kind of "outsiders' real estate tour" of their own.

"We wanted to see if we could actually encourage people to live in all parts of the community," says Nancy Gagnier, executive director of the South Orange-Maplewood Community Coalition on Race.

After a commuter rail line directly connected the area with Manhattan in 1996, diverse families increasingly began settling here from Manhattan, Brooklyn, Queens, Jersey City and Hoboken, Gagnier says. "They're looking for that step out into the suburbs that doesn't fully remove them from an urban feel and has a level of diversity."

The change had many locals worried about white flight to more far-flung suburbs. The coalition hired the same consultant who helped Shaker Heights, Ohio, stay integrated. They offered home improvement loans in at-risk neighborhoods and aggressively marketed South Orange and nearby Maplewood as appealing places to live.

"I guarantee you, you ask any person walking down the street, 'Why did you move here?' or 'What's the community's best asset?' and they'll use the term 'diversity,'" Gagnier says.

In addition to housing policy, much of the shift to suburbs by immigrant groups can be traced to a subtle change in attitude, says David Dante Troutt, the founding director of the Rutgers Center on Law in Metropolitan Equity (CLiME). He's the author of the 2014 book *The Price of Paradise: The Costs of Inequality and a Vision for a More Equitable America.*

As cities gentrified and urban housing grew more expensive, immigrants whose forerunners had long settled in cities began to rethink that idea, deciding "the city is no longer the place to be," Troutt says. Add troubled urban schools to the mix, he says, and the result is an explosion of ethnic enclaves, comprised of new immigrants, outside central cities.

"It's fascinating, and it holds all sorts of promise," he says. "It both contradicts American ideas about immigration and demographics and supports many long-standing ideas about it, including the belief that the American dream is found in the ownership of a single-family home in the suburbs."

He says much of the diversity of places such as South Orange will depend on how strongly local attitudes support diverse kinds of housing. "It's still a delicate balance," he says. "Let's not kid ourselves. Even discussion of building workforce housing in some of these progressive towns will meet with a vitriol and an opposition that you can expect from the most affluent, conservative places."

In nearby Montclair, N.J., he says, residents fought to block four lower-cost units from being built in one neighborhood. In another case, in Marin County, Calif., in 2011, filmmaker George Lucas decided to sell some land to a developer of affordable housing, but neighbors fought the move, saying they feared the development would bring in "lowlifes," "drug dealers" and "criminals."

At the time, an annual household income up to $88,000 qualified buyers for affordable housing, Troutt says. "The public commenters who came in and railed against these prospective tenants in these vitriolic terms were talking about people who were making as much as assistant district attorneys, who were in fact prosecuting criminals and lowlifes and drug dealers," he says. "What it suggests to me is that people are much more careful to either hide or overcome their racial animus—but what they are much less reflective about is their class animus, that it is almost OK to speak in hate-speech-like terms about people who we regard as our economic inferiors."

Not every corner of the country is changing rapidly, or even in the same direction. Nearly 200 counties, or about 6 percent, saw their Diversity Index fall in the past decade.

For a glimpse of what the USA looked like in 1970 and still looks like in some places, drive around Idaho, South Dakota or Wisconsin. If you want to see what the USA might look like in 2040, when the Diversity Index is projected to reach 65, look at Denver, Albuquerque, Austin or Phoenix, which already have reached that level.

The changes are so widespread they have even reversed the trend in some places. Counties along the Texas border—notably El Paso—have become less diverse as Hispanics have grown to make up more than 90 percent of the population.

The second wave of immigration is putting its own stamp on the makeup of communities across the country.

Access to transportation and a wider geographical swath of jobs means immigrants are not just showing up in big coastal cities and staying for generations. They're moving to "new destinations," as demographer Jacob Vigdor calls these places—not just suburbs but rural parts of the South, Midwest and West.

The black American experience, forged early on by slavery that brought millions from Africa, also is diversifying. Almost 10 percent of blacks are new immigrants from Caribbean or African countries, especially Haiti, the Dominican Republic and Jamaica. Some must learn English as a second language and face other challenges typical of immigrants.

While this second wave brings tensions and battles over school districts, religion, public spaces, law enforcement and affordable housing, it also brings new energy: The immigrants have higher birth rates, ensuring a steady supply of workers for future generations. They bring new role models, new foods and traditions, new sports, a tremendous entrepreneurial energy and, perhaps most significantly, intact, religiously devout families that place a heavy emphasis on education.

In other words, true Americans.

"We should be really happy that we have this large minority growth in the United States," says Brookings Institution demographer William Frey, author of the upcoming book *Diversity Explosion: How New Racial Demographics Are Remaking America.*

Frey says "new minorities"—Hispanics, Asians and multiracial Americans—are arriving as the USA's white population is growing quite slowly and actually declining for the younger part of the population. "So it's in fact a tonic," he says. "We're going to need this as we look ahead."

"We should be so thankful that they're here," demographer William Frey says of immigrants boosting the USA's diversity.

With the new growth in diversity, Frey says, should come a new attitude about ethnic and racial minorities. "This is everybody's business to make sure we have a productive multi-ethnic population in the United States," he says. "And we should be so thankful that they're here, because if we didn't have the immigration and the fertility of these groups in the last 20 years, we would be in the same situation as Japan or a lot of European countries, which are facing a declining labor force and an aging population."

Frey puts it rather bluntly, noting that Census projections show that in about 10 years, the USA's white population will not only be crowded out—it'll start to shrink. "A lot of people don't realize this," he says. "It's the full-scale demographic scope of all this that's really important for us to get our arms around because it's really important for our future as a country."

2. Immigrant Population Growing Faster Than Natives in Metro Areas

Mike Maciag

The nation's major metropolitan areas have long served as hubs attracting steady streams of immigrants from all over the world seeking opportunities. Now, as some cities lose residents and the native population ages, migration from abroad has overtaken homegrown and domestic population shifts in many urban areas.

A *Governing* analysis of new census estimates found that 135 metro areas experienced an increase in international migration surpassing domestic population growth. In each of these regions, net international migration exceeded the combined net domestic migration and natural change (births and deaths) between the 2010 Census and last summer.

As Americans moved out of the Rust Belt and other areas, those from outside the U.S. took their place. The Detroit metro area saw more than 50,000 residents move away since 2010, but added more than 21,000 via international migration. Similarly, the Cleveland-Elyria, Ohio, area recorded a net domestic migration loss of 27,000 residents, but attracted nearly 8,000 from abroad.

In fact, 37 growing metro areas would have lost total population had it not been for new residents from overseas. Such metro areas include New York City, Trenton, New Jersey, and Reading, Pennsylvania.

International migration has historically accounted for the bulk of the

Originally published as Mike Maciag, "Immigrant Population Growing Faster Than Natives in Many Metro Areas," *Governing*, March 26, 2013. Reprinted with permission of the publisher.

population growth in many of the nation's coastal cities. The New York City, Los Angeles and Miami metro areas, for example, each welcomed more than 100,000 international residents over the two-year period.

But some regions not traditionally known as international destinations have attracted new groups of foreigners. Jeanne Batalova, a senior policy analyst with the Washington, D.C.–based Migration Policy Institute, said many such areas saw a noticeable uptick in their immigrant populations beginning in the 1990s.

Latino groups living in New York City boroughs began to branch out to other areas of the state, and across state borders to New Jersey and Pennsylvania. Those initially settling around Los Angeles also moved to Nevada or Arizona, lured by lower costs of living.

"A number of hot spots emerged," Batalova said. "The primary driving forces were that immigrants were looking for new jobs, lower costs of living and educational opportunities for their children."

Once immigrant communities in these areas established themselves, word got back to those living abroad, then international migration followed. These networks, according to Batalova, act as the "oil of the migration machine."

Each metro area offers its own unique opportunities for immigrants.

Cities like Boston boast world-renowned colleges and universities, while Minneapolis and Detroit are home to large refugee populations.

Silicon Valley also continues to be a destination for college-educated immigrants working in the technology sector. The San Jose metro area, which includes Santa Clara and Silicon Valley, saw a net increase of about 30,400 immigrants since the 2010 Census, according to estimates.

Monica Limas, interim director at the San Jose-based Center for Employment Training, said the region's high-tech companies recently jumpstarted hiring, so foreign employees likely account for much of the increase. Many of these educated workers migrated from India, and the center assists large numbers of Latino and Vietnamese immigrants as well.

The recession, coupled with stepped-up border enforcement efforts, slowed international migration in recent years, Batalova said. The Pew Hispanic Center estimates the number of unauthorized immigrants living in the U.S. is slowly declining after reaching a peak of 12 million in 2007, mostly driven by a sharp decrease in the flow of immigrants from Mexico.

To lure immigrants, an increasing number of local governments have set up special offices or programs specifically targeting them.

Officials in Dayton, Ohio, established a Welcome Dayton plan in 2011 that's since evolved to include programs such as grants for new business owners and an international soccer tournament. In Baltimore, Mayor Stephanie Rawlings-Blake signed an order requesting social service and law enforcement agencies not to ask anyone about their immigration status.

Earlier this month, Philadelphia Mayor Michael Nutter created an Office of Immigrant and Multi-Cultural Affairs, slated to provide immigrants with access to city services, local nonprofits and educational programs. The office is likely to stay busy once it's up and running, given that the surrounding metro area has added more than twice the number of residents from international migration than net domestic migration and natural changes since the 2010 Census.

Michigan, the only state losing population in the 2010 Census, has also rolled out the red carpet for immigrants.

"Welcoming Michigan," a project of the Michigan Immigrant Rights Center, focuses on making four communities in the state more immigrant-friendly. Susan Reed, a supervising attorney for the center, says local officials need to first communicate the benefits of immigrants, especially to those who fear they'll take their jobs.

In a state like Michigan—with severe job losses—this can be a difficult task.

"Some people just feel a sense of loss of what the Michigan economy has been through and that we can't afford to be welcoming," Reed said.

Immigrants, though, often use their unique skill sets to startup businesses and create employment opportunities. What's more, these groups help to subsidize agriculture and other industries with low-wage jobs.

"It's really engaging the community in a dialogue about the tensions, such as tensions around language, delivery of service or religion," Reed said.

Data

The international migration data represents estimates, not hard population counts. The Census Bureau, according to its methodology, bases its estimates on immigration/emigration of the foreign born, net migration between Puerto Rico and the U.S., migration of natives in and out of the country and movement of those serving in the Armed Forces. So, not all residents included in the census migration estimates are foreigners.

Nearly every metro area across the country recorded positive net international in-migration, with only three experiencing declines since 2010. Of 381 metro areas, 187 registered negative net domestic migration and 139 reported more deaths than births, according to estimates.

Not surprisingly, major urban hubs home to large minority communities welcomed that largest numbers of international residents. The following 10 metro areas had the largest net international migration since the 2010 Census:

New York–Newark–Jersey City, NY-NJ-PA: 269,067
Los Angeles–Long Beach–Anaheim, CA: 112,503
Miami–Fort Lauderdale–West Palm Beach, FL: 111,181
Washington–Arlington–Alexandria, DC-VA-MD-WV: 79,564
Houston–The Woodlands–Sugar Land, TX: 54,391
Chicago–Naperville–Elgin, IL-IN-WI: 52,120
Boston–Cambridge–Newton, MA-NH: 50,950
San Francisco–Oakland–Hayward, CA: 49,077
Dallas–Fort Worth–Arlington, TX: 42,805
Atlanta–Sandy Springs–Roswell, GA: 40,013

A total of 135 of these areas recorded faster international migration than domestic growth, led by New York City.

3. Asian Immigrant Numbers Surpass Latino Numbers
Rebecca Trounson

Asian Americans are now the nation's fastest-growing racial group, overtaking Latinos in recent years as the largest stream of new immigrants arriving annually in the United States.

In an economy that increasingly depends on highly skilled workers, Asian Americans are also the country's best educated and highest-income racial or ethnic group, according to a new report from the Pew Research Center.

In fact, U.S. Asians, who trace their roots to dozens of countries in the Far East, the Indian subcontinent and Southeast Asia, are arguably the most highly educated immigrant group in U.S. history, the study shows. And although there are significant differences among them by country of origin, on the whole they have found remarkable success in their new land.

"These aren't the poor, tired, huddled masses that Emma Lazarus described in that inscription on the Statue of Liberty," said Paul Taylor, the research center's executive vice president.

In fact, the Asian newcomers' achievements are likely to change the way many Americans think about immigrants, typically as strivers who work hard in the hope that their children and grandchildren will have easier lives and find greater success in this country, Taylor said.

For U.S. Asians, especially those who arrived in recent years, the first generation itself is doing well, outpacing Americans as a whole when it comes to education, household income and family wealth, according to the report released Tuesday.

Asian Americans also tend to be more satisfied than most Americans with their own lives, the survey found, and they hold more traditional views than the general public on the value of marriage, parenthood and hard work.

As a whole, Asian Americans are more likely than the general public to prefer a big government that provides more services. They also lean Democratic and a majority approves of President Obama's job performance.

Although the first large wave of Asian immigrants came to the U.S. in the early 19th century, the population grew slowly for more than a century, held down by severe restrictions and official prohibitions, some explicitly racist. Most Asian Americans now living in the U.S. arrived after 1965 legislation that allowed immigration from a wider range of countries.

Asian Americans now make up nearly 6 percent, or 18.2 million, of the U.S. population, the latest figures from the U.S. Census Bureau show. Nearly three-quarters were born abroad, and about 8 million came to this country in the last 30 years.

Geographically, nearly half of all U.S. Asians live in the Western states. California, the traditional gateway for Asian immigrants, has by far the largest number, almost 6 million. Of the major Asian subgroups, in fact, only those from India are relatively evenly distributed throughout the country, with the largest share, 31 percent, living in the Northeast.

Asian immigration has grown rapidly in recent years, with nearly 3 million arriving since 2000. At the same time, Latino immigration, especially from Mexico, has slowed sharply, mainly because of the weakened U.S. economy and tougher border enforcement.

As a result, the number of newly arrived Asian immigrants has outpaced Latinos each year since 2009, according to Pew's analysis of census data. In 2010, for instance, 36 percent of new U.S. immigrants were Asian, compared with 31 percent who were Latino.

The most recent immigrants have arrived even as the economy has boomed in many Asian countries and the standard of living has risen. Taylor said the reason many Asians move to the U.S. include shifts in U.S. immigration policies, changes in their home countries and U.S. labor needs for science, engineering and math graduates.

The Pew study combines recent census and economic data with an extensive, nationally representative survey of 3,500 Asian Americans. The interviews, conducted from January to March, were done in English and seven Asian languages.

Chinese Americans are the largest Asian immigrant group, with more than 4 million who identified as Chinese, followed by Filipinos, Indians, Vietnamese, Korean and Japanese.

U.S. Asians as a whole are more satisfied than most Americans with their lives overall (82 percent compared to 75 percent), with their personal finances (51 percent compared to 35 percent) and with the general direction of the country (43 percent compared to 21 percent).

More than half of adult Asian Americans say that having a successful marriage is one of the most important things in life; 34 percent of all American adults agree. Asian Americans are more likely than American adults in general to be married (59 percent compared to 51 percent) and their newborns are less likely than U.S. infants as a whole to have an unmarried mother (16 percent compared to 41 percent).

Experts praised the study, saying that it was likely to change views of U.S. Asians for scholars and the public alike.

"This really opens up a conversation and sheds light on a community that is extremely heterogenous and very complex," said Tritia Toyota, a former Los Angeles television reporter who is now an adjunct professor of anthropology and Asian studies at UCLA.

Karthick Ramakrishnan, an associate professor of political science at UC Riverside, also noted that in terms of their education, recent Asian immigrants are an elite group. More than two-thirds of recent adult immigrants are either college students or college graduates, the study showed. So, he said, experts should be careful when comparing their characteristics with other Americans.

"This is a select group even in their own countries," he said.

4. Not-So-Comprehensive Immigration Reform

Samuel Kleiner

As immigration reform is stalled in Congress, progressives should look to the states and cities to take action to help incorporate immigrants into the fabric of American society. Ultimately, we need an integrated system with federal, state and local action on immigration. But we can't wait for Congress to take the lead.

In October, California Governor Jerry Brown signed the TRUST Act, which barred California police officers from turning over undocumented aliens arrested for non–violent crimes to federal authorities. Brown said that he "not waiting" for Washington to act, an argument that was strikingly similar to Governor Brewer's claim in enacting SB1070 that Washington's "decades of inaction" necessitated local policy. Our political leaders of all stripes have characterized local immigration policy as a necessity in light of federal inaction. The Supreme Court ruled in 1979 in *DeCanas v. Bica* that the "power to regulate immigration is unquestionably exclusively a federal power." By and large, states have only sought to justify their action in immigration as a necessity stemming from the failure of the federal government.

While SB1070 certainly left a sour aftertaste for thinking about the role of immigration localism, its Constitutional problems are not inherent to immigration localism. SB1070 was enacted in 2010 during a period of hyperbolic media alarmism about the growth of illegal immigration. These types of anti-immigrant measures are the aberration; the high legal bills

Originally published as Samuel Kleiner, "Not-So-Comprehensive Immigration Reform: What Can Local Governments Do?," *Tucson Weekly*, January 24, 2014. Reprinted with permission of the author.

and the blow to business triggered a backlash that pushed its architect, State Senator Russell Pearce, out of office. With that chapter behind the state, it is time to think about a more constructive path forward for immigration localism.

At its core, immigration is a multifaceted phenomenon that is different in different parts of the country. Immigration has largely been driven by economic factors, with immigrants choosing to settle in parts of the country where work was readily available and there is a community that they can belong to. In Arizona, for instance, undocumented immigrants make up for 6 percent of the population whereas in another border state, Montana, undocumented immigrants were less than .1 percent of the population. Of course, the reason for the disparity is that illegal immigration flows from Mexico and Central America and has congregated in the Southwest with more recent growth in the Southeast. Immigration and the ensuing public policy issues in healthcare, education and a myriad of other issues are as varied as the different communities in our nation. The federal government is not in a great position to be able to address the local nuances of immigration in an efficient manner.

There is a value to local experimentalism in designing immigration policy. Justice Louis Brandeis noted, a "state may, if its citizens choose, serve as a laboratory; and try novel social and economic experiments without risk to the rest of the country." There is a value to debating and hashing out a compromise to immigration at a local level where the citizens can help to determine what solutions fit with their local needs. Though they may err in the ideal solution, the democratic process is self-correcting and the courts serve a role in policing the limits of anti-immigrant restrictions.

In fact, the growth of political activism amongst the immigrant community is closely tied to placing power over immigration in local hands. While immigrants cannot have a significant voice at the federal level, they are politically empowered at the local level. The growth of political organizations in Arizona such as 'Team Awesome' that seek to mobilize the political power of the Hispanic population has been part of a desire to have more of a voice in the debate over the local immigration debate. Locality matters in drumming up the voice of the immigrant community. "It is easier to get someone to vote for [local candidates] than it is to vote for something they can't really see," said Stanford Prescott, a Team Awesome organizer in Latino sections of Phoenix. Rather than looking to the federal government as a source to preempt state action, advocates for immigrants should be embracing local immigration policy for driving immigrant political participation.

The immigration challenges that Arizona faces are different than the ones that a non-border state faces. While Governors Brewer and Brown have cast aspersions on immigration localism as a response to the failure in Congress, we need to embrace a local approach to immigration as an important objective. We want a customized immigration policy, so long as it respects the rights of the immigrants, that fits the needs of the state and of its cities.

Long thought to be the exclusive providence of the federal government, immigration is actually an issue where localism is greatly needed. Arizonans who care about immigration shouldn't wait for an inert Congress to act; we should look to our progressive mayors and, someday, a progressive Governor for action that can move the ball forward on immigration.

5. Costs Mount for Counties as Immigration Reform Languishes

Charles Taylor

In Deep South Texas, Brooks County officials are seeing one of the seldom-mentioned consequences of a broken immigration system all too often.

Chief Deputy Benny Martinez recalls the sheriff's office receiving a 911 call: A woman, lost in a remote area of the 944-square mile county—her husband gravely ill.

It's dark and the wife, an undocumented immigrant, doesn't know where she is. Her cell phone is dying. The only advice the sheriff's office can give is to turn off her phone, to conserve its battery, and call back after daybreak, when she could, perhaps, identify a landmark. Morning came too late. The man had died amid the scrubby brush land.

His was one of the 300 bodies to be recovered in the last three years, Martinez said, and the county of 7,200—one of the poorest in the state—must "eat" the associated costs. It does not touch the Mexican border, but is one county, Hidalgo, removed.

"It's difficult in the sense that it creates a hardship on the office because not only do we have to process those bodies, as mandated by law, but we also still have everything else that comes along with it," Martinez said, "whether notifying family members or family members calling in from various states throughout the U.S. or countries, whether it be from central America or Mexico."

While immigration reform is stalled in Congress, Brooks and other

Originally published as Charles Taylor, "Costs mount for counties as immigration reform languishes," *County News*, published by the National Association of Counties Research Foundation, May 5, 2014. Reprinted with permission of the publisher.

border and near-border counties find themselves caught in the middle of a seemingly unresolvable dilemma.

In 2013, the sheriff's office spent more than $155,000 out of its $615,000 budget on transport, autopsies and fees related to migrant death investigations.

Martinez said there is no federal aid to help—which the letter was requesting—and the county's budget is already stressed. Last fall, elected officials and the sheriff took 10 percent pay cuts; other county employees were cut 3 percent.

County officials wrote members of their congressional delegation in December in a cry for help.

"It is now a daily practice for the Brooks County Sheriff's Department to respond to stranded, vulnerable, weak and many times deceased immigrants in the punishing desert-like terrain of Brooks County," County Judge Raul Ramirez wrote in a letter, signed by all four members of the Commissioners Court.

In another non-border county, Pinal County, Ariz., the county Board of Supervisors has put the Immigration and Customs Enforcement (ICE) on 100-day notice that it will cease to house ICE detainees unless payments to house them can be increased.

The existing per diem of $59.64 was agreed upon in 2006, according to county officials, but it's been a money-losing proposition ever since— costing approximately $3.5 million a year.

County Manager Greg Stanley, who was not county manager at the time the deal was inked, said the true cost of housing ICE detainees is closer to $75 per day.

"We'd still like to come to an agreement," Stanley said, "and locally we have a really good relationship with the local ICE office." The county is open to continuing negotiations. But if a deal can't be worked out, he foresees "pretty significant" staff cuts.

Southeast of Pinal County, Cochise County—an actual border county— has seen its first-responder resources strained by illegal-immigration-related duties.

"We're pretty much a pass-through community here," said Bill Miller, fire district chief and chair of the Cochise County EMS Association. Fire districts in the county, funded by local taxes, are absorbing the costs of responding to undocumented immigrants.

"They come over the Huachuca Mountains and they figure it's a short-cut into the large cities such as Tucson and Phoenix," he said. "In reality it's not." On the mountain, nighttime temperatures can dip below freezing; in daylight hours the mercury can top 100 degrees.

Miller said smugglers known as "coyotes" often mislead their human cargo into thinking they are being dropped off closer to big cities than they actually are. "Sometimes they just abandon them; they just drop them off and say, see those lights? That's Phoenix."

In a group of "20, 40, 50" immigrants, if some lag behind because of age or medical problems, the rest of the group will leave them behind.

"So what will end up happening is that they get distressed," he said, "and they'll try to find their way down through the mountain or they find a hiker; they'll call for assistance. And that's where your EMS providers, our fire department providers will have to call out our tactical rescue teams to go up there and remove them from the mountain."

Such rescues can take several hours even up to half a day, he said, depending on their complexity.

"Border patrol will assist us in getting them off the hill; they're very cooperative about that, but they're not placing them into custody," Miller said. "We'll transport them into to the hospital, and typically what ends up happening, we eat the transport cost," which can run to $1,500 per ambulance trip—much higher if a medevac helicopter is involved.

"Our best-case scenario would be, we'd like to get reimbursed from the federal government, and our federal government charges the Mexican government," he said. "It's beyond me how they would do that."

6. For Mayors, It Is About Integration, Not Immigration

Paul Pontieri

At the 2011 Congress of Cities and Exposition in Phoenix, I helped lead a workshop featuring segments from the PBS documentary "Not In Our Town: Light in the Darkness," about the community response to an anti-immigrant hate crime killing in my town. The session, sponsored by NLC's Municipal Action for Immigrant Integration program (MAII) launched a productive conversation with mayors and other city leaders about how to effectively address these complex challenges. I will appear at a film screening and discussion on February 8, 6:30 p.m. at Scottsdale Community College Performing Arts Center in Scottsdale, Arizona.

In our personal and national lives, we recognize certain events as "game changers"—a parent's death, the birth of a first child, JFK's assassination, the 9/11 attack—after which life can never be as it was before. Yet when I became mayor of the Incorporated Village of Patchogue, a suburban community of 12,000 residents located about halfway between New York City and "the Hamptons," I couldn't foresee that November 8 would mark the anniversary of such an event for me and the residents I serve.

I couldn't foresee that, on that date in 2008, seven high school students from an adjoining community would pile into a car and drive to Patchogue looking for Latinos to assault. In the wake of the volatile and pervasive immigration debate, they saw what they called "beaner hopping" as a sport

Originally published as Paul Pontieri, "A Local Perspective: For Mayors, It is About Integration, Not Immigration," www.nlc.org/media-center/news-search/a-local-perspective-for-mayors-it-is-about-integration-not-immigration. February 6, 2012. Reprinted with permission of the National League of Cities and author.

to be engaged in with friends after dark. They killed Marcello Lucero, an Ecuadorian immigrant who had lived in Patchogue for 15 years. This single act changed how I view and do my job and taught me that local leadership is about integration, not immigration.

We in local government believe that immigration issues should be solved at the national level by the President and Congress. Regardless of our feelings about the viability, success or failure of any efforts, we know that our communities face real challenges that are not based on "shoulds," but rather on "hows."

We know that we cannot resolve the immigration debate at the local level. In fact, the debate itself has created a sense that "these people" are expendable, and discriminatory behavior like "beaner hopping" is acceptable despite the reality that immigrants are inextricably interwoven into our communities in many ways.

When I first heard of the murder and spoke to the police, it was clear that this would go well beyond the borders of our 2.2-square-mile village. I have always believed that the mayor is the face and voice of the village and that how I respond to a situation determines how the community responds. I went first to our local library, the place where citizenship classes are given and ESL is taught. It is a safe and welcoming place for immigrants, and I had held meetings in the past with Latinos on how to become involved in the village. I knew that we needed to calm their fears, listen to their concerns and bring them together with the police in an environment where trust could be built.

During the following weeks, I visited restaurants, construction sites and walked the streets of our downtown and neighborhoods talking to members of the community, both Latino and Anglo. I assisted in organizing forums in local houses of worship in an attempt to uncover and discuss frustrations in all segments of the village. I went to the site of the murder, which had become a shrine and talked to the people gathered there.

While these encounters were not always comfortable, I learned a great deal about this tiny village in which I'd grown up and which had almost imperceptibly been changing. For example, I met a Latino man who lived across the street from my mother. I was shocked to learn that he had been there for 23 years. Do we not see them or do they wish not to be seen? My growing belief that leaders have a responsibility to integrate all residents into the community, regardless of immigration status, was underscored.

In concert with various other organizations, a vigil was held the following week that about 750 people attended. There was every opportunity for the community to divide and for each to blame the other. I felt that I had to be the one to bridge that potential divide. I met with the ambassador to the United States from Ecuador and showed him a photograph of short men with tanned skins and shovels paving the streets of Patchogue in the 1920s. They were from Calabria, Italy; my grandfather was in the foreground of that faded picture. Today, Latinos are building our communities.

The ambassador and I spoke at the vigil, and the community responded. We followed with community meetings. Patchogue Medford High School provided programs to bring the groups together. A Unity Coalition was formed, chaired by New York State's Commissioner for Human Rights, Galand Kirkland, to discuss and provide opportunities for an open discussion on what needed to be done to foster the integration of the Latino community into the greater Patchogue community.

From this came a Unity Celebration that brought more than 1,000 people to the Patchogue Theatre for a night that celebrated our diversity. One group worked on a quilt; a table was provided at our summer street fair; the Lucero Foundation was formed; meetings continued with the police. I also visited Gualaceo, Ecuador, the home of Marcello Lucero, and was greeted warmly and openly. Gualaceo's Mayor Tapia has now visited Patchogue and the Ecuadorian community here.

Importantly, we held a public hearing on the language we as public officials would use when discussing the immigration issue. Terms like "illegal immigrant," "aliens" and "boarder babies," when used in any context, devalue people or groups in a manner that causes anger and distrust. The resolution passed that March night in 2009 directs the Village Board to consider the language used when discussing immigration issues.

Despite our national identity as a melting pot, the integration of immigrants into any community is difficult in the best of times. Patchogue began the process in earnest on the heels of a tragic murder, with the press and outside political pressure taking the issue beyond our borders. At times, it seemed that the scrutiny was impossibly unfair.

For me, however, the result is a solidly forged belief that my responsibility is to my residents, regardless of their immigration status. Men and women working, raising families, learning our customs and adhering to our laws deserve their mayor's support as they attempt to integrate into any city, town or village. Mayors cannot afford to focus on the wrong aspect of the immigration debate: Patchogue's story should serve as a powerful cautionary tale.

7. The Immigration Debate We're Not Having

Susan K. Urahn

The push for immigration reform certainly is making headlines and fostering spirited debate, but what is being overlooked in our national discussion is the critical role state and local governments play in managing the influx of new arrivals—legal and unauthorized.

In 2012, the U.S. Supreme Court reaffirmed that it is the role of the federal government to decide whom the country admits, how long they stay and the circumstances under which they're removed. But this leaves a considerable role for states and localities to manage the complex education, language, health and public-safety issues that come with immigration.

Some states with a history of handling immigrant arrivals, notably California, New York and Texas, have been integrating them for many years. But for other states with new and quickly growing immigrant populations, managing these challenges is a more recent development. These states are waking up to the social, fiscal and economic effects of immigration—and sometimes attempting to respond without the benefit of past experience and good data about what works or doesn't.

In 1990, about 20 million people, nearly 8 percent of the U.S. population, were foreign-born. Today that number is around 40 million, accounting for approximately 13 percent of the population and including about 11 million unauthorized immigrants. And unlike in decades past, there now are substantial foreign-born populations in nearly all 50 states and the District of Columbia.

Originally published as Susan K. Urahn, "The Immigration Debate We're Not Having," *Governing*, October 2, 2013. Reprinted with permission of the publisher.

Whether states have long-standing or new immigrant communities, state laws and policies for dealing with them differ widely. Some laws focus on controlling immigration by penalizing employers who hire unauthorized workers or requiring police to check the status of people they believe may not be here legally. Other laws focus on integrating immigrants into communities regardless of status, and provide drivers' licenses, in-state college tuition, health care and other services.

States and localities also are involved in providing English classes to non-native speakers. In some jurisdictions, law-enforcement agencies offer language or cultural sensitivity training to officers, reasoning that it is in the community's interest to encourage all residents to report crimes and testify in court.

Yet federal and state laws often overlap. Changes in federal treatment of immigrants, for example, can affect state and local governments. Consider the Obama administration's Deferred Action for Childhood Arrivals program, which offers a two-year reprieve from deportation for certain unauthorized people who were brought here as children and meet other eligibility criteria. For young immigrants, obtaining school records is one of the steps required to prove they qualify for the program. But not all jurisdictions were ready for the flood of requests. California schools faced a particularly large workload, and localities including Fresno, Los Angeles and San Diego put new procedures in place or partnered with community groups to solve the problem. Localities with smaller immigrant populations also found innovative solutions. Des Moines, Iowa, for instance, set up a website specifically to help immigrant students and their families with the paperwork.

Comprehensive immigration reform that includes enhanced enforcement and legalizes certain unauthorized immigrants would entail both costs and benefits for states and localities. If additional newly legalized residents are incorporated into the American mainstream and the formal economy, then there will likely be additional tax revenue, new talent and greater cultural diversity, but also possibly increased demand for social services.

The immigration debate is an emotional one. Myths and misinformation abound. That, along with America's changing demographics, calls for a deliberative, fact-based public discussion about immigration. There is also a need for dialogue between states and the federal government alongside solid research about how federal, state and local immigration policies intersect. The bottom-line question for governments at all levels: If comprehensive immigration reform is enacted, are they prepared?

8. It's Okay That Congress Won't Act on Immigration

Cristina Rodriguez

It's official: Congress won't take up immigration reform this year. Today, President Barack Obama said he'll use executive actions to change policies unilaterally.

It's a disappointing, if unsurprising, outcome. But advocates for reform have reason to hope. States and cities long have shaped the country's immigration policy, and can continue to do so.

Take New York. Just last week, the New York City Council made a splash in the immigration world by allocating $4.9 million to free legal assistance for non-citizens in deportation proceedings. It also created a municipal identification card available to everyone, regardless of immigration status.

In Albany, advocates introduced a bill that goes further, granting unauthorized immigrants the right to vote and sit on juries. Although that measure is probably aspiration more than reality, it provides a counterpoint to the Arizona-style enforcement crackdowns.

Such immigration federalism necessarily will entail ideological battle, between pro-enforcement and pro-integration strategies. But partisans on both sides should be willing to let states and localities take immigration policy in different directions.

State and local authority in this domain is limited, but it exists. When it comes to enforcement, state and local police historically have played a role alongside the federal government. In 2012, the Supreme Court trimmed this role by striking down most of Arizona's notorious Senate Bill 1070. But

Originally published as Cristina Rodriguez, "It's okay that Congress won't act on immigration. States can do a lot on their own," *Washington Post*, June 30, 2014. Reprinted with permission of the author.

the court also left space open for local immigration policing. As the administration emphasized throughout the litigation, the federal government depends on cooperation from state and local police. Nothing in the court's decision precludes Congress from authorizing greater state and local involvement.

And, the court recognized police authority to inquire into immigration status, subject to civil rights constraints. States also have considerable authority to define the parameters of their own political communities, as well as significant freedom to use their resources to benefit immigrants, regardless of status.

Given these parameters, what should immigration federalism look like today?

On the enforcement end, where enthusiasm for enforcement remains, states should focus on combating racial profiling and curbing distrust of police in immigrant communities. This should be complemented by training for police in the details of immigration law and in how to interact with immigrant communities.

At the same time, some jurisdictions have rejected enforcement cooperation altogether. States such as California and Connecticut, and cities such as Chicago and Washington, D.C., actively resist federal requests for assistance. State and local ordinances constraining police cooperation continue to proliferate, especially as controversy over federal enforcement builds. Enforcement enthusiast should acknowledge these moves as legitimate, too.

Critics might worry that this localized activity is creating an incoherent patchwork; no doubt the federal government prefers not to be challenged from both directions. But in reality, these mixed agendas offer examples of how state and local action can contribute to the national debate over immigration enforcement by highlighting what is at stake in concrete terms. Like Arizona's law, the anti-enforcement measures reflect a rejection of current federal policy and may well force the federal government to rethink its enforcement strategies. There is no "final" answer to the enforcement question—only an ongoing debate.

Today, numerous states and localities practice an affirmative integrative federalism. Republican and Democratic states alike make available in-state tuition to unauthorized college students. Municipal identification cards such as the one recently adopted in New York enable even unauthorized immigrants to open bank accounts, sign leases, get library cards and access other services.

State and local bureaucracies are also interested in and capable of implementing the immigration laws, and they could be enlisted productively not just in enforcement, but also in future legalization and integration programs, and even in the process of selecting and admitting immigrants. For example, the Republican governor of Michigan and Utah's state legislature have floated the idea of recruiting immigrants to help revitalize local communities. Though this idea would require federal authorization and may prove to be misguided, it reflects the possibilities for reform that open up when we recognize states and localities as legitimate players, rather than label them as out of their league.

Immigration federalism will ultimately be a limited tool and cannot substitute for a federal policy. Only Congress (not the states, or even the president) can provide today's unauthorized population with the ultimate security of legal status (or adopt direct means of restricting immigration). And in some cases a uniform immigration policy will be necessary.

But because the United States consists of overlapping political communities with varied views on immigration, federalism offers a framework for productive debate, as well as a set of institutional mechanisms for working toward compromise. When imagining a better system, we should take advantage of these alternative forms of lawmaking to channel the complexity of the immigration question, even if it means embracing contradictions.

This essay is adapted from "Law and Borders," published in the summer 2014 issue of *Democracy: A Journal of Ideas*.

9. Elderly Immigrants in the United States

Paola Scommegna

In 2010, more than one in eight (11.9 percent) U.S. adults ages 65 and older were foreign born, a share that is expected to continue to grow. The U.S. elderly immigrant population rose from 2.7 million in 1990 to 4.6 million in 2010, a 70 percent increase in 20 years. This chapter highlights recent studies of older immigrants in the United States, conducted by National Institute on Aging (NIA) supported researchers and others.

Elderly immigrants are a diverse group, from a wide range of life circumstances. Some are highly trained professionals who immigrated early in their careers; others are the recently arrived elderly parents of naturalized citizens; and some immigrated with their families when they were young children. Understanding both the unique characteristics of elderly foreign-born adults and the challenges some of them face is important as policymakers and planners address the well-being and health of the United States' aging population.

Demographic Trends

Fueling the growth of the U.S. immigrant population ages 65 and older are two trends—the aging of the long-term foreign-born population and the recent migration of older adults as part of family reunification and refugee admissions (Leach 2009). This ongoing migration makes projecting

Originally published as Paola Scommegna, "Elderly Immigrants in the United States," *Today's Research on Aging*, no. 29 (Washington, D.C.: Population Reference Bureau, 2013). Reprinted with permission of the author and publisher.

the future size of the elderly immigrant population challenging. One projection estimated that the number of U.S. immigrants ages 65 and older will quadruple to more than 16 million by 2050 (Treas and Batalova 2007, cited in Leach 2009).

Latin America has replaced Europe as the leading birth place of America's older immigrants. In 2010, a larger share of older foreign-born adults were of Latin American origin (38 percent) than of Asian (29 percent) or European (28 percent) origins (Wilmoth 2012). In 2010, a majority of immigrants ages 65 and older (60 percent) had entered the United States before 1970. Analysis of American Community Survey data suggests that 10 percent of immigrants ages 65 and older had been in the country fewer than 10 years in 2010 (Batalova 2012).

Most U.S. immigrants who settle in this country after age 60 are sponsored by their adult children who had immigrated to the United States as young adults. Beginning in 1965, family reunification provisions in U.S. immigration policy gave naturalized U.S. citizens the opportunity to petition for their parents' entry outside the usual quota restrictions. The annual number of late-life immigrants (ages 60 and older) admitted to the United States has grown but has varied from year to year, from 40,000 in 1986 to more than 86,000 in 2010, with a high of nearly 101,000 in 2006, according to Wilmoth's (2012) analysis of Department of Homeland Security data.

Long-term immigrants who arrived as children or young adults and are "aging in place as long-standing U.S. residents" tend to face challenges similar to their U.S.-born peers (Wilmoth 2012). By contrast, immigrants who migrate after age 60 are often a "potentially vulnerable population" due to limited English language proficiency, little or no U.S. work experience, and weak ties to social institutions. They face rules barring them from participating in most entitlement and welfare programs unless they become naturalized citizens, but their language skills and age are often a barrier to naturalization. Compared to immigrants who arrive earlier in life, late-life immigrants are more likely to be female, to have low education levels, to have limitations in physical functioning, and to be widowed.

The length of time immigrants have spent in the United States is key to their acquiring English language skills, which contribute directly to their ability to use health care and other social services (Leach 2009). More than two-thirds of recent older immigrants (71 percent) did not speak English well in 2006, compared to just about one-third of long-term older immigrants (31 percent). Late-life immigrants with limited English skills must depend heavily on family members, putting them at risk of isolation and depression (Wilmoth 2012).

Recent older immigrants are more likely than long-standing immigrants to settle outside traditional destination cities, such as New York, Los Angeles, and Miami (Leach 2009). Late-life immigrants are contributing to growing immigrant populations in rural areas and small towns in midwestern and southern states, including Minnesota, Kansas, Georgia, and North Carolina. English proficiency is particularly important for functioning in rural areas; bilingual staff in health care settings, senior service agencies, and legal aid organizations are rare in many places (Gurak and Kritz 2013).

Economic Circumstances

Foreign-born elderly tend to have less personal income than U.S.-born elderly, on average. But overall, by any number of measures, family or household income (unadjusted for household size) is higher for the foreign-born elderly than for the U.S.-born elderly. This likely reflects both the living arrangements of the elderly immigrants and higher levels of labor force participation for elderly immigrant men who have been in the United States for fewer than 10 years. Extended-family living, more common among immigrant groups, tends to boost household income because multiple earners are often present. In addition, family income captures not just the income of the elderly person but also, for dependent elderly, income of other family members. Similarly, household income captures income from all per sons at the same address.

National averages mask wide differences by country of origin. One study that examined average household income in the 2006 to 2008 period for adults ages 60 and older found that certain immigrant groups had incomes substantially higher than their U.S.-born peers, including older Indian, Filipino, and Chinese immigrants (Gurak and Kritz 2013). Household income for older Mexicans was substantially lower than that of their U.S.-born peers during the period.

Borjas (2009) found that both the relative wages and skills of U.S. immigrants have declined since the 1950s, raising concerns about what economic resources immigrants will have in their old age. His analysis showed growing disparity in the average personal income of immigrants ages 65 and older and their U.S.-born counterparts. The income gap between immigrant and U.S.-born elderly widened from 5 percent in 1970 to 30 percent in 2007. A growing income gap also is evident within the immigrant population, with older immigrants who had lived in the United States for fewer than 10 years having far less annual income than those who had been in the United States for 10 years or longer.

Reliance on a different mix of economic resources in old age accounts for some of the income differences between immigrant and U.S.-born elderly. Borjas (2009) found that in 2007 U.S.-born elderly were considerably more likely than immigrant elderly to receive Social Security benefits, investment income, and retirement benefits such as pensions. These differences may be a result of the high proportion of immigrants originating from less economically developed countries. These immigrants tend to lack "human capital necessary to obtain jobs that provide pensions, may lack adequate health insurance, and often have a harder time accumulating resources for retirement" (Gerst and Burr 2012).

Immigrant elderly were more likely to be employed than U.S.-born elderly (30 percent versus 18 percent in 2007) (Borjas 2009). Gerst and Burr (2012) suggested this reliance on earned income "implies a heavier dependency on continued employment in later life." The need to continue working makes the economic well-being of immigrant elderly more vulnerable to labor market fluctuations and health problems than if they had greater access to pensions and Social Security benefits.

Older immigrants' higher employment rates are driven in part by incentives related to Social Security program eligibility (Borjas 2011). Analysis of 30 years of Census data (1970–2000) shows that as retirement age approaches, the employment rate of foreign-born men declines more slowly than that of U.S.-born men. Before their late 50s, foreign-born men tend to have lower employment rates than U.S. born men, but after their early 60s immigrant males tend to have higher employment rates. This "crossover point" is related to Social Security benefit eligibility rules that require workers to be employed for at least 10 years in the United States. Once the 10-year minimum is met, foreign-born workers tend to retire. By age 70, U.S.-born and immigrant men have similar labor force participation rates. The retirement of recently arrived elderly immigrant men will contribute to already rising Social Security program costs.

A preliminary study of Social Security beneficiaries found that about 10 percent of Latin American immigrants born between 1915 and 1918 returned to Latin America to live (Vega 2013). Lower Social Security benefits do not appear to increase the likelihood of Latin American immigrants returning to their country of origin. Latin American-born immigrants with lower benefit levels due to miscalculation of benefits had similar migration patterns as other Latin American immigrants. Poverty and few or no retirement benefits, however, may contribute to return migration (Vega 2013; Van Hook and Zhang 2011, cited in Vega 2013). Immigrant elderly also receive public assistance at more than twice the rate of U.S.-born elderly (13 percent versus 5 percent in 2007) (Borjas 2009). Virtually all of the older immigrants' public assistance income came through the Supplemental Security Income (SSI) program—a federal program providing supplemental payments to elderly, blind, and disabled people who have little or no income—suggesting that a sizeable share of immigrant elderly have extremely limited economic resources. Gerst and Burr (2012) found that 11 percent of elderly Asian immigrants and 15 percent of elderly Hispanic immigrants were receiving SSI, based on 2006 to 2010 American Community Survey data. The 1996 welfare reform law restricts the use of federal welfare programs, preventing most legal permanent noncitizen residents from receiving SSI benefits. Naturalized immigrants do not face the same restrictions. If more of the elderly foreign-born were to become naturalized citizens, the share of elderly immigrants receiving SSI would likely be higher. Not surprisingly, immigrant elderly were more likely to have incomes below the poverty line than U.S.-born elderly. In 2010, 8 percent of U.S.-born elderly lived below the poverty line.

Living Arrangements

Compared with their U.S.-born peers, elderly immigrants are more likely to live in extended-family households, especially those who arrived in the United States after age 60 (Wilmoth 2001; Wilmoth, De Jong, and Himes 1997, cited in Wilmoth 2012). Older adults are usually classified as residing in an extended-family household if they live with at least one relative other than a spouse or a young child. Extended-family households often are established as a response to economic need, providing a way to conserve limited income and assets. Extended-family living may also reflect cultural preferences among some immigrant groups, "shaped by long-standing practices of filial piety" (Wilmoth 2012). Such households may be established to provide intergenerational support, such as child care, or to address "concerns about their aging relative's health status or social isolation." For late-life immigrants, the extended-family living arrangement may represent the support provided by the adult child who sponsored a parent's immigration. However, Vietnamese immigrants ages 50 and older participating in focus groups expressed fear of losing independence and becoming a burden to their families; Chinese and Latino focus group participants (both U.S. born and immigrant) also voiced these same worries (Laditka et al. 2011).

Levels of extended-family living vary widely among immigrant groups. In 2000, based on analysis of Asian and Hispanic immigrants ages 60 and older from 11 countries of origin, the most extended-family living occurred among Indians, Vietnamese, Filipinos, Dominicans, and Mexicans (Gurak and Kritz 2010). About 50 percent in each of these immigrant groups lived in extended families, making them roughly four times more likely to do so than U.S.-born non–Hispanic whites.

Analysis of 2000 Census data showed that older immigrants who lived in extended-family households were more likely to be unmarried, to have lower levels of education and income, and to have more disabilities than immigrants who did not (Gurak and Kritz 2010). Assimilation plays a strong role in living arrangements: Older immigrants were less likely to live in an extended-family household if they had a high level of English language proficiency, lived outside of areas where their immigrant group traditionally settled, and immigrated at younger ages. When the researchers controlled for the economic resources of older Vietnamese and Mexicans (groups that tend to have lower income levels), the difference in extended-family living compared with U.S.-born older non–Hispanic whites narrowed considerably, but not as much as when assimilation measures were taken into account. Some groups, however, tend to have high levels of both economic resources and extended-family living (such as Indians and Filipinos), suggesting that cultural preferences continue to play an important role in housing decisions.

Results of a study that focused on differences within the elderly U.S. Hispanic population in 2000 underscore the role of assimilation in influencing living arrangements (Burr, Mutchler, and Gerst 2010). Compared to elderly U.S.-born Hispanics, elderly foreign-born Hispanics in 2000 were more likely to live in crowded housing (more than one person per room) even after demographic and socioeconomic characteristics were taken into account. This study found that among elderly foreign-born Hispanics, the lower their levels of English language proficiency and the shorter the length of time they had been living in the United States, the more likely they were to live in a crowded household. Additionally, renters were more likely to live in crowded settings than owners. The researchers found no link between living in an ethnically segregated area and crowding. They did find that with all else equal (including income and the cost of housing), living in an urban area with a relatively large Hispanic population increased the likelihood of crowding, suggesting that elderly immigrant Hispanics may place a higher value on physical proximity to other Hispanics than on larger living quarters.

Living With and Caring for Grandchildren: Immigrants 65 and older are much more likely than U.S.-born elderly to live with their grandchildren. In 2007, about 14 percent of immigrant elderly lived with at least one grandchild, compared with just 4 percent of the older U.S.-born elderly population (Terrazas 2009). However, among grandparents living with their grandchildren, older immigrant and U.S.-born elderly were equally likely to have primary responsibility for caring for these children.

Nursing Home Residence: Gurak and Kritz (2010) studied older Asian and Hispanic immigrants from 11 countries and found that they were much less likely than older U.S.-born non–Hispanic whites to reside in nursing homes, group homes, or other types of group quarters. In 2000, 5 percent of U.S.-born non–Hispanic whites ages 60 and older lived in group settings, compared to only about 1 percent of older immigrant Hispanics and Asians. Additionally, a study of older Hispanics (both immigrant and U.S.-born) in five southwestern U.S. states found those who had spent time in a skilled nursing facility were much more likely to use English as their primary language, suggesting that language assimilation plays a role in the use of institutional care (Finley et al. 2013).

Life Expectancy and Health

Mortality statistics show that immigrants tend to live longer than their U.S. counterparts. One recent analysis explored the magnitude of these differences. Dupre, Gu, and Vaupel (2012) examined newly available Medicare records linked to Social Security Administration files for more than 30 million Medicare-eligible U.S. elderly in 1995, the most recent year for which these data are available. Compared to Medicare-eligible U.S.-born adults, Medicare-eligible foreign-born adults had lower mortality at nearly every age between 65 and 100. The study demonstrated that the U.S. foreign-born elderly population contributed to an increase in overall U.S. life expectancy. In particular, U.S. foreign-born adults "were among the longest-lived older adults in the world" when compared to older adults in other industrialized countries. Additionally, among the Medicare-eligible, foreign-born U.S. blacks had the longest life expectancy of any group examined. This "exceptional longevity" stands in "contrast to the well-documented disadvantages and correlated health risks among U.S.-born blacks."

Better health is at the root of these life expectancy differences, and research continues to find that, overall, immigrants tend to be healthier on arrival than their U.S.-born peers (for more information, see "The Health and Life Expectancy of the Older Blacks and Hispanics in the United States," *Today's Research on Aging* 28, June 2013). These health advantages include higher levels of cognitive functioning at the time of migration (Hill et al. 2012). Studies of cellular function also find evidence of better health among new immigrants (Kaestner et al. 2009). These differences reflect the "healthy migrant effect"—that is, immigrants who are able to make the trip are "healthier, wealthier, and more educated" than the compatriots they leave behind (Wilmoth 2012). Also, U.S. immigration policies give preference to immigrants with high levels of education and do not admit people with infectious diseases and other undesirable characteristics.

Once in the United States, cultural factors—such as better health habits and stronger networks of social support—may offer protection from some diseases and lead to longer lives. Immigrants often have healthier diets and smoke less than the U.S.-born population (Osypuk et al. 2009; Blue and Fenelon 2011). Some immigrant communities are characterized by high levels of family contact and mutual assistance, with religious participation playing an important role (Taylor, Chatters, and Jackson 2007; Jackson, Forsythe-Brown, and Govia 2007). But these health advantages are often reduced over time as immigrants become more assimilated and adopt more typical U.S. diets and lifestyles, particularly among immigrants with low income and education levels (Gallo et al. 2009; Lutsey et al. 2008). There is also evidence that some immigrants leave the United States to return to their birth place when their health deteriorates, resulting in measured population health outcomes that are better than they would have been if the returning immigrants had remained in the United States (Palloni and Arias 2004; Turra and Elo 2008; Riosmena, Wong, and Palloni 2012).

Studies find that immigrant adults (ages 18 and older) have lower medical expenditures than U.S.-born adults, even among those immigrants who are fully insured (Tarraf, Miranda, and González 2012; Ku 2009). Among adults ages 65 and older, immigrants and the U.S.-born population tend to have similar levels of health care expenditures (Mohanty et al. 2005). Some immigrant groups' attitudes toward cognitive decline and diseases such as

Alzheimer's may prevent them from seeking appropriate health care and taking steps to prevent loss of mental function (Laditka et al. 2011). Vietnamese immigrants ages 50 and older participating in focus groups said that cognitive loss was a normal part of aging rather than the result of a disease; Chinese and Latino participants (both U.S.-born and immigrant) also viewed mental decline as an expected part of the aging process.

Disability

While some immigrant groups in the United States have fewer chronic diseases in old age than their U.S.-born peers, there is growing evidence that important segments of the immigrant population are reaching older ages with more physical limitations and disability than their U.S.-born counterparts (Zhang, Hayward, and Lu 2012). A study based on 2000 Census data found that older Asian immigrants face a greater likelihood of having a disability than U.S.-born non–Hispanic whites (Mutchler, Prakash, and Burr 2007). Specifically, Asian immigrants were more likely than U.S. born elderly to have difficulty going out alone shopping or to a medical appointment and to have problems performing personal care such as dressing, bathing, and getting around the house. Elderly Vietnamese immigrants tended to have the highest disability levels, likely reflecting their arrival as refugees and limited economic resources. One study of foreign-born Hispanic men found that their disability levels start, manual labor likely took a physical toll that became evident later in life, the authors suggested.

Gurak and Kritz's (2013) study of older rural immigrants found that all major groups examined except Mexicans were less disabled and had fewer health limitations than the U.S. born rural population in both 2000 and 2008. Older rural Mexicans immigrants, however, had almost twice as many limitations as other immigrant groups. Another study based on 2006 American Community Survey data found that one in four Mexican immigrants ages 55 and older had functional limitations (any long-term condition limiting walking, climbing stairs, reaching, lifting, or carrying), a disability level the researchers called "disturbingly high" (Thomson et al. 2013). In addition, among Mexican immigrants, the longer they had lived in the United States, the more likely they were to have a problem with physical functioning. When the researchers took into account education and income, however, they found that Mexican immigrants were less likely to have limitations in physical function than U.S.-born non–Hispanic whites.

Finally, limited English language proficiency appears linked to high levels of physical limitations. Findings from these studies suggest that older Mexican immigrants have high levels of health care needs, driven in part by low socioeconomic status and manual labor, and that this group could benefit from bilingual health care service providers and preventive care.

Conclusion

The growing share of foreign-born elderly in the U.S. population faces greater economic challenges than the U.S.-born elderly population, on average, but they may also have some advantages in terms of longevity and social networks. Findings with respect to longevity suggest that the immigrants live longer, but this is balanced by high rates of disability among some segments of the foreign-born elderly. Low personal income and laws restricting noncitizen access to federal programs may prevent some immigrants from seeking preventive care. Limited English language skills of both the elderly and their caregivers may be an additional barrier to health services, particularly institutional services. Better transportation and more accessible community health services could help low-income immigrant elderly "age in place" in their communities as they say they prefer, saving human service costs and improving quality of life (Vega and González 2012). It remains unclear whether immigrant living and caregiving arrangements are the result of preferences or barriers to accessing services.

REFERENCES

Batalova, J. (2012). "Senior Immigrants in the United States." *Migration Information Source*, Migration Policy Institute.

Blue, L., and Fenelon, A. (2011). "Explaining Low Mortality Among U.S. Immigrants Relative to Native-Born Americans: The Role of Smoking." *International Journal of Epidemiology* 40, 3: 786–93.

Borjas, G. (2009). "Economic Well-Being of the Elderly Immigrant Population." Paper presented at the 11th Annual Joint Conference of the Retirement Research Consortium, Washington, D.C., August.

_____. (2011). "Social Security Eligibility and the Labor Supply of Elderly Immigrants." *Industrial and Labor Relations Review* 64, no. 3 (2011): 485–501.

Burr, J., Mutchler, J., and Gerst, K. (2010). "Patterns of Residential Crowding Among Hispanics in Later Life: Immigration, Assimilation, and Housing Market Factors." *The Journals of Gerontology Series B: Psychological Sciences and Social Sciences* 65, 6: 772–82.

Dupre, M., Gu, D., and Vaupel, J. (2012). "Survival Differences Among Native-Born and Foreign-Born Older Adults in the United States." *Public Library of Science One* 7, 5: e37177.

Finley, M., et al. (2013). "Characteristics of Mexican American Elders Admitted to Nursing Facilities in the United States: Data From the Hispanic Established Populations for Epidemiologic Studies of the Elderly (EPESE) Study." *Journal of the American Medical Directors Association* 14, 3: 226.e1–4.

Gallo, L., et al. (2009). "Do Socioeconomic Gradients in Subclinical Atherosclerosis Vary According to Acculturation Level? Analyses of Mexican-Americans in the Multi-Ethnic Study of Atherosclerosis." *Psychosomatic Medicine* 71, 7: 756–62.

Gerst, K., and Burr, J. (2012). "Welfare Program Participation Among Older Immigrants." *Public Policy & Aging Report* 22, 2: 12–16.

Gurak, D., and Kritz, M. (2010). "Elderly Asian and Hispanic Foreign- and Native-Born Living Arrangements: Accounting for Differences." *Research on Aging* 32, 5: 567–94.

_____. (2013). "Elderly Immigrants in Rural America: Trends and Characteristics." in *Rural Aging in the 21st Century*, ed. Nina Glasgow and E. Helen Berry. New York: Springer.

Hayward, M., et al. (2011). "Does the Hispanic Paradox in Mortality Extend to Disability?" paper presented at the MacArthur Foundation Research Network on an Aging Society, Palo Alto, CA.

Hill, T., et al. (2012). "Immigrant Status and Cognitive Functioning in Late-Life: An Examination of Gender Variations in the Healthy Immigrant Effect." *Social Science and Medicine* 75, 12: 2076–84.

Jackson, J., Forsythe-Brown, I., and Govia, I.O. (2007). "Age Cohort, Ancestry, and Immigrant Generation Influences in Family Relations and Psychological Well-Being Among Black Caribbean Family Members." *Journal of Social Issues* 63, 4: 729–43.

Kaestner, R., et al. (2009). "Stress, Allostatic Load, and Health of Mexican Immigrants." *Social Science Quarterly* 90, 5: 1089–111.

Ku, L. (2009). "Health Insurance Coverage and Medical Expenditures of Immigrants and Native-Born Citizens in the United States." *American Journal of Public Health* 99, 7: 1322–28.

Laditka, J., et al. (2011). "Older Adults' Concerns About Cognitive Health: Commonalities and Differences Among Six United States Ethnic Groups." *Ageing and Society* 31, 7: 1202–28.

Leach, M. (2009). "America's Older Immigrants: A Profile." *Generations* 32, 4: 343–49.

Lutsey, P., et al. (2008). "Associations of Acculturation and Socioeconomic Status With Subclinical Cardiovascular Disease in the Multi-Ethnic Study of Atherosclerosis." *American Journal of Public Health* 98, 11: 1963–70.

Mohanty, S., et al. (2005). "Health Care Expenditures of Immigrants in the United States: A Nationally Representative Analysis." *American Journal of Public Health* 95, 8: 1431–38.

Mutchler, J., Prakash, A., and Burr, J. (2007). "The Demography of Disability and the Effects of Immigrant History: Older Asians in the United States." *Demography* 44, 2: 251–63.

Osypuk, T., et al. (2009). "Are Immigrant Enclaves Healthy Places to Live? The Multi-Ethnic Study of Atherosclerosis." *Social Science and Medicine* 69, 1: 110–20.

Palloni, A., and Arias, E. (2004). "Paradox Lost: Explaining the Adult Hispanic Mortality Advantage." *Demography* 41, 3: 385–415.

Riosmena, F., Batalova, R., and Palloni, A. (2012). "Migration Selection, Protection, and Acculturation in Health: A Binational Perspective on Older Adults." *Demography*, article ID 1533–7790 (online).

Tarraf, W., Miranda, P., and González, H. (2012). "Medical Expenditures Among Immigrant and Non-Immigrant Groups in the U.S.: Findings From the Medical Expenditures Panel Survey (2000–2008)." *Medical Care* 50, 3: 233–42.

Taylor, R. Chatters, L., and Jackson, J. (2007). "Religious Participation Among Older Black Caribbeans in the United States." *The Journals of Gerontology* Series B: Psychological Sciences and Social Sciences 62, 4: S251–56.

Terrazas, A. (2009). "Older Immigrants in the United States." Migration Policy Institute Spotlight, May.

Thomson, E. F., et al. (2013). "The Hispanic Paradox and Older Adults' Disabilities: Is There a Healthy Migrant Effect?" *International Journal of Environmental Research and Public Health* 10, 2: 1786–814.

Treas, J., and Batalova, J. (2007). "Older Immigrants." in *Social Structures: The Impact of Demographic Changes on the Well-Being of Older Persons*, ed. K. Warner Schaie and Peter Uhlenberg. New York: Springer.

Turra C., and Elo, I. (2008). "The Impact of Salmon Bias on the Hispanic Mortality Advantage: New Evidence From Social Security Data." *Population Research and Policy Review* 27, 5: 515–30.

U.S. Census Bureau (2012). "The Foreign-Born Population in the United States: 2010." *American Community Survey Reports* ACS-19, May.

Van Hook, J., and Zhang, W. (2011). "Who Stays? Who Goes? Selective Emigration Among the Foreign-Born." *Population Research and Policy Review* 30, 1: 1–24.

Vega, A. (2013). "The Impact of Social Security on Return Migration Among Latin American Elderly in the U.S." paper presented at the annual meeting of the Population Association of America, New Orleans, April.

Vega, W., and González, H. (2012). "Latinos 'Aging in Place': Issues and Potential Solutions." in *Aging, Health, and Longevity in the Mexican-Origin Population*, ed. Jacqueline L. Angel, Fernando Torres-Gil, and Kyriakos Markides. New York: Springer.

Wilmoth, J. (2001). "Living Arrangements Among Immigrants in the United States." *Gerontologist* 41, 2: 228–38.

_____. (2012). "A Demographic Profile of Older Immigrants." *Public Policy & Aging Report* 22, 2: 8–11.

_____, De Jong, G., and Himes, C. (1997). "Immigrant and Non-Immigrant Living Arrangements Among America's White, Hispanic, and Asian Elderly Population." *International Journal of Sociology and Social Policy* 17, 1: 57–82.

Zhang, Z., Hayward, M., and Lu, C. (2012). "Is There a Hispanic Epidemiological Paradox in Later Life? A Closer Look at Chronic Morbidity." *Research on Aging* 34, 5: 548–71.

Part II

Practices and Experiences

10. A Safe Haven in New Haven
Michele Wucker

As Washington tussles over the fate of the nation's estimated 12 million undocumented immigrants, municipal governments are taking sides. Places like Morristown, N.J., and Danbury, Conn., are cracking down. Others, like New Haven and New York City, are embracing their undocumented workers.

City councils can't change the federal government's failed immigration policies, but they can choose whether to offset or intensify the damage. According to the Migration Policy Institute at New York University, United States municipalities passed 34 laws last year tightening the screws on undocumented immigrants; 56 more such measures are pending.

But the costs of the crackdown cure—high legal fees, damage to local businesses, scarce police resources wasted, the negative impact on public safety of keeping undocumented immigrants underground and the social division—are far worse than the supposed illness.

The officials pushing these crackdowns say they are doing so because of the burden imposed on government services by illegal immigrants. But if businesses close for lack of customers or workers, a town's tax base will fall and it will have to reduce the services that it provides.

Last year, Riverside, N.J., voted to fine anyone who knowingly rents to or hires illegal immigrants, becoming one of the first municipalities to pass such an ordinance. Many of those towns now complain that immigrants—with and without papers—have packed up and left, causing worker shortages. And businesses have had to close because of a lack of customers.

These policies have imposed other costs in the form of steep legal fees. In New Jersey, Freehold Borough ended up agreeing to pay as much as $278,000 to settle a lawsuit over an anti-loitering law aimed at preventing day laborers from soliciting employment in public places. In a similar case in New York, legal bills for the village of Mamaroneck are estimated in the hundreds of thousands of dollars.

The direct and indirect costs of cracking down did not escape the notice of Long Island's Suffolk County legislators, who in late March voted down a similar anti-loitering bill. Almost immediately after the defeat, calm-headed proposals surfaced for setting up designated hiring sites while addressing residents' quality-of-life objections.

Yet recent federal immigration raids in East Hampton, N.Y., including one on a household of American citizens of Ecuadorean descent, are evidence of unresolved tensions on Long Island. In Morristown and Danbury, where residents are deeply divided about whether local police officers should be enforcing federal immigration rules, protests have erupted.

A much better approach would be for municipalities to follow New Haven's lead. This summer, the city expects to become the first place in the nation to allow undocumented immigrants to apply for municipal identification cards identifying them as city residents. The cards, equipped with a debit chip, will be useful for all residents by facilitating access to municipal services like the public beach, the library, the dump and parking.

New Haven is also providing financial literacy and tax filing help to immigrants. It expects the ID's to reduce crime by widening access to bank accounts so that residents do not have to hide money in mattresses or carry it on them, making them easy targets for muggers.

Furthermore, officials hope that their "don't ask, don't tell" policy, which prevents the police from inquiring about immigration status, will encourage undocumented residents to feel more comfortable reporting crimes and coming forward with information. What's more, it will allow law enforcement to focus scarce resources on fighting violent crime, a task that police officers widely prefer to chasing illegal immigrants.

New Haven and the dozens of other so-called sanctuary cities—which include Newark, New York and Trenton—base their approach on the theory that bringing undocumented residents out of the shadows benefits everyone.

Morristown and Danbury could learn from New Haven's sensible approach. Identifying residents, encouraging them to trust the police and providing access to needed services makes sense.

New Haven understands that citizens themselves benefit when all residents feel they have a stake and are not pariahs. A place is far better off when people want to come to it than if they are fleeing in fear, and when practical solutions take precedence over mean-spirited non-solutions.

11. Philadelphia's Open-Door Immigrant Policy

Tod Newcombe

Philadelphia Mayor Michael Nutter's administration has taken an unabashed pro-immigrant stance, welcoming all with no questions asked. It may sound a bit extreme, but the move by the City of Brotherly Love reflects an open-arms approach to immigrants in urban areas—and there's a reason for this open-door policy. Immigrants have been good for cities throughout history, and that symbiotic relationship continues today.

In Philadelphia, the immigrant story has become a prominent feature of life: Foreign-born residents make up 9 percent of the population in the metro region, which has the fastest-growing immigrant base among its peers, according to a 2008 Brookings Institution report.

Despite the fact that four in 10 immigrants now move directly to the suburbs when they arrive in America, they remain a key source of economic development for inner cities. In 2005, Harvard Business School professor Michael Porter wrote a report showing that 5.5 million immigrants had been a catalyst for development and investment in inner cities, spurring job growth in 10 inner cities that outpaced job growth in their broader metropolitan areas. Other studies have come to the same conclusion: Cities with thriving immigrant populations tend to prosper the most.

In Dearborn, Mich., Arab immigrants have become a lifeboat for the local economy. Overall, the Arab-American community is now 200,000 strong in southeastern Michigan and produces $7.7 billion annually in salaries and earnings, according to a 2007 Wayne State University study.

Originally published as Tod Newcombe, "Philadelphia's Open-Door Immigrant Policy," *Governing*, January 2011. Reprinted with permission of the publisher.

As the influx of Arab-Americans expands and their impact on the region's economy continues to grow, downtrodden Detroit is looking to entice them into its inner core, the one area where Arabs haven't set down roots.

One way Detroit hopes to make that happen is by setting up an economic development center that specializes in recruiting immigrant investors. Known in government circles as an EB-5 investment visa regional center, it allows immigrants who are willing to invest at least $500,000 in cities with high unemployment, permanent resident status in return. Detroit will join 80 other cities in setting up such a program.

In November, the National League of Cities released a report on how 20 cities have integrated immigrants into city life. Recognizing the policy vacuum at the national level, the report, *Municipal Innovations in Immigrant Integration*, provides examples of ways municipalities have figured out how to move immigrants into the mainstream. Some examples come from the nation's largest cities, but others—such as Littleton, Colo.—have used a simple but effective grassroots approach that involves volunteers who help steer immigrants onto a path of self-reliance and citizenship.

Meanwhile, back in Philadelphia, local leaders are doing what they can to make the city an immigrant hub. Some of their ideas have been controversial, such as pushing city services and jobs into immigrant neighborhoods. But as Israel Colon, the city's director of multicultural affairs, explained to *Governing* in a July 2010 interview, immigrants aren't going away. So rather than try to drive them out, as some cities have, Nutter's administration wants to rely on them, no matter their resident status, to help the city grow and prosper.

12. Make San Francisco a Sanctuary for Illegal Immigrants

Peter Fimrite

Mayor Gavin Newsom vowed Sunday to maintain San Francisco as a sanctuary for immigrants and do everything he can to discourage federal authorities from conducting immigration raids.

The mayor cannot stop federal authorities from making arrests, Newsom told about 300 mostly Latino members of St. Peter's Church and other religious groups supporting immigrants. But no San Francisco employee will help with immigration enforcement.

"I will not allow any of my department heads or anyone associated with this city to cooperate in any way shape or form with these raids," Newsom declared. "We are a sanctuary city, make no mistake about it."

The Board of Supervisors first declared San Francisco a "sanctuary city" in 1989. The designation, which many U.S. cities across the country took on during the 1980s, has no legal meaning.

U.S. Immigration and Customs Enforcement officials have since May 2006 conducted raids across the country, including arrests in San Rafael, Oakland, Richmond, San Pablo, Santa Clara and other cities across the Bay area. Immigration officials have said they were executing arrest warrants for immigrants who had committed crimes or were in the country illegally and had ignored final deportation orders.

Originally published as Peter Fimrite, "Newsom Pledges to Make SF a Sanctuary for Illegal Immigrants," *San Francisco Chronicle*, April 22, 2007. Reprinted with permission of the publisher.

Related Stories

In the course of serving deportation warrants, the officials said, other people whom officers suspected of being illegal immigrants were questioned and then arrested. Of at least 65 Marin County residents arrested in March, for example, just five had been ordered deported.

The raids, many of which conducted at private homes before dawn and some of which caught up legal immigrants and even citizens, have created an uproar in the Bay Area. Politicians and community leaders have demanded they end, saying some immigrants parents are now afraid to send their children to school or leave home.

Immigration agents on Friday arrested 13 foreign nationals who were working illegally at Eagle Bag Corp. in Oakland, a packaging manufacturer whose clients include the U.S. military. The arrests there of immigrants suspected of using counterfeit documents to obtain jobs were not related to the recent raids.

San Rafael Mayor Al Boro in March called on California's U.S. senators, Democrats Barbara Boxer and Dianne Feinstein, to push the immigration agency to change how it is enforcing immigration law because he believed children were the ones being hurt.

Marches and rallies are planned in coming weeks in Redwood City, San Francisco, Oakland, San Jose, Sacramento and other cities.

Porfirio Quintano was one of those who pleaded with Newsom, Senator Carole Migden and Assemblyman Mark Leno during Sunday's meeting to do what they can to make San Francisco safe for immigrants.

The 42-year-old immigrant from Honduras said his Richmond home was raided in 2003 by federal immigration agents based on what turned out to be bad information.

"We are victims," said Quintano, adding that his wife and two daughters, then ages 4 and 10, live in fear of another raid, even though they are in the country legally. "They were looking for somebody unrelated to us, but they lined us up against the wall and held us for an hour. It was terrifying, especially for our daughters."

Newsom, Migden and Leno all vowed to work with other cities and legislators to put a stop to what they said was blatant intimidation of immigrants.

"Our action is to stand strong in opposition to these raids ... to make sure that we are not contributing in any way, shape or form," Newsom said. "Even legal immigrants are fearful. This just sends a chill to a lot of people. There are a lot of cities that want these raids. That's where the federal government should be spending their time."

13. Looking the Other Way on Immigrants

Anthony Faiola

HIGHTSTOWN, N.J.—After federal agents launched a massive raid on an apartment complex here two years ago, other illegal immigrants in this quiet town near Princeton University grew so wary of the law, authorities say, that many began hiding behind headstones in a local cemetery when patrol cars approached.

But these days, the immigrants of Hightstown are more likely to be the ones calling the cops.

In the aftermath of a series of raids in 2004, the town council in this historic borough of 5,300—transformed in recent years by an influx of at least 1,300 Latin Americans—unanimously approved a sort of immigrant bill of rights. Joining a growing list of cities enacting a no-questions-asked policy on immigration status, Hightstown now allows its undocumented residents to officially interact with local police and access city services without fear of being reported to federal authorities.

It has opened new lines of communication here, officials say. One illegal immigrant at the complex where the raids were staged called on the police recently to help place a family member in alcohol rehabilitation; others have reported domestic abuse, extortion, theft and other crimes. Some are calling the town's pro-immigrant mayor for advice on City Hall weddings and landlord troubles. Hightstown has added services aimed at immigrants, including free bilingual computer classes last month. Noting the shift, one Spanish-language newspaper recently dubbed Hightstown the "Paradise Town" of New Jersey.

"People are talking about how the police here can be trusted, so I called them right after I was mugged," said Julio, 33, a Guatemalan illegal immigrant who was assaulted in Hightstown last year. He said he was robbed several times in Texas before moving to New Jersey three years ago, but was too fearful to call law enforcement there. Here, "they came out to meet me, made a report and gave me a ride home. They haven't caught the guys who did it, but at least I didn't feel like I was the one who committed a crime."

As Congress once again prepares to consider immigration bills, the debate is already playing on the nation's Main Streets, with liberal enclaves extending protections to illegal immigrants as conservative locales seek to push them out.

The country is deeply divided on immigration, with 29 percent of respondents in a December Washington Post-ABC News Poll calling immigrants "good" for their communities and an equal number describing them as "bad." About 39 percent said they make no difference.

With federal authorities enlisting local law enforcement agencies to act as their "eyes and ears" on the ground, a number of towns have responded with highly publicized zero-tolerance policies on illegal immigrants. In Hazelton, Pa., the Illegal Immigration Relief Act—passed last year but being challenged in federal court—denies licenses to businesses that employ illegal immigrants, fines landlords $1,000 for each illegal immigrant discovered renting their properties and requires that city documents be in English only. Other towns have deputized police officers to act as local immigration cops.

But equally fervent are a less well-known but fast-growing number of "sanctuary" cities and towns—from Seattle to Cambridge, Mass.—where local authorities are effectively rejecting the federal government's call for tougher enforcement and instead bestowing a measure of local acceptance.

In New Haven, Conn., for example, officials have prohibited police from asking about an immigrant's legal status, and in July the city will introduce municipal identification cards, providing undocumented immigrants with a "locally legal" form of ID that will make it easier for them to apply for bank accounts and sign rental leases. Overall, at least 20 cities and towns have approved pro-immigration measures over the past three years, according to the D.C.–based Fair Immigration Reform Movement. Analysts and advocates say almost as many—including at least five in New Jersey, where about one in 17 residents is an illegal immigrant—are considering similar resolutions.

"What we're seeing is a surge in immigration policy at the local level," said Michael Wishnie, a Yale University law professor who has worked with New York City on pro-immigration measures. "What they have in common is that mayors are basically saying, 'Look, this is a major issue for us, and if Congress can't fix it, we will.' "

Initially coined by immigrant groups in the 1980s, when a number of cities approved local laws granting a haven to the victims of civil wars in Central and South America, the term "sanctuary city" has been adopted in recent years by opponents of pro-immigrant ordinances. They argue that the new crop of towns approving such measures is effectively sanctioning illegal immigration.

"You have cities facilitating the violation of federal law and tying the hands of their police forces in terms of when they can or can't ask about legal status," said Steven A. Camarota, research director for the Center for Immigration Studies. "You're also talking about a group of people who often work off-the-books but are getting access to expensive city services. It's not fair to everyone else paying the bill."

Hightstown Mayor Robert Patten, who hails from the core German-Irish stock in this heavily Democratic town, sees things differently. The town square, once peppered with empty storefronts, is brimming with new Latin American restaurants and remittance centers. Last year, the town closed the streets for an Ecuadorian festival that brought together hundreds of residents.

"Most of us know this town would have a heck of a time trying to run itself these days without the immigrants," said Patten, a Republican. "They're working at the grocery stores, the fast-food places, they're opening businesses and keeping this town alive and young. We're just being practical by telling them, 'Look, we want you in our community, and we want you to feel like you belong.'"

Patten and his wife, Kathy, have taken Spanish classes and given their personal phone numbers to immigrants. The mayor helped secure the release of one Hightstown immigrant seized by immigration authorities in 2005 in a case of mistaken identity.

At a city-sponsored health fair at Hightstown High School last month, dozens of immigrants showed up for free medical checks by a local doctor, while a local police officer roamed the halls to engage residents. "¿Como esta?" Patten repeated in American-accented Spanish as he went through the crowd, receiving pats on the back, hugs and kisses.

"I feel I can get help in this town," said Sonia, a 34-year-old from Ecuador who, like all illegal immigrants interviewed here, declined to give a last name. After getting an HIV test, she was in line to take her infant son for a doctor's visit. "These are things I could never afford. I don't have health insurance, and I'm afraid to go to the county hospital. I don't know what kind of paperwork they ask for. I feel more comfortable here. No forms. No questions. You just have to come in."

As police have promised to refrain from asking about immigrants' legal status, authorities say communication between undocumented residents and local law enforcement officials has markedly improved. Although police here concede that they must cooperate with federal agents possessing outstanding warrants for illegal immigrants, they say they will arrest immigrants or report their undocumented status only if they are caught committing a criminal offense.

Maria, 23, who arrived in Hightstown from Ecuador two years ago, was persuaded by a bilingual volunteer police liaison to call police after $3,000 was stolen from her family's apartment last November. Most of the undocumented families here, whose status makes it difficult to open bank accounts, keep the money they earn—from jobs in a local packaging factory—at home, living in constant fear of robbery.

"We are so vulnerable because of our status that the idea of calling the police is still a little frightening," Maria said. "But we realize now that if we don't, there's no chance of justice. And if we do, they are going to at least try to help us—not arrest us for being victims."

14. How Language Fits
Into the Immigration Issue
Ryan Holeywell

When Palermo Galindo immigrated to the United States as a 15-year-old, he knew almost no English. What he did know were the challenges that came with being a stranger to his new community, country and language. Thirty years later, Galindo is helping others overcome those struggles by serving the city government of Fort Wayne, Ind., as liaison to the Hispanic and immigrant communities. Among his tasks are promoting health services and English language classes that are available to immigrants. "I'm the result of a lot of people investing in [me]," Galindo says. In his new role, he's helping the city make a similar investment.

Not long ago, there was no need for a job like Galindo's. But that was before Fort Wayne and its environs experienced dramatic changes. From 2000 to 2010, the Hispanic population of Allen County—of which Fort Wayne is the seat—grew nearly 10 times as fast as the population at large, according to the Census. That echoes a similar demographic shift occurring nationwide for all immigration groups. From 2000 to 2010, the number of people living in the U.S. who speak English "less than very well" increased by 3.9 million.

While immigration is a federal issue, integrating immigrants and bringing them into the fold of American civic life is a local challenge. It's no longer confined to places like California, New York or Texas—places that have a long history of absorbing diverse populations. In 21 states, the limited-English population grew by more than 25 percent over the last

Originally published as Ryan Holeywell, "How Language Fits Into the Immigration Issue," *Governing*, January 2012. Reprinted with permission of the publisher.

decade, and during that same time period "61 counties crossed the threshold of having a population of more than 5 percent limited-English speakers," according to the Census.

In some of those places, the influx of newcomers has caused controversy, with one of the flash points being language. For immigrants, learning English can give them the keys to the kingdom, opening the doors to educational and economic opportunity. Nonspeakers of the country's common language can find themselves isolated in their new communities—and resented by their neighbors. Some localities are actively working to help newcomers learn the language while temporarily providing them with services in their native tongue. But others take a different outlook, as evidenced by the proliferation of "English-only" policies approved by localities in an effort to save money and drive away a population viewed as burdensome.

"Now, almost every city in the country faces demographic changes in their communities," says Ricardo Gambetta of the National League of Cities. "It's important for local officials to have the political will to make a change in their communities."

One of the places that have adjusted to change is Marion County, Ind., which includes Indianapolis. The number of limited-English speakers was a scant 3.4 percent of the population in 2000. Ten years later, that population has more than doubled even as the county overall grew by only 5 percent. "It's a population that can't be ignored," says Carlos May, who serves as Indianapolis' director of Latino Affairs. As he points out, newcomers who don't speak English are going to be working in the area, driving cars and sending their children to school. "If they're going to do that, we want them to feel included," May says. "It's going to affect us economically."

Many of May's efforts focus on making the city more accessible to residents who only speak Spanish. He hosts a public access television program called Somos Indianapolis—"We are Indianapolis"—designed to inform non–English speakers about civic issues. He started the annual Indiana Latino Expo, which is now run by a nonprofit, that offers business seminars, education fairs and health information to immigrants.

May says it's in the local economy's best interest for immigrants to feel engaged and at home in the city. That way, they'll spend money in Indianapolis, rather than send it home to their native countries. If an immigrant can get an education and earn a higher salary, he argues, that brings a benefit to the area as a whole. "We want them to reinvest here, pay sales tax and add to the tax base."

To integrate immigrant populations into the community, a growing number of cities and counties are setting up cabinet-level offices and councils that recommend ways a city can better serve its people. A major tool in that endeavor is the recognition of language obstacles. Azadeh Khalili, former deputy commissioner of New York City's Office of Immigrant Affairs (OIA), says that the OIA deals with many issues, but "language access is the key." Typically, immigrants can learn English in three to four years if they attend classes regularly. But during that learning period, governments need to find ways to communicate with them. Without language access, Khalili says, "most immigrants feel the services of the government aren't accessible to them."

An executive order from 2000 requires the federal government and governments that are recipients of federal aid—including virtually every locality—to provide services to people who speak limited English. But communities have latitude in how to implement those rules, and the extent to which they want to provide services beyond the minimums required by law. One technique being used in some cities is to track which aspects of government have the most contact with non–English speakers and prioritize how they can improve, says Margie McHugh, co-director of the Migration Policy Institute's (MPI) National Center on Immigrant Integration Policy.

Many local governments also sign contracts with translators to work onsite or by phone. A popular option is Language Line Services, a company many governments pay in order to gain telephone access to translators. The company can provide translators for 170 languages. Experts say translation services are crucial and prevent inappropriate situations, like having a police officer rely on an accused abuser to translate on behalf of his victim or having a Spanish-speaking parent take her child out of school to help with translation.

Those services are typically used by front-line workers who have the most interaction with the public, including police, staffers who work at the desks where residents pay utility bills, and clerks working at departments that provide residents with documents and records. A growing number of communities are also requiring those types of positions to be filled by bilingual employees, greatly eliminating the need for translators.

Others are finding creative ways to bridge that language gap. In the Minneapolis suburbs of Brooklyn Center and Brooklyn Park, the police departments are recruiting young people from non–English speaking communities into a cadet program, in which the department pays for a portion of the students' schooling while they work part time. They also move to the front of the line for job openings. In Winston-Salem, N.C., all fire trucks are stacked with cards that allow fire and EMS crews to ask simple questions of Spanish-speaking residents during emergencies. (The words on the cards are written phonetically to help with pronunciation: "koo-on-dough romp-e-oh el aug-wah," or, "when did your water break?")

The perceived expense of translation can create issues. Three years ago in Nashville, Tenn., anti-immigration groups were able to force an ultimately unsuccessful ballot measure that would have made English the metro government's official language. During their campaign, the group's supporters said it was necessary to help the city save money since some $100,000 a year was being spent on translation. To Mayor Karl Dean's relief, the measure was defeated. The cost of translation, he says, "is not the biggest economic issue facing the city by any means."

Nor is it a big economic hit in Loudoun County, Va. There, the population of limited-English speakers more than tripled to an estimated 27,124 over the past decade. But phone interpretation, in-person interpreters and other translation services cost the county only $54,000 in fiscal 2011.

Proponents of language access say that's money well spent. There would be, they say, inevitable inefficiencies if government officials insisted on interacting solely in English, regardless of their constituents' language. But it is worth noting that despite the federal mandate from 2000, there are no dedicated federal grants for localities to provide language services, nor is there a federal office charged with coordinating issues like immigrant integration or language access. Some think that should change. "The federal government's responsibility isn't just the conditions and terms of people coming into this country," says Michael Fix, senior vice president and director of studies at MPI. "It's also determining their success."

Some cities have taken the lead on educating adult non–English speakers. That role has traditionally been reserved for the school system. But English as a Second Language (ESL) programs for adults have historically had poor results. Many immigrants don't have the sort of stable schedule that can allow them to attend classes—usually the result of working multiple jobs. In Littleton, Colo., the city runs a program from its library that pairs adult students with volunteers who work one-on-one with immigrants on English classes and preparation for citizenship exams. Alejandra Harguth, who leads the program, says those efforts have become enormously popular in a city where an estimated 5 percent of the population has trouble with English. "Immigrants started coming out of the woodwork," Harguth says. "They weren't hiding, but then we had this resource."

At the same time, many communities are actively working to create obstacles for immigrants. One of the primary tools: English-only laws that make a locality's "official" language English and prohibit the translation of some official documents and services. In many cases, those laws are a response to the perceived ills caused by the growing population of undocumented immigrants. But those laws may be putting legal residents in the crossfire too. An Urban Institute study found that 60 percent of legal immigrants who are eligible for citizenship had limited-English proficiency.

In the first decade of this century, more than 100 towns, cities and counties approved policies that are hostile to immigrants, according to a study cited by MPI's Fix. Among the most popular anti-immigrant policies were language laws, which were considered by about 61 localities and approved by a third of them. Localities have also enacted policies designed to crack down on day laborers, penalize landlords for renting to illegal immigrants and force employers to use a federal database to verify workers' legal status.

In many cases, local leaders cite the expense of providing services to illegal immigrants as the reason behind those policies. A 2007 study by the Congressional Budget Office notes that illegal immigrants generally aren't eligible for federal aid programs such as food stamps, Social Security, Temporary Assistance for Needy Families or Medicaid (except for emergencies). But some state and local services—mainly law enforcement, health care and education—must be provided, regardless of an individual's immigration status, according to federal law. The report goes on to note that most of the time, the costs of those programs that can be attributed to illegal immigrants amount to less than 5 percent of those programs' total expenditures. Some local leaders see that as a significant figure.

In Frederick County, Md., about an hour outside of Washington, elected leaders are pursuing efforts to ratchet up policies designed to drive illegal immigrants from the community, including an English-only law. "If we're not mandated by the state or federal government to produce a document in any other language, we're not going to do so," says Blaine Young, president of the county commission.

The county's new approach comes at a time when more residents are likely to need language assistance. According to Census estimates, Frederick County's limited-English population nearly tripled over the last decade to more than 8,500 residents.

Based on a survey that the school system conducted at Young's request, he estimates that 5 percent of Frederick County students are the children of illegal immigrants. He doesn't believe authorized residents should have to subsidize the cost of education for illegal immigrants' children. Young says he is trying to preserve quality of life in Frederick, which has suffered largely due to the abundance of poor neighborhoods that are home to illegal immigrants. "Frederick County gets labeled by some as the most unfriendly county in the state of Maryland when it comes to illegal aliens," Young says. "We don't run from that. We wear it as a badge of honor."

Francisco Lopez, who leads a coalition of immigrant-rights advocacy groups in Oregon, says it's not surprising that the increasing visibility of immigrants is creating tensions. "Suddenly the good old small town looks different than it used to," Lopez says. "It's a big change, not just in Oregon, but around the country."

While some cities have embraced the change, more work remains. "There are some municipalities that are doing the right thing," Lopez says, "but there are some that are still struggling. They're not up to the challenge yet, especially in the rural areas." In those cases, Lopez would like to see localities partner with local nonprofits to help with language and integration issues.

The demographic shifts are forcing communities to look at more than just language policies as they try to integrate their new residents. There may be laws and procedures that unintentionally discriminate against some immigrants. In New York, Khalili says, her office worked to overturn a policy that required street vendors to have proof of their permanent resident status (no requirement existed for restaurant owners). In Boulder, Colo., the city tweaked a rule that was intended to prevent overcrowding of college students in group homes but was instead causing stress for immigrant families. "[Localities] need to pull people together across agencies," says McHugh of MPI's Center on Immigrant Integration Policy. "Having a coordinated approach is really a significant factor for being successful."

Many communities are hosting civics classes for immigrants to educate them on everything from how elections work to how to register a business. In Louisville, the city's Office of Globalization coordinates with various agencies on giving non–English speakers access to housing, medical services and jobs. "People who speak broken English—usually people won't give them the time of day," says Suhas Kulkarni, who leads the office. "If they have somebody to work as a go-between for interviews ... it's extremely helpful."

As the language barrier falls, newcomers become integrated into a community, New York's Khalili and Indianapolis' May argue. Communities that have embraced their non–English speaking newcomers are finding that, in the long run, these immigrants become taxpaying contributors to their new home.

15. Wanted: Language and Cultural Competence

Elizabeth Kellar

What second language do 23 percent of the public school children speak in Beverly Hills, California? If you answered, "Farsi," you would get this question right on a future quiz show!

Increasingly, city and county governments are making a quiet investment to gain a better understanding of the cultural differences among their residents. The city of Beverly Hills found that the Persian population who had settled in the community had a low trust in government, a limited tradition of voting, and seldom participated in public hearings. Many of these new residents also feared assimilation. It was common for multiple generations to live under one roof; traditions for women were different from American ways. Unfortunately, domestic violence was an issue, too.

When a Persian American was elected to the city council for the first time in Beverly Hills' history, he spearheaded outreach efforts to this community of recent immigrants. The city's Human Relations Commission began a cultural awareness effort that included showing pictures of the communities and the housing that they had left behind.

Some city staff could speak Farsi and interpret; others familiarized themselves with the customs of this population. Instead of waiting for their Farsi-speaking residents to come to a city council meeting, city staff members went to the synagogues where many of the immigrants worship. There, it was possible to hold conversations, share important information, and establish relationships.

Reprinted with permission from the January/February 2005 issue of *Public Management (PM) Magazine*, published and copyrighted by ICMA (International City/County Management Association), Washington, D.C.

We can position our communities to be more globally competitive and prepared by encouraging our employees to develop language skills and by supporting language educational programs for children and adults. Did you know that 2005 is the Year of Foreign Languages?

Think and Speak Globally

Local governments have learned to think globally in a world that brings international opportunities and challenges to their doorsteps. They know that successful economic development strategies require more sophistication than ever to attract and retain businesses that have global markets. Likewise, homeland security issues often involve cross-border cooperation, including mutual aid agreements and intelligence sharing.

As Dr. David S.C. Chu, U.S. Undersecretary of Defense, said in his opening remarks at the first National Language Conference in June 2004, we need a "permanent change in our approach to the peoples and cultures of the rest of the world ... our need to understand the world is a prime national security concern.

"National security concerns have taken us from the streets of Manhattan to the mountains of Afghanistan and to the resort cities of Bali. Our economy has brought workers here to America and sent jobs to 100 countries around the world. Our health is affected by conditions and events in China, Britain, Africa, and South America. Criminal cartels and corrupt officials hundreds of miles beyond our borders have an immediate impact on our streets, in our schools, and our homes. Within one generation, we have become integrated into the world as never before."

Security and Safety Issues

While all local governments have security issues, border communities have special challenges. Consider Laredo, Texas, the largest land port in the United States for people and goods arriving from Central and South America. Every day, 10,000 trucks bring parts and supplies across the border for GM, Ford, and Chrysler, and 30,000 people cross its four bridges, a process that takes one and one-half hours on a normal day and two hours when Code Orange is in effect.

When the temperature reaches 105 degrees outdoors, government officials don't just worry about security-they also worry about the health of the people waiting in line, especially if they lack sufficient water.

Laredo is a booming city, having doubled its population in the past 10 years, from 100,000 to more than 200,000. Old Laredo, its sister city across the border in Mexico, has a population of 600,000. Laredo Fire Chief Luis Sosa is well aware of the strategic importance of his gateway city and also of how reliant he is on his colleagues across the border.

If he has a serious emergency, the closest support from any U.S. locality, state government, or federal government agency is 150 miles away. Laredo knows it cannot wait for the U.S. Cavalry to arrive, so it has built relationships with Old Laredo across the border. Laredo sees its bilingual staff as a critical asset.

The mutual aid agreement between Laredo and Old Laredo includes an understanding of hazardous-materials responses and SWAT tactics. Chief Sosa notes that, with three or four bomb threats each month, the two border cities have learned to work together seamlessly.

He explains that Laredo has translated all of its fire academy requirements into "street Spanish," which is geared to the education levels of the first responders, many of whom do not have a high school education. The translations have been done by Laredo staff, none of whom received extra compensation for this work.

Because Laredo has a staff who enjoy sharing knowledge and user-friendly Spanish-language materials, staff members have trained their counterparts in other parts of Mexico, Venezuela, Peru, Colombia, Nicaragua, and Panama. Their expenses have often been paid by the host country, although they also have sought grants from the donor community. Because 90 percent of Laredo's population is Hispanic, many of them third-generation immigrants, the city has a Spanish-English Web site (www.cityoflaredo.com).

Multicultural Reality Can Challenge Small Communities

Manchester, New Hampshire, is home to 8 percent of the state's immigrants and 80 percent of the children enrolled in English-as-a-second-language classes. You will find a significant population of Russian immigrants in West Hollywood, California, and Afghanis have settled in Fremont, California. But when some 1,200 Somalis arrived in Lewiston, Maine, over an 18-month period, the city was at first overwhelmed.

A community of 36,000, Lewiston made national news when then-

Mayor Laurier Raymond, Jr., wrote an open letter asking local Somali residents to "communicate with out-of-state Somalis and discourage them from considering Lewiston as a destination" (Nadeau 2003). As Assistant City Administrator Phil Nadeau recounts in a study of the rapid immigration into Lewiston, citizen concerns about the costs of settling the new immigrants prompted the mayor to write the letter. The new immigrants had limited English-speaking skills and had different cultural, social, and religious practices from others in the community. There had been only 700 minority residents in Lewiston in 1990.

Although the mayor's letter sought only to slow down the relocation effort so the city could catch up with the needs of new residents, it sparked an international controversy. Amid the unwelcome attention came a decision by a white supremacist group to hold a public meeting in Lewiston. Nadeau notes that "what was largely a local matter evolved into a national policy debate on general immigration and refugee resettlement" (Nadeau 2003).

Lewiston got a crash course in becoming a global community and had to take it under the glare of national and international media. In the beginning, it found help from the nearby city of Portland, which also has a significant Somali immigrant population; the state of Maine was not equipped to offer assistance.

Lewiston city officials quickly focused on improvements in social service programs, housing, employment training, language education, and health services. They hired a Somali staff member to help interpret and manage social services cases. The Portland Department of Health and Human Services and Catholic Charities Maine also offered critical expertise and free training to Lewiston staff.

Finally, Nadeau and Sue Charron, director of social services, decided to produce a Limited English Proficiency (LEP) manual "to instruct city employees on how to work with linguistically challenged people and how to use the AT&T Language Service when local interpreters were not available" (Nadeau 2003).

In time, the cities of Lewiston and Portland teamed together to form the Portland-Lewiston Refugee Collaborative and were successful in securing grant funds from the U.S. Department of Health and Human Services' Office of Refugee Resettlement (DHHS/ ORR) with which to manage some 900 immigrant cases in 18 months. The cities in the collaborative quickly overcame many administrative, budgetary, policy, and political barriers to work together effectively.

Lewiston also invited the U.S. Department of Justice to assist the community in October 2002, a move that resulted in aggressive monitoring of nondiscrimination policies and compliance training. When Nadeau describes the training and programs as legitimate and necessary costs, he notes that compliance costs are usually budgeted incrementally. This was not an option in Lewiston because of the unusual circumstances.

There have been numerous positive developments since Lewiston has had more time to absorb and assist its new immigrant population. Nadeau describes a more international feel and flavor to downtown Lewiston, with the addition of a Somali mosque, two Halaal general stores, and a new Somali restaurant.

The state government has become more focused on immigrant and refugee issues, and the cities of Lewiston and Portland have continued to work together on support programs such as an employment network. The Lewiston city government now is better prepared to help individuals who are hearing- or speech-impaired or who do not speak English. Although city staff still do not have the language skills, Nadeau says the cultural training has made them more effective.

Strengthening Cultural Competence

If you want to understand another culture, the best way to do so is to live and work in that culture. ICMA has organized city-to-city and county-to-county partnerships for a number of years, pairing a community from a developing country with one from the United States or another developed country. The professional staffs from the United States are reimbursed for travel and expenses from donor agencies, which allows American staff members to make multiple visits and to assist their partner communities over a period of one to three years.

Working with the United States Agency for International Development (USAID) and other international agencies, the partnerships allow local officials to address common problems, drawing on the resources of their U.S. counterparts to find solutions. Many of the partnerships focus on developing the economic potential of a city in a developing country in a way that protects and improves environmental conditions.

Once the official assignment has been completed the relationships may continue for years. Those who have participated in the partnerships say that the experiences helped them grow and gave them a new appreciation of the challenges that others face.

In an interview with Elizabeth Nelson, reporter for the Charlottesville, Virginia, *Daily Progress*, conducted on August 8, 2003, Pleven, Bulgaria, Mayor Nayden Zelenogorski said that "any country with as many applicants for citizenship as the United States must be doing something right." Charlottesville, Virginia, City Manager Gary O'Connell said that he gained a new perspective on local history and the role of a city council in representing its constituents when he thought about the issues from another country's point of view.

O'Connell added that visiting Pleven and seeing the disrepair in streets, sidewalks, and buildings also reminded him of the need to keep up with maintenance.

Recognizing the importance of cultural competence, ICMA is launching a new, Web-based international training program designed to introduce city and county managers to the requirements of international consulting work. The courses will be offered in a series, with an introductory course providing an overview of international work, followed by more in-depth courses for those who want to strengthen their ability to work overseas.

Lost Without Translations

Languages are the front door to another culture, and many local governments are recognizing this fact. The Salinas, California, Police Department is 50 percent bilingual; the rest of the officers take a "survival Spanish" course from an instructor in Santa Clara County. There is a skilled translator at every city council meeting.

Salinas City Manager David Mora took a Spanish immersion class in Costa Rica to improve his language skills. Like many Americans who have assimilated, his generation did not grow up with the notion that bilingual skills were important. Perhaps, this will change.

While the United States has not made progress in promoting multiple language skills in its educational programs, the demand for cultural competence and language skills is growing in government and industry. Since many U.S. communities have populations of immigrants who have retained their language skills, these immigrants, part of a heritage community, may be one pool that can help bridge the gap.

When ICMA was asked to recruit city officials to assist in reconstruction and democracy efforts in Iraq, Cameron Berkuti, an Iraqi-American public works director from Mesa, California, applied. He took a leave of absence and is still working in Kirkuk, where his bilingual skills have been invaluable.

In the meantime, as cities and counties look for ways to communicate with residents speaking 40 to 50 different languages, they use translation services, rely on employee volunteers, or recruit and train employees in needed languages.

In Leesburg, Virginia, one employee offered free language instruction to city staff during lunch. With the assistance of a software program, Oakland, California, is composing a computer-based dictionary with multiple language capability to reduce the amount of time required of translators to produce ballots and other legal documents in the required languages.

Hiring and developing talent is a critical strategy to meet community needs. As Sheryl Sculley, assistant city manager of Phoenix, Arizona, says, "All factors being equal, we will hire the person with competency in a second language." Phoenix also offers premium pay to employees who gain certification in a second language. To make it more convenient for employees to gain language skills, Phoenix contracts with a county agency for language training services in 25 languages.

A Critical Leadership Skill

Cultural competence is a critical leadership skill, and there are numerous ways in which the local government management profession can develop it. Gaining overseas experience and learning languages are clearly helpful. Communities can become more globally competitive and prepared by encouraging their employees to develop language skills and supporting language educational programs for children and adults. Did you know that 2005 is the Year of Foreign Languages? The momentum for change is building.

Ambassador W. Robert Pearson, director general of the U.S. Foreign Service and director of human resources for the U.S. Department of State, spoke of the challenges facing the Foreign Service at the National Language Conference. He used a Chinese aphorism, "Shou zhu dai tu," which means "Sit by the stump and wait for the rabbit," to remind the audience that we should not rely on luck to develop the workforce of the future.

"We need people with sound judgment and developed character so that they can do the right thing in an emergency overseas ... and among them we want people with very strong language skills."

He could have been talking about the next generation of city and county managers!

REFERENCES

Nadeau, Phil. (2003). "The Somalis of Lewiston: Community Impacts of Rapid Immigrant Movement into a Small, Homogeneous Maine City." University of Southern Maine Edmund S. Muskie School of Public Service Capstone Report (October 20, 2003).

16. Providing Language Access Services in a Global Economy

Anuj Gupta and *David Torres*

The nation's economic crisis is having a significant impact on demographic trends. Evidence suggests that the economy is slowing the national immigration growth rate and possibly causing reverse migrations to countries of origin. Nevertheless, historical data indicate that immigration trends are not affected in the long term by economic downturns, and prerecession demographic prognostications are likely to regain their relevancy as the economy recovers.

These predictions point toward the bulk of the U.S. population growth occurring through immigration during the next 40 years. A 2008 study by the Pew Research Center, for example, predicts that more than 80 percent of the country's population growth during the next half century will be due to immigration. The implication for local government managers and their communities is significant.

Local governments interested in staying in the forefront of changing demographics and meeting the needs of their diversifying constituents must figure out how to provide services to limited English proficient (LEP) individuals. A strong language access program can play a significant role in accelerating the integration of the newest Americans and, potentially, in encouraging population growth.

Building a high-caliber language access program has been a priority for the city of Philadelphia. During the past year, the city has taken steps to improve and expand language accessibility in an extremely difficult fiscal

Reprinted from the May 2010 issue of *Public Management (PM) Magazine*, published and copyrighted by ICMA (International City/County Management Association), Washington, D.C.

environment. This chapter describes improvements made in the language access program, results of these efforts, and steps that managers can consider in developing a similar program to deliver world-class local government services.

Establishing a Mandate

On August 11, 2000, President Bill Clinton signed Executive Order 13166, which required recipients of federal funds to provide meaningful service access to LEP individuals. Although the federal executive order established a solid legal baseline by requiring language accessibility, implementation was still the sole responsibility of state and local governments.

Philadelphia took its first step toward local implementation by executing its own mandate in 2001. Philadelphia's executive order required city agencies to determine the resources necessary to provide meaningful access to federally funded city services and to develop language access plans.

Before this, the city provided language access services, but sparingly. An executive order in 2003 from the mayor also drove the inception of "Global Philadelphia"—the city's formalized language access program. To assist in the implementation of those plans, the 2003 order was followed in 2007 by a specific directive issued by the city's managing director, detailing the content that each agency's language access plan should contain.

The 2007 directive serves as a step-by-step blueprint for city agencies in creating their plans. It details (1) the citywide approach toward creating language access plans, (2) departmental responsibilities necessary toward plan completion, and (3) specific items that must be included in each plan.

Recognizing the import of the issue and wanting to expand Philadelphia's commitment to language accessibility, Mayor Michael Nutter signed a second executive order in June 2008. This executive order reinforced the previous one by mandating all city departments, agencies, boards, and commissions to develop language access plans and to assess and improve any existing plans regardless of whether they receive federal funding or are overseen by the managing director.

This significantly expanded the purview of the program by extending the mandate to several independent city agencies, some of which provided few to no language services. Collectively, these measures have set a tone that language access matters and departments need to pay attention to it in delivering services.

Measuring Progress and Maintaining Accountability

Establishing an executive mandate is just the first step. The mandate is useless unless managers are actively held accountable and their progress measured. Philadelphia's experience was a case in point. Although the first mayoral executive order was signed in 2001, in 2008 when the Nutter administration took office, incoming officials learned that a number of departments had either never drafted language access plans in accord with the executive order or had shelved what had been drafted.

To address this issue, staff decided to make language accessibility a subject that would be reviewed with regularity (currently quarterly) through two mechanisms: quarterly meetings with language access point persons from all city departments and Mayor Nutter's version of the CitiStat program, which is called PhillyStat.

Language access staff organize quarterly meetings with departmental language access point people who are called global ambassadors. These meetings are used to tell departments of any changes in the access program, stay abreast of departmental needs, and provide departments with technical assistance when necessary. These meetings are internal and are open only to those invited by the access staff to ensure open discussions.

The second tool for improving accountability is PhillyStat. The PhillyStat staff and language access team regularly identify three or four departments that are either laggards or are establishing best practices toward implementing their responsibilities. The goal of these sessions is to track, in a data-driven format, what departments are doing to provide language access and also to encourage cross-departmental collaboration.

Using PhillyStat to measure language access progress also allows the public and stakeholders to hold the administration accountable, as all PhillyStat sessions are open to the public, televised, and streamed across the Internet.

There are benefits to using PhillyStat to track language access. First, department heads now understand that language access is a priority and that efforts must be made to comply with the executive order. As evidence, the Philadelphia Water Revenue Bureau, which mails thousands of monthly water bills to account holders, recently updated its standard bill format to include a tagline in eight languages instructing customers that assistance is available.

Second, many departments that ignored or struggled with implementation of their access requirements have made progress as a result of the focus on their efforts. The Department of Recreation, for example, attended the first PhillyStat language access session and reported that not only had the department not provided language accessibility at any of its facilities but had irretrievably lost its access plan.

In less than a year since that session, the department has drafted a new plan, equipped 29 recreation facilities with telephonic interpretation access, and trained facility managers on how to provide children with translation service.

Finally, including language access in the PhillyStat review process has allowed departments to learn from one another and share best practices. The police department has received wide acclaim for a certified interpreter training program it has been administering for several years. This program allows bilingual officers to attain an industry-accepted level of interpreter proficiency that expands the department's capacity to serve LEP customers in the field.

After attending a PhillyStat language access session, the fire department committed to replicating the police program. For the first time, the city has certified bilingual interpreters within the fire department's ranks and is on course to certify nearly 80 additional interpreters.

A PhillyStat-like program is by no means the only method to ensure accountability and measure progress of a language access program. The method chosen, however, should ultimately set up regular reporting to the city's chief executive, the chief administrator, or someone in a similar position. Without this executive-level oversight, language access can often be overlooked, particularly in difficult fiscal times.

Establish Community Partnerships

In many places, community-based organizations stand on the front line in providing services to immigrants. Whether because of a deep-rooted mistrust of government originating in their homelands or the inability to properly access government services, recent immigrants often turn to community organizations to fill the void. In Philadelphia, such organizations as Community Legal Services, the Hebrew Immigrant Aid Society, the Welcoming Center for New Pennsylvanians, and the Pennsylvania Immigrant and Citizenship Coalition provide critical services, including job placement, health-care services, and legal representation to immigrant and ethnic communities. They are able to provide these services successfully in part because they have developed strong, trusting relationships with the communities served. Accordingly, leveraging these organizations, their knowledge of the immigrant communities, and their established relationships is an important ingredient toward building a successful access program.

These partnerships can take many forms. At a basic level, the local government should engage in ongoing dialogue with the relevant local organizations to better understand language access needs throughout the community. In Philadelphia, we began by inviting partner organizations to attend and observe our PhillyStat language access sessions. This allowed organizations to better understand the city's deficiencies, strengths, and overall direction. It has also allowed the same groups to consistently provide constructive feedback and simultaneously act as champions of the change where improvements were made.

We also have invited the same organizations to attend the quarterly language access meetings held with department language access point persons. This provides another mechanism for sharing information with the community organizations, and it allows the organizations to stay abreast of initiatives in development.

In addition to maintaining an ongoing dialogue, language access managers should use the community organizations as focus groups to test new ideas. Philadelphia staff members have relied on partner groups to review the language of translated documents, provide feedback on cultural competency curricula, and determine the efficacy of such new initiatives as the city's language access cards.

The relationship cannot be a one-way street. In addition to ensuring that LEP customers can access services, a locality can also take steps to expand the capacity of community organizations to provide services. In Philadelphia, we used the purchasing power of government to negotiate new language access contracts that required selected vendors to provide city rates to any nonprofit organization headquartered in Philadelphia.

In some cases, this has reduced service fees for nonprofits by up to 75 percent. Not only has this initiative strengthened the relationship between the city and nonprofit organizations, but it has also expanded language accessibility throughout the city. Nonprofit directors have commented that they can provide their clients with appropriate language assistance without worrying about the additional cost.

Nearly every community will have organizations analogous to our partners. Managers should make overtures to these organizations and build relationships where they do not exist. The local government and LEP community will reap the benefits for years to come.

Make Language Access Visible

An access program works only if clients understand how to use it. The Philadelphia staff have made improving the visibility of program information a high priority. Increasing signage and placing it in areas of high foot traffic was one of the first steps taken. We started by placing telephonic access signs at all primary points of entry for the city's three central buildings, constituting the majority of city government office space (including city hall). Now, if an LEP customer enters any of the city's central office facilities, telephonic interpretation is available to help guide the customer to the desired destination or answer any other questions.

The city also created its first website (www.phila.gov/globalphiladelphia) for language access. It serves as a clearinghouse for basic information about the program, the interpretation and translation services provided, department language access plans, and contact information for the global ambassadors. The site includes contact information for nonprofit organizations serving immigrant and ethnic communities.

It also provides a welcome message from the mayor that is translated into five different languages and provides a translated tagline connecting LEP residents to the city's 311 nonemergency call center. In the future, the site will include a library of translated informational material that customers and providers can access from work or home.

Consistent with the goal of improving visibility, two best practices resources were developed: the Translation Station and the Language Access Card. The Translation Station is a desktop "point to your language" translation tool used during interactions with LEP customers and city staff. It provides basic written phrases to assist in identifying the purpose for the customer's visit and is translated into seven languages.

Translation Station was first developed by the Free Library of Philadelphia and has now been tailored to the department of licenses and inspections. It can be found at the department's counter service areas and has proven to be a great communication tool. In the future Translation Station will also be made available in other departments with counter service.

The Language Access Card is a multilingual customer service tool that a customer can present during an interaction at a city agency. It serves as a prompt and a reminder to staff of an individual's need for interpreter services and provides instruction on how to obtain interpreter services over the phone and at a city agency. These cards, commonly referred to as "I speak cards," are widely used in other communities and have been adapted to Philadelphia in five languages. Language access staff have leveraged their existing relationship with community organizations to distribute them. They are also made available at city facilities.

A new access resource called the Field Guide will be launched soon. Similar to Translation Station, this guide will be a pocket-sized "point to your language" translation tool to be used by staff during interactions with customers outside of city facilities. It will also provide basic written phrases to identify (1) an individual's spoken language, (2) who the city staff person is, (3) the purpose of the person's visit, and (4) several possible follow-up actions. The resource is currently being tailored specifically to the role of field inspectors.

These initiatives have helped increase usage rates of access services. Although much more work could be done if resources were infinite, these simple steps have expanded program awareness without requiring the dedication of additional resources.

17. Tips for Testing and Certifying Multilingual Employees

Jason Reed

An effective language access program consists of language services that are: (1) available and timely; (2) clearly and accurately provided by someone who has demonstrated proficiency in two or more languages; and (3) cost effective. In Washington State, the Department of Social and Health Services (DSHS) has determined that the best way to achieve timely, accurate, and cost-effective language services is through the use of multilingual employees.

What Are Some of the Benefits of Utilizing Multilingual Employees?

- Language services are more readily available compared to accessing services through contract. Issues associated with customer or contractor cancelations and no-shows can be avoided.
- Language services are provided directly to customers, reducing the potential for miscommunication.
- Language services can be much more cost effective, even when paying multilingual skill incentive pay to employees.

Originally published by the Migration Policy Institute, an independent, nonpartisan think tank dedicated to the study of movement of people worldwide.

Are Multilingual Employees the Right Choice for Your Organization?

Factors to consider when determining whether multilingual employees are right for your organization include:

- Language demographics: consider the non–English language demographics of your service delivery area and identify/track customers by primary language.
- Frequency of contact with limited English proficient (LEP) customers: how often are employees in direct contact with customers in your organization? Be sure to consider initial customer contact, including requests for information and walk-ins.
- How will multilingual employees be utilized: would multilingual employees in your organization provide services directly to customers or would they function as a third party interpreter and/or translator for other staff?
- What skills will be needed: would multilingual employees use written language skills, oral language skills, or both?
- Ability to hire full-time equivalent (FTE) staff: does your organization have the ability to hire new staff or reassign the responsibilities of or replace existing monolingual staff?
- Availability of qualified multilingual staff: do existing or potential employees have sufficient multilingual skills to perform their duties effectively in the necessary non–English language?

Once you have determined that multilingual employees are right for your organization, these same questions will help you determine the right framework for assessing an employee's multilingual skills.

How Should Your Organization Determine the Language Skills of Your Multilingual Employees?

There are both formal and informal approaches for assessing an employee's non–English language proficiency. Informally, when reviewing a person's resume, you may look at whether a candidate has education in a non–English language, experience working with LEP individuals, or any non–English language certification that s/he may possess. In an in-person interview, you may choose to conduct a portion of the interview in the non–English language.

What Standard Does Washington State DSHS Use to Test Its Current Employees and New Recruits with Multilingual Assignments?

Given our caseload and the types of services that we provide, in addition to a legal mandate, DSHS opted to develop our own formal testing program.

DSHS provides comprehensive language testing in Cambodian (Khmer), Chinese-Cantonese, Chinese-Mandarin, Korean, Lao, Russian, Spanish, and Vietnamese. Testing is available for seven different "position clusters" or job classification types. Most positions require testing of both written and oral language skills.

The written test is composed of five sections:

- A multiple-choice non–English language vocabulary test.
- A multiple-choice non–English language reading comprehension test.
- A non–English language written summarization exercise
- An English to non–English language translation exercise.
- A non–English to English language translation exercise.

The oral test is composed of a sight translation exercise and a consecutive interpretation exercise.

It is important to note that ensuring the quality of multilingual employees does not begin or end with a test. Training and continuing education before and after testing is also necessary to maintain a multilingual employee's language skills.

Who Is Required to Take the Test?

According to Washington State law, DSHS policies, and the consent decree between DSHS and Legal Services, all DSHS employees serving in a multilingual capacity are required to obtain certification status by successfully passing a bilingual fluency test. Bilingual duties are not assigned to staff without proper certification.

What Type of Pay Differential Do Multilingual Employees Receive?

There are a few options available for remunerating multilingual workers:

- Pay a flat monthly rate for all multilingual employees (e.g., $40/ month).
- Pay per multilingual encounter.
- Provide a salary increase.

In DSHS, we provide a salary increase equivalent to 5 percent of the employee's salary provided s/he has met eligibility and testing requirements. In Washington State, pay has been negotiated with labor unions and is not intended for additional workload. Instead, multilingual employees receive additional incentive or assignment pay because of their non–English language proficiency.

What Other Language Skills Testing Does DSHS Offer?

In addition to testing its multilingual employees, DSHS conducts language skills testing for the following candidates:

- Contracted interpreters providing oral interpretation services to DSHS social service programs.Comprehensive language and interpreter skills testing in Cambodian (Khmer), Chinese-Cantonese, Chinese-Mandarin, Korean, Lao, Russian, Spanish, and Vietnamese. Screening of language and interpreter skills in all other languages.
- Contracted translators providing written translation services to DSHS social service programs.Comprehensive translation skills testing in Cambodian (Khmer), Chinese, Korean, Lao, Russian, Spanish, and Vietnamese.
- Medical interpreters providing oral interpretation services to DSHS clients in medical settings.Comprehensive language and

interpreter skills testing in Cambodian (Khmer), Chinese-Cantonese, Chinese-Mandarin, Korean, Lao, Russian, Spanish, and Vietnamese. Screening of language and interpreter skills in all other languages.

- Licensed agency personnel whose agency is providing services to DSHS under contract. Comprehensivelanguage skills testing in Cambodian (Khmer), Chinese-Cantonese, Chinese-Mandarin, Korean, Lao, Russian, Spanish, and Vietnamese.

Related Documents

Department of Social and Health Services (DSHS), State of Washington (2006). *Bilingual Employee Test Information*. Washington State: DSHS.

Department of Social and Health Services (DSHS), State of Washington (2007). *Professional Language Certification Examination Manual*. Washington State: DSHS Language Testing and Certification.

Department of Social and Health Services (DSHS), State of Washington (2008). *Dual Language Assignment Pay*. Washington State: DSHS.

18. Welcome Mat

Rob Gurwitt

On a sunny fall afternoon, Rafael Ramos pulls up in front of a modest house in a working-class neighborhood of New Haven, Connecticut. He hops out and heads for the open door of a street-level apartment. A young man and woman standing outside with their two toddlers eye him warily, but when Ramos asks in Spanish if he can enter, they invite him in.

Ramos is deputy director of the city's housing code enforcement division, and he is not happy with what he sees in the tiny, two-room dwelling: The sole source of heat is a small, wall-mounted device that malfunctions easily and is a threat for carbon monoxide; a second exit at the back of the family's shared bedroom is boarded up. In deliberate Spanish, he explains the problems and begs the couple not to use the cheap heater. As the husband enlists a neighbor to help him knock through the back exit and create an opening for safety, Ramos pulls out his cell phone, calls the landlady and tells her about the violations he's found. He hangs up, shaking his head. "I'll give her 30 days to deal with the heating," he says, "because these people are not going to survive after October with that furnace."

Other than the possibility that Ramos will be forced to condemn the apartment in a few weeks, one small thing is striking about this encounter—how little tension there is. The couple are illegal immigrants from Ecuador, not the sort one would expect to welcome official notice. Yet, says Ramos, pretty much every renter he deals with in this immigrant-heavy section of the city, known as Fair Haven, treats him civilly. "I knock on the door, identify myself, ask if I can come in, and they're always, 'Sure, you want

Originally published as Rob Gurwitt, "Welcome Mat," *Governing*, November 30, 2008. Reprinted with permission of the publisher.

some coffee?' In other parts of the city, people are, 'What do you want? Go away!'"

Ramos' reception in Fair Haven, where a significant portion of the city's estimated 12,000 to 15,000 illegal immigrants live, is due in no small part to the fact that City Hall has gone out of its way to make friends there. At countless community meetings and door-to-door encounters over the past couple of years, police and city officials have told residents that their immigration status is a point of municipal indifference. In a 2006 "general order," the police department announced it would not ask about immigration status "unless investigating criminal activity," and even then wouldn't check the legal status of crime victims or witnesses—only suspects. It declared it would not make arrests based on warrants issued by U.S. Immigration and Customs Enforcement (ICE).

Nothing has signaled New Haven's unusual approach toward illegal immigrants more dramatically, though, than what it did last year: It began issuing what it calls the "Elm City ID Card" to anyone who can prove residence in the city, regardless of how they got there. There is no question that a significant portion of the 6,900 people who had taken advantage of the offer by this past October were in the country illegally. "If you whip out this card, there's no way of telling where you're from," says Kica Matos, New Haven's community services director, who helped create the program. "It just says that you live in New Haven."

Nothing related to immigration is simple these days. The failure of Congress to come to grips with the illegal immigrant problem has, as New Haven's mayor, John DeStefano, puts it, "dumped this issue as a practical matter into the laps of hometowns across America." Some have responded with a hard-headed approach, passing ordinances that call for fines or jail time for property owners who knowingly rent to illegal immigrants or employers who hire them. Around the country, 63 state and local police agencies have signed memoranda of agreement to have ICE train their officers in enforcing immigration laws, and more are on a waiting list to do so. At the same time, other communities have gone in the opposite direction, joining the sanctuary city movement that makes it a matter of policy not to check immigration status except in criminal cases.

New Haven, though, remains the only city in the country to take the sanctuary impulse further and offer an ID card and the symbolic acceptance that it confers. This step has won it the intrigued attention of other cities, from nearby Hartford to San Francisco and Richmond, California, that are grappling with how to shape their own responses to illegal immigrants. It also has earned New Haven the scorn of federal immigration officials and landed it square in the sights of anti-immigrant activists, who remain a persistent thorn in City Hall's side.

A small group of mostly white suburbanites, who call themselves the Community Watchdog Project, have harried Matos and DeStefano on the card in particular and the overall policy of welcoming illegal immigrants. "The people he claims he's helping, he's not helping at all," says Lou Gold, a private investigator who is the father of the group's founder, Dustin Gold. "He's helping the people who rent them apartments, or sell them cigarettes, or make them work 60 hours a week in the back of the kitchen."

Yet despite the CWP's doggedness, what may be most noticeable about the card a year and a half after its introduction is how muted it has become as a citywide issue. In recent hearings on whether to accept foundation funding for the second year of the program, members of the Board of Aldermen spent most of their time praising the card.

Still, it would be hard to call the program a raging success. Although nearly 6,000 adult cardholders is hardly an insignificant number, that's a minority of the illegal immigrants in New Haven. And while the card appears to have boosted immigrants' use of the public libraries and made them more comfortable about talking to the police, it has not helped many immigrants make use of the city's banks, which was a key goal.

To backers of the idea, though, the card's greatest effect may never be measurable: the extent to which it eases the burdens of daily life for immigrant residents and for city officials such as Rafael Ramos. "They see someone like Rafael Ramos as either someone who will help them or do nothing, but he won't hurt them," says Robert Solomon, a Yale University law professor who runs a legal clinic. "That's how we should feel about city employees. We have a percentage of our population that was afraid to do things, and now they're less afraid. They're more a part of the community than they were without the card."

Point of Entry

You get a sense of why this is important in New Haven when you realize that there are two basic sources of urban dynamism in the city these days. The first is on the fringes of downtown, where Yale has undertaken several prodigious—at least, for a city of 124,000—building projects. The other is Fair Haven.

Set off from the rest of the city on three sides by the Mill and Quin-nipiac rivers and on the fourth by train tracks and an interstate highway, Fair Haven has long been a neighborhood apart and a point of entry for immigrants and residents of humble means. Waves of Polish, German, Italian and Irish settled there, filling its tenements until, in the 1950s and '60s, many of them moved out and were replaced by Puerto Ricans and African Americans. By the 1970s, Fair Haven was down at its heels, its major thoroughfares of Grand Avenue and Ferry Street lined with tattered storefronts that housed thrift shops, liquor stores and all-night convenience stores that attracted drug traffic.

Today, Grand Avenue surges with the life of a home away from home: Latin music pulsing from open doorways and cars; restaurants serving Peruvian, Ecuadoran and Mexican food; money-transfer businesses; markets that stock hard-to-find foods that the giant C-Town supermarket around the corner—which carries plenty of goods from Latin America—doesn't sell. "We've cleaned up the drug and prostitution problems in this corridor," says Angelo Reyes, a Fair Haven native who did some time in jail himself for drug dealing, came out determined to turn around his life and neighborhood, and now owns a few choice pieces of Grand Avenue, which he is bent on revitalizing. "We've got better businesses and better jobs here, now. And a lot of Latinos are choosing to stay and put a foundation down."

The influx of immigrants from all over Latin America—both legal and illegal—has put Fair Haven on a more promising track, but it remains predominantly a working-poor and working-class neighborhood. Outside the immigrant community, says Lieutenant Luiz Casanova, who commands the police district substation there, the chief issue has been crime related to the drug trade. "The undocumented folks are not part of that problem," he says. "When I first took over the district almost four years ago, what I noticed was that we had a large community within our community that was being overlooked—they were being victimized. We had several murders of undocumented folks, we had assaults and home invasions. The bad element knew they didn't trust the banks or couldn't put their money in the banks."

The Elm City ID card had its genesis in that problem, and specifically in a 2005 meeting that a couple of immigrant advocacy groups held with police and Mayor DeStefano. One of those groups was run at the time by Kica Matos, the current community services director. At the meeting, one immigrant stood up to say that undocumented residents hesitated to cooperate with police because they knew they'd be asked for identification and were nervous about not having any. "What if the city issued IDs?" he asked.

Students in a legal clinic at Yale Law School did some research and concluded that an identity card rooted in proof of residency would be legal under both state and federal laws. Even so, delayed by DeStefano's unsuccessful 2006 gubernatorial campaign, the card didn't make its debut until July of last year.

When the city finally did introduce it, there was an explicit attempt to broaden its appeal beyond immigrants, mostly by emphasizing that it could be useful for all residents. And it is. The Elm City ID can be used to get discounts from retailers, buy time on parking meters and gain entrance to the city's beach, golf course and parks. "It's turned into a Chamber of Commerce promotion," scoffs card opponent Dustin Gold.

Yet from the card's first days, it's been seen within the community at large mostly as a tool for immigrants to use. Two days after it was introduced, people hoping to apply for one were arriving before dawn to stand in a line, made up overwhelmingly of immigrants, that eventually stretched down the block.

DeStefano is adamant that the card should be seen as a "resident's" card, not designed for any particular group, but he doesn't dispute how it's actually used. "In a community, we all have rights, but we also have responsibilities," he says. "Here in New Haven, what this meant was we had this population that was sort of in a gray area, and it was prohibiting enforcement of the social contract in the sense that people weren't reporting crime because they were afraid to talk to the police. That's not just bad for the victims of crime, who might be illegal undocumented residents; it's bad for the person who's been living next door for 30 years, that you've created an environment of lawlessness. You've created this population that is—because of their fears and the status the federal government has created for them— afraid to interact with us. But we work best when everyone's on the same team. And that's what this was about: getting everyone on the same team."

The Other Side

For the die-hard opponents involved with the Community Watchdog Project, the very idea that the city would want to be on the same team with Latinos in the country illegally is close to treasonous. When the Office of New Haven Residents—the department responsible for issuing the Elm

City cards—held a "Family Day" at City Hall in September, about 20 people affiliated with the CWP showed up to protest. Their ire at the city ballooned when they noticed that, across the street on the New Haven Green, the Mexican flag was flying just underneath the American flag. "It's intimidating to us," muttered Armand Serio, an anti–ID-card activist from next-door West Haven. "It's just to make us upset."

As it turns out, the flag was a leftover from a celebration of Mexican Independence Day the week before. But enough hate mail flowed into City Hall in the wake of the event—"You need to get your head out of your proverbial rectal area and become an American," one e-mailer told DeStefano—that the mayor called his own little rally by the city's flagpole to point out that Italian, Irish, Polish, Ukrainian and other flags also had flown there in celebration of New Haven's immigrant makeup.

Matos and DeStefano both label the Watchdog Project and its followers "a hate group." Dustin Gold, a graphic and Web designer from suburban North Branford who created and runs the CWP, insists that it doesn't hate anyone: It is merely worried about the effects of being too soft on illegal immigrants. "On one hand, you have people breaking into the country who are undercutting wages," he says. "On the other hand, they are being used and exploited, and whether they realize it or not, they are helping reconstitute a slave class in this country. My biggest beef is with politicians who encourage it and businesses that take advantage of it."

Gold and his allies have gotten their fair share of media coverage as the only organized opposition to the ID card. They tried to deep-six the card by filing a Freedom of Information request for the names and addresses of cardholders, but were turned down by the state Freedom of Information Commission. The CWP appealed, but its lawyer failed to file the appeal within the legal time limit.

A more pointed riposte to DeStefano's policy has come from Danbury, a city of 79,000 about 35 miles northwest of New Haven. There, the city council voted last February to join the so-called ICE ACCESS program, which trains police officers in immigration enforcement. "The message is, if you come into the United States of America, you've got to follow the law," says the city's Republican mayor, Mark Boughton, who has debated DeStefano on the matter several times.

"We can't undermine federal law by doing things like providing ID cards and rights and benefits for people who don't go through the process correctly." Danbury, too, has a large immigrant population, especially of Ecuadorans, and Boughton contends that his city's more hard-edged approach hasn't made them afraid of the police. "I hear that excuse every day as an excuse to undermine federal law," he says. "But my experience has been that people aren't afraid to approach the police to report a crime." On the other hand, there is anecdotal evidence from New Haven that a significant number of Ecuadorans has been moving there from Danbury—and, indeed, Ecuador chose New Haven for its first new consulate between New York and Boston.

Mayors and top senior officials on all sides of the issue concede Boughton's point that the presence of a large population of illegal immigrants hits city government's front lines. But many dispute that the hard-nosed approach can work. "They're here already," Ramos says of the illegal immigrants he visits. "They're here. Should we not protect their health and safety while they're here? Are we going to close our eyes? We can't turn our backs on them."

In the end, the differing approaches of cities such as New Haven and Danbury will likely be judged less on the grounds of ideology than on their day-to-day impact on people such as Ramos and the families he works with. So far, that's been hard to measure in New Haven. "The empirical data generally on the undocumented population is terrible," says Michael Wishnie, a Yale law professor who has spearheaded the legal work supporting the card. "If someone says, 'What was the crime rate in Fair Haven and the crime-reporting rate in the five years before the ID, and what's the crime rate and crime reporting rate after?' people don't have those numbers. It's not because New Haven is special: No city has those numbers."

Several Yale departments are working with the city to develop more solid data. Luiz Casanova, the police supervisor in Fair Haven, says he has seen a 17 percent drop in the overall crime rate in his district since the city began using its more tolerant approach in 2006. The card's effect, he says, "is hard to measure, but it does give folks a sense of belonging, it gives them, I guess, ownership of the community. It puts folks at ease when you go to them and ask them, 'Do you have any ID?'"

James Welbourne, the city librarian, says that concrete statistics on library usage are hard to come by, since ID-card account numbers are indistinguishable from regular library-card numbers. His staff, however, tells him that the card has brought many more customers. "Hispanic families are coming into the library, and particularly the neighborhood branches, for services; they all have the ID card with them when they check out books or access the computers. We've also seen increased interest in the library's offerings of ESL classes."

If there is one area where the card has disappointed its architects, it's in banking. So far, only four banks in New Haven have agreed to accept the card for identification, and even those four accept it only as a secondary form of ID. A potential depositor still needs a driver's license or Social Security card, which makes it difficult, if not impossible, for an illegal immigrant to open an account. Matos, DeStefano and others are counting on the launch next year of a new community-development bank to help Elm City Card holders move out of the margins of the financial system.

What is certainly clear is that places such as New Haven will be crafting their approaches to illegal immigration for a long time to come. "Cities and counties around the country have to think about local measures to address the realities of new immigrant populations and how institutions like libraries, the police, fire departments, hospitals and schools can adapt to the realities of those populations—whatever happens in Congress," says Wishnie. "I don't think the ID card is going to sweep the nation, but given the dispersion of new immigrants into communities that hadn't seen new immigration for a hundred years, what I hope does sweep the nation is the question, 'Well, that's what worked for New Haven. Now what might work for us?'"

19. Who We Are
Center for Popular Democracy

Who Needs ID?

The ability to provide proof of identity is a basic necessity that many Americans take for granted. Access to widely accepted forms of ID such as passports, drivers licenses and social security cards is a privilege that attends other privileges—privileges of race, of class and of citizenship. But, increasingly, identification requirements gate-keep almost every aspect of daily life. Without the right form of ID you may not be able to open a bank account or even cash a check, see a doctor at a hospital, register your child for school, apply for public benefits, file a complaint with the police department, borrow a book from a library, vote in an election, or even collect a package from the post office. Ironically, the very people who are most in need of such basic services are also those who have the most difficulty obtaining the proof of identity that will allow them to access those services. In addition to serving practical urgencies, identification cards also have a symbolic importance as a sign of membership in the community. Cities that offer ID to their residents regardless of immigration status are making a powerful statement of welcome and inclusion.

Goals of Municipal ID Card Programs

- Improve community safety by making it easier for those without state-issued ID to interact with local authorities.

Originally published as Center for Popular Democracy, *Who We Are*, December 2013. Reprinted with permission of the publisher.

- Improve access to financial services by providing a form of ID that will allow those without other forms of identification to open bank accounts.
- Mitigate impact of racial profiling.
- Make symbolic statement of welcome and solidarity to immigrant residents.
- Promote unity and sense of membership in the local community among all residents.

Types of Documents Accepted by Municipal ID Programs

To Prove Identity

Some Combination of the following is usually sufficient:

- US or Foreign Passport
- US Driver's License
- US State ID
- US Permanent Resident Card (Green Card)
- Consular Identification (CID)
- Certified Copy of US or Foreign Birth Certificate
- Social Security Card
- National ID Card with photo, name, address, date of birth, and expiration date
- Foreign Driver's License
- US or Foreign Military Identification Card
- Current Visa issued by a government agency
- US Individual Taxpayer Identification
- Number (ITIN) authorization letter
- Educational Institution Identification Card: elementary, middle, secondary and post secondary schools

To Prove Residency

Usually municipalities require that the below documents have been issued within the previous thirty days.

- Utility bill
- Local property tax statement or mortgage payment receipt

- Bank account statement
- Proof of a minor currently enrolled in a local school
- Employment pay stub
- Jury summons or court order issued by a state or federal court
- Federal or state income tax or refund statement
- Insurance bill (homeowner's, renter's, health, life or automobile insurance)
- Written verification issued by a homeless shelter that receives City funding confirming at least 15 days residency.
- Written verification issued by a hospital, health clinic or social services agency that receives City funding confirming at least 15 days residency.

Many of the municipalities featured in the case studies below made a point of designing their ID cards to be useful and attractive to all residents, even those who already have more traditional forms of identification. One potential danger of municipal IDs is that they may brand their holders as undocumented. To avoid this "scarlet letter" effect, it is important for local ID programs to be used by as many people in as many different situations as possible. Some of the incentives that cities are using to encourage residents to apply for the card include discounts at local businesses and city-operated attractions and venues, and the option to use the ID card as a prepaid debit card or to access public transportation. Some cards also include the holder's emergency contact information and some medical information.

A useful, recognizable and widely relied upon municipal ID card can promote a sense of city unity, which benefits all residents. And when undocumented immigrants are able to access the services they need to take care of themselves and their families, to find and keep employment, and to participate in neighborhood life, that has positive social and economic consequences for the entire community.

Common Features of Municipal ID Cards

- Photograph of Card Holder
- Name, Address and Date of Birth of Card Holder
- City Name and Logo
- Card Number
- Signature line
- Expiration date

OPTIONAL CARD FEATURES

- Gender of Card Holder
- Phone Number of Card Holder
- Mastercard/Visa Logo (for cards with banking functions)
- Medical Information
- Emergency Contact Information
- Bar Code

MAKING ID CARDS FRAUD RESISTANT

Municipalities have used some combination of the following strategies to ensure that ID cards could be difficult to forge:

- Card is made of certain stock thickness and material
- Card stock inventory is laser engraved with a serial number
- Cards include fine-line pattern background
- Embedded watermark
- Foil stamp of city seal
- Ultraviolet Ink
- Holograms
- Tamper-proof magnetic stripe
- Tamper-proof signature panel

Case Studies

Richmond, California: The Richmond City Council unanimously approved its municipal ID card program in July, 2011. Several community groups advocated for the program, which was spearheaded by Councilwoman Jovanka Beckles and had strong support from Mayor Gayle McLaughlin.

The issues that drove Richmond to launch a municipal ID program for undocumented residents mirror the concerns of other localities that have adopted municipal id programs: lack of access to services, fear of reporting crime, and increased prevalence of crime against undocumented immigrants. There was some resistance to Richmond's municipal ID program from constituents concerned about the possibility of identity fraud and the potential for increased pressure Richmond city resources, but these concerns did not have much political traction.

Although any person who can prove residency in Richmond for 15 of the previous 30 days is eligible to receive a card, Richmond specifically designed its ID program for vulnerable community members included immigrants, children, the indigent, survivors of domestic violence, and the homeless.

To prove identity Richmond residents will need to present one of the following documents: a U.S. or foreign passport; a driver's license issued by any state or territory of the United States; a state identification card; a U.S. Permanent Resident Card (green card); a CID; a photo ID issued by another country that is treated by that country as an alternative to a passport that has both the photograph and date of birth and meets the standards set by Richmond's Program administrator for reliability and authenticity. Alternatively, applicants can present any two of the following documents as long as one of them contains a photograph and birth date: a national identification card with photo, name, address, date of birth, and expiration date; a foreign driver's license; a U.S. or foreign military identification card; a current visa issued by a government agency; an ITIN Number authorization letter; an identification card issued by a California educational institution, including elementary, middle, secondary, and post-secondary schools; a certified copy of a U.S. or foreign birth certificate; a court order issued by a state or federal court to verify a person's identity; or a Social Security card. For applicants 13 and under Richmond will also accept medical and school records as proof of identity.

To prove residency, applicants can present any one of the following documents: a utility bill dated within the last 30 days; a written verification confirming at least 15 days residency within the last 30 days issued by a County or State run homeless shelter; written verification issued by a County or State run hospital health clinic or social services agency; a local property tax statement or mortgage payment receipt dated within the last 30 days; proof of a minor currently enrolled in a school in the City of Richmond; an employment pay stub dated within the last 30 days; a jury summons or court order issued by a state or federal court dated within the last 30 days; a federal or state income tax or refund statement dated within the last thirty days; or an insurance bill (homeowner's, renter's, health, life or automobile insurance) dated within the last 30 days. Card applicants can also rely on documents bearing the name of his or her spouse in conjunction with a copy of their marriage certificate.

The card will cost $15 for the general population, and $10 for low income residents. Looking to Oakland as a model, Richmond also plans for the card to have the capacity to act as a prepaid debit card. Richmond has awarded the contract to administer the program to SF Global LLC, the same company that operates the Oakland program (see discussion below). The ordinance establishing the ID program also directs the Richmond City Manager to appoint a Program Administrator to oversee the program. The ID cards were scheduled to launch in May or June of 2013, but of this writing has yet to officially begin.

Oakland, California: The Oakland Municipal ID card program, formally adopted by the Oakland City Council in June, 2009, is unique among existing ID programs in that it can also be used as a debit card. The purpose of including the debit card function is to give banking access to people who can't provide the documentation necessary to open an account at most large national banks. While the debit card aspect of the Oakland ID is an obvious benefit to those who would otherwise be carrying around large amounts of cash, there are significant fees associated with using the card in this way, including 75 cents for each debit transaction, a monthly charge of $2.99, and $1.75 for each call to customer service. Although these fees are a disincentive for low income families, they are still lower than those associated with most prepaid debit cards currently on the market. Adding the debit function to the ID card has also proven logistically complicated and time consuming, and ultimately delayed the launch of the ID program until March of 2013. Nevertheless, the debit card function is proving to be a draw. As of August 2013, Oakland had issued about 3,000 IDs and had received applications for about 4,800 more. Of current card holders, about two-thirds are using the debit feature. As noted above, New Haven, Richmond, and Los Angeles are now looking to add a debit feature to their municipal ID programs.

Councilmember Ignacio De La Fuente initiated the push for an Oakland ID card, and found broad support on the Oakland city council as well as from Mayor Jean Quan. While much of the political discussion in the lead up to the ordinance adopting the program focused on public safety arguments, officials have also been very explicit that the intention of the card is to make all residents, including undocumented residents, feel welcome and included. In 2007

Oakland adopted a resolution declaring itself a sanctuary city, and the local immigrant rights community views the ID program as one way the city is making good on the promise of refuge. The Oakland ID is accepted by local authorities as a valid form of identification, and residents are using their cards in interactions with police, as well as at libraries, health clinics, banks and other local businesses.

According to the city's website, applicants wishing to use the banking function of the Oakland card must present either their Social Security Card or one of the following: a current U.S. passport; U.S. Permanent Resident Card; a current U.S. driver's license; a current U.S. state-issued ID; a current U.S. military service ID; a current U.S. Tribal ID Card; a current Mexican Matricula Consular ID; any other U.S. government-issued ID which is current and contains a photograph; a current foreign passport. Those wishing to use the Oakland card solely for identification purposes may also rely on any of the following which may be current or expired: a national ID card issued by a foreign government; a foreign passport; a foreign driver license; a foreign military service ID; or a consular ID.

To prove residency, applicants must present one of the following, dated within the previous thirty days: a utility bill; a local property tax statement; a mortgage payment statement; a bank account statement; an employment pay stub; a jury summons notice; proof of a minor currently enrolled in a local school; written verification from a city run shelter or social service agency of at least 15 days residency.

The cost of Oakland's ID is $15 for adults and $10 for seniors. Oakland contracts the ID card program out to SF Global LLC. A Program Administrator, housed in the City Clerk's office, oversees the program for the city.

New Jersey: In New Jersey, ID cards have been a growing trend since 2008, when Asbury Park issued the first local card in the state. As in New Haven, Asbury Park was galvanized to action by the death of an undocumented community member who was killed during a robbery attempt. Municipal, county and religious leaders, area business owners, law enforcement and local residents came together to discuss ways of addressing the vulnerabilities of immigrants living in Asbury Park. The group agreed that, while not a complete solution to the community's problem, photo ID cards containing the name, birth date, address, and phone number of the cardholder would help improve access to services and ease communication between residents and local authorities. Having an Asbury Park ID would also enable people to leave other forms of identification, such as foreign passports or birth certificates—which for some would be difficult or impossible to replace if lost—at home. The local coalition engaged the local police to secure buy-in for the ID program, and to ensure that officers would know about and accept the cards as legitimate forms of ID in interacting with the community. The first cards were issued in April 2008. Though the Asbury Park card is issued not by the city itself but by the Latino Network, a non-profit advocacy group, the card is widely used and accepted in the community today.

The success of the Asbury Park card inspired Trenton to adopt its own local ID program. The impetus for the campaign there came from a group called the Tremendously Trenton Coalition, which formed with the goal of facilitating the integration of immigrants into civic life. The ID card program launched in May 2009, and the city issued more than 1,500 cards in its first year. The cards were distributed by the Latin American Legal Defense and Education Fund (LALDEF). LALDEF also administered Princeton's ID card program, which started in May of 2010, and eventually helped to expand access to the cards across all of Mercer County. The Mercer County card has now supplanted the individual Princeton and Trenton cards, and is designed not only for undocumented people, but for the homeless, the elderly, and people re-entering society after a period of incarceration.

To obtain a Mercer County ID, an individual must prove residency in Mercer County by presenting a lease or utility bill or by having a landlord vouch for their residency, and show some form of photo ID from an official office, employer, or school. The photo ID may be current or expired, domestic or international. The card costs $10 for adults and $5 for youth and seniors.

Thanks to intensive relationship building that LALDEF and the community did in advance of launching the program, the Mercer County card is now recognized and accepted by law enforcement agencies, healthcare providers, the board of social services, courts, recreational locations, libraries, and retail establishments.

The most recent NJ locality to start issuing ID cards is Freehold, NJ. The Freehold cards are modeled on the Mercer County card, but are currently available only to members of CASA Freehold, an organization that helps newly arrived immigrants integrate into the community through employment opportunities, work health and safety, wage theft claims, and education about immigration. CASA began issuing the cards in November 2012 to all its members, and the card is accepted by law enforcement and other local authorities as well as banks, schools, and businesses in Freehold.

Conclusion

Municipal ID's are giving people easier access to local services and institutions, reducing fear of police interaction, and fostering a sense of belonging and shared identity. While Congress struggles to pass comprehensive immigration reform legislation, there are many innovative policy strategies that local governments can use in to protect and empower their constituents. Municipal ID card programs are one such approach, and the trend is growing.

20. Driver's Licenses Will Be "An Incredible Relief"

Kate Linthicum

Claudia Bedolla never leaves home without making a calculation: Is this trip worth the risk?

Bedolla has a car but no driver's license. She hasn't been eligible for one in California, having never obtained legal immigration status since arriving from Mexico at age 10. If she were stopped by police, she could be fined hundreds of dollars for driving without proper documentation and have her car impounded.

So she makes choices. A drive to the grocery store or to pick up her kids from school is deemed essential. Nearly everything else is not.

"It stops us from doing so many things that most people do, like driving to the beach or going to Magic Mountain," said Bedolla, 36, who is raising five U.S.-born children in Pomona. "I don't even go to my kids' games, because I'd rather not risk it."

Beginning Friday, Bedolla will have a chance to change that when California becomes one of 10 states to allow immigrants in the country illegally to apply for special licenses.

She and her husband are among tens of thousands who have already made appointments with the Department of Motor Vehicles to apply for licenses. "It's an incredible relief," said Bedolla. "Now we won't have to worry every day."

Supporters of the law say it will alter immigrants' attitudes toward law enforcement and increase levels of civic engagement.

Originally published in *Los Angeles Times*, December 31, 2014. Copyright © 2014. *Los Angeles Times*. Reprinted with Permission.

to change everything," said Ben Wood, an organizer at the
ɔmic Opportunity Center, a nonprofit that assists day laborers
dozens of groups across the state offering license test prepa-
es for immigrants. "Once people are able to lose a little bit of
ey had of being on the road, that will increase participation."

Politics

Immigrants can soon get driver's licenses, but it's been a long road.

License applicants will have to provide documents to verify their iden-
tities and prove they reside in California. They will each also have to submit
a thumbprint, pass vision and written exams and schedule a behind-the-
wheel driving test. The special licenses will feature text explaining that they
are "not acceptable for official federal purposes," such as boarding an air-
plane.

The agency has been working for more than a year to prepare for the
1.5 million applications expected in the first three years of the program. An
extra $141 million has been budgeted to handle the influx, with the DMV
opening four new offices and hiring an additional 900 employees.

The cost has been a point of contention for critics, some of whom also
complain that the new program rewards immigrants who broke the law
with "quasi-amnesty."

Democrats in the Legislature, who argue the program will improve
traffic safety by requiring immigrants who are already driving to study the
rules of the road, pushed through the law allowing special licenses in 2013
after a decades-long battle.

Claudia Bedolla

Claudia Bedolla, who was brought to the U.S. illegally at age 10, has been
careful about when she chooses to drive (Gina Ferazzi / *Los Angeles Times*).

In the past, many people in the country without permission had been
able to obtain California driver's licenses because applicants did not have
to prove they had legal immigration status. That changed in 1993 with the
passage of a law that required any first-time applicant to provide a Social
Security number.

The new law may be a boon to the auto insurance industry. Some companies are targeting advertising to those who are eligible for the licenses.

"This is a whole new population of individuals who will now be entering the market and shopping for insurance," said Madison Voss, a spokeswoman for the California Department of Insurance. About two dozen insurance companies in California have sold insurance to unlicensed immigrants for years, Voss said.

Robert Correa, a broker at Guidance Insurance Agency in Highland Park, said that about 20 percent of his clients don't have licenses. In a city as sprawling as Los Angeles, many immigrants have no choice but to drive, he said.

Ascencion Jimenez, who hauls metal to junkyards in his small Nissan truck, says he has paid about $6,000 in traffic tickets, including for multiple violations for driving without a license. In the 18 years since he came illegally from Mexico, he has avoided driving after dark, knowing that it takes no more than a broken taillight or a stop at a DUI checkpoint to attract the attention of police.

Jimenez said he hopes a license will make him eligible for cheaper insurance. Most companies charge a premium—often more than $200 a year—for unlicensed drivers.

Jimenez has a DMV appointment Jan. 24 and has been practicing for the driving test online. Although he drives every day, the written test questions "aren't easy," he said.

"Once people are able to lose a little bit of the fear they had of being on the road, that will increase participation" (Ben Wood, organizer, Pomona Economic Opportunity Center).

Immigrant advocates are pushing people to study, noting that in Nevada, a large percentage of immigrants flunked the written test in the first few weeks a new driver's license was offered there. Advocates are also working to ensure that immigrants with poor literacy skills and those who speak obscure indigenous languages are not excluded from the process.

"This is an issue this community has always faced," said Arcenio Lopez, who works with the Mixteco/Indigena Community Organizing Project, a group that represents indigenous workers in Ventura County who hail from Mexican states such as Oaxaca and Guerrero.

Jaime Garza, a spokesman for the DMV, said that the written license test is available in 31 languages but there is not sufficient demand for tests in indigenous Mexican dialects. Those who do not speak English or Spanish can request a translator, he said.

Other groups are addressing the fears of some immigrants who may be used to life in the shadows.

Aquilina Soriano-Versoza, director of the Pilipino Workers Center of Southern California, said many in her community are excited about the opportunity to drive legally, "but there are others who are wary of identifying themselves in any way to the government."

Filipinos have not applied for immigration relief opportunities, such as President Obama's Deferred Action for Childhood Arrivals program, at the same rate as other immigrant groups, she said.

But the ability to drive is essential for many Filipinos, she said, especially those who work as caregivers and have to travel late at night.

Judy, a 41-year-old who came illegally from the Philippines and did not give her last name because she fears backlash from immigration authorities or her employers, said a license will give her more freedom.

She relies on the bus or an expensive carpool to get to her three jobs, which she works seven days a week. Judy lives in the San Fernando Valley, sending money to her three children and husband back home. She has friends in Manhattan Beach, but the distance means she rarely can go there.

With a license, she said, she'll be able to visit them.

21. Toil and Trouble
Jonathan Walters

It's just after six o'clock on a crisp February morning in the Village of Brewster, New York, one of a string of small towns that dot a busy commuter rail line leading into Manhattan, 50 miles to the south. The dark outlines of Main Street's one- to three-story commercial buildings are silhouetted against a pink and purple dawn sky. Despite the early hour, there is a general stirring downtown. Descending from the hill above the village's commercial row is a steady stream of men in work clothes, hooded sweatshirts and ball caps pulled down to just above their eyes.

It's the beginning of the daily procession of immigrant workers—most of them from Guatemala and most of them undocumented—as they take their places along Main Street in clusters ranging from three to more than a dozen. They stand curbside waiting to be picked up by the small convoy of trucks and SUVs that circulates through Brewster seven mornings a week, contractors and homeowners looking for a day's work out of men willing to do dirty, hard jobs for wages that most American workers wouldn't even consider.

The scene that unfolds nearly every morning in Brewster is mirrored in hundreds of municipalities, both large and small, across the country. Groups of men—from places such as Mexico, Guatemala, Ecuador, Columbia and El Salvador—up early in the morning, gathering at casually established pickup points, hoping to make enough money to live and perhaps send to family back home. And while many Americans seem comfortable with the concept of cut-rate labor when it comes to home renovation or grounds-keeping, they seem decidedly less sanguine about the conse-

---

Originally published as Jonathan Walters, "Immigrants Toil and Trouble," *Governing*, April 2006. Reprinted with permission of the publisher.

quences of such economics, the most fundamental of which means playing host to a new and very different group of residents in and around their communities.

And so in villages, towns and cities from New York to California, the day labor phenomenon is bringing with it predictable tensions crime. To date, local governments have been the front line in dealing with the issue. The ways they have managed it are as varied as the communities experiencing the phenomenon, but the approaches can be broken down into three general categories: ignore it, crack down, or adapt and manage.

Overt Conflict

A quiet bedroom community of about 2,000 people, Brewster was one of those places that for a decade more or less ignored the issue. But as its undocumented day-laborer population began to swell (some estimate it to be as many as 600 to 1,000), tensions inevitably ratcheted up. Complaints about intimidating groups of strange men on the sidewalks watching women walk by, public drunkenness, homelessness and other objectionable behaviors simmered.

The situation heated up further last fall when a day laborer was found passed out on the grounds of a local elementary school. It boiled over in early January, when a Putnam County sheriff rounded up eight day laborers who were playing soccer on the grounds of the same elementary school during school hours. They were all arrested for trespassing. One was reported to federal immigration authorities and faces deportation. With the arrests, Brewster became one more pinpoint on the national map of places where the battle over day laborers had broken out into the open.

Why streams of immigrants have arrived in the United States to take jobs that most Americans don't seem to want isn't much of a mystery. Ask any day laborer why he's here and at least some part of the answer will include that work here pays incredibly well by the standards of their home countries. Eduardo, a 32-year-old, undocumented worker who first arrived in Brewster 11 years ago, and who now lives just to the south in the Village of Mount Kisco, says he has managed to carve out a specialty in tree work, which earns him as much as $25,000 per year, more than half of which he sends back to his family in Guatemala. He makes that much, he says, "because the work is very dangerous." While Eduardo says he now has a steady employer, initially he too was part of the small army of young men in Brewster standing on the sidewalk willing to take just about any work that came their way.

According to a recent study of the day-labor phenomenon, Brewster has its equivalent in more than 500 other communities nationwide—where roughly 120,000 laborers gather every day to try to find work—or, more accurately, where they hope work will find them. Three-quarters of those workers are here illegally. About half work directly for homeowners, and just over 43 percent for contractors. The jobs they do masonry, although most appear to be basic, hard and often dangerous. The study documents a fairly high level of abuse of day laborers at the hands of employers—the most common form being failure to pay owed wages, but ranging up to outright neglect when it comes to workplace danger and on-the-job injuries. It also touches on some issues related to how day laborers are treated by the communities in which they live and work, noting frequent instances of hostility from both police and local merchants. Nonetheless, at least 63 communities have tried to defuse the tension by setting up organized sites where they can gather and wait for work.

The concept of day-labor centers isn't one that's quickly accepted by most communities. Many localities have resisted this approach, believing that it will only draw more illegal workers to their town. Other communities have decided (or have been compelled to decide, in part through legal action) that it makes more sense to at least create a safe place where workers can get a hot cup of coffee, use a bathroom and perhaps benefit from some other centralized services.

Central Site

Port Chester, which sits on Long Island Sound just below the Connecticut border, is one of those places that decided on its own to deal with the growing problem of congregating day laborers. About a dozen years ago, day laborers discovered Port Chester as a handy jumping off point for work opportunities in affluent Westchester County, New York. And while a number of gathering points had been created informally by day laborers, one of the favorites was the centrally located and bustling commuter rail station downtown. It was a situation bound for trouble as it put heavy commuter traffic into direct conflict with heavy contractor traffic, and forced well-paid white-collar commuters to work their way through a small army of hard-looking Latino immigrants.

"We saw the need several years ago," says Port Chester Mayor Gerald Logan, a Republican who is in the middle of his third two-year term. "And I mentioned it in an article in the local newspaper." As it turned out, Logan wasn't the only one thinking about the issue. Tim Ploch, the pastor at the local Holy Rosary Catholic church, also noticed, and after reading the mayor's comments in the paper, stepped up to offer his parish as the site for a day-labor center.

With an identified site on the table, the Westchester Hispanic Coalition agreed to help staff the center and coordinate programs. In stark contrast to the situation in Brewster, day laborers in Port Chester now head for a single, central site where contractors know to go when they need help. The location is handy because it's within walking distance of where many day laborers live, and is also close to the train station—some day laborers take the train to Port Chester because it's known as a work center. Perhaps equally important, it's just down a main road from a Home Depot. "So contractors can swing over to Home Depot and then swing by here," says Soraya Principe, director of the center. (In many localities Home Depots have become ground zero for conflicts over the day-laborer issue. In fact, a handful of local governments are now demanding that Home Depots and other big-box construction supply outlets create day-labor shelters on site as a condition of site plan approval.)

The center at Holy Rosary, which gets no government money, is roomy, warm and well lit. At one end, hot coffee and pastries are being served. For those who don't get work on any given day, the center offers English classes taught by volunteers. Workers who use the center also have access to services offered by the Westchester Hispanic Coalition, including help with immigration authorities or in tracking down contractors who fail to pay promised wages. Principe says the coalition enjoys about a 50 percent recovery rate.

Port Chester, though, is the clear exception when it comes to how various communities have dealt with day laborers. The official reception has been rough in a lot of places. Last September, undercover police posing as contractors arrested 30 day laborers in Houston for violating a local ordinance against soliciting work in the roadway. Last November, police in Farmingville, New York, on Long Island, arrested several day laborers for trespassing (Farmingville also has witnessed assaults on day laborers). Last December, Oconee County, Georgia, sheriff's deputies swept into a Home Depot parking lot and arrested 31 day laborers for loitering. And early in January, five day laborers were arrested in Cicero, Illinois, part of a group of 40 men in a Home Depot parking lot waiting for work. The same month, the new mayor of Morristown, New Jersey, Donald Cresitello, vowed to crack down on the overcrowding of illegal immigrants in local housing, a phenomenon known as "stacking."

Stacking is frequently cited as one of the most common and potentially dangerous public safety side effects of the day-laborer phenomenon. The high rents in Brewster (a small studio apartment goes for around $1,000 per month) make it tempting for landlords to carve houses and apartments into ever-smaller, more numerous units. Still, buildings that are carved up into multiple units can be firetraps, and also put a strain on local utilities. Some localities have beefed up inspections of properties where stacking is suspected. Others have passed local laws requiring landlords to regularly report on their tenant loads. Brewster has gone to a stricter monitoring of water use as a way to identify the practice.

While some localities try to crack down on day laborers, others are going after contractors, on the grounds that it's illegal under federal law to hire undocumented immigrants. In East Hampton Village, New York, police last fall started taking down the license plate numbers of vehicles picking up day laborers, threatening to report the contractors to federal authorities. In Riverside, California, police are enforcing "red curb" zones—where it is illegal to pull over and pick anybody up—at traditional day-labor gathering sites.

Militant Response

As the day-labor issue has seen increasing numbers of local flashpoints, there's also been a national backlash in the form of groups urging tough action against illegal immigrants, in general, and day laborers, in particular. Last January, immigration control activists organized "Stop the Invasion" day, which saw about 40 groups demonstrating in 20 states, from New Jersey to California.

Even some local officials are starting to lean toward the militant. "Mayors and County Executives for Immigration Reform," a coalition of local officials, is pressuring the federal government to act. "It's local governments that are experiencing the fallout of a failed federal policy," says one of the effort's founders, Mayor Mark Boughton of Danbury, Connecticut. "We're all left to our own devices to try and manage this flow of people without any support or backup from the feds, and you're seeing communities get into these bitter, divisive fights. Until we secure the borders, we're wasting our time. Things like hiring halls and day-laborer centers, that's just managing a policy and system that has spun out of control."

It is not hard to understand why there is so much tension—and even hostility—around the whole day-labor phenomenon. No local politician or chamber of commerce president would argue that groups of undocumented workers clustered along downtown sidewalks is a good thing for business, public safety or the civic image. Jane Neri, who runs a consignment shop on Main Street in Brewster, says she's seen a 70 percent decline in business over the past few years, as more day laborers have begun to congregate and then hang around downtown if not hired that morning.

Neri, who on this particular morning is complaining that she just had to clean vomit off her storefront window courtesy of a day laborer, says that her customers have told her they are afraid to run the gauntlet of men who now congregate on the sidewalks outside her shop. She doesn't blame all day laborers, just a hard-core group that seems uninterested in co-existing with the rest of the community, she says. In talking to those on both sides of the issue, the operative emotion does seem to be fear. Mayra, who manages a laundromat on Brewster's Main Street, an unofficial gathering site for day laborers, says that the young men who frequent her place—virtually all of them undocumented—are afraid, too, especially in the wake of the school arrests. "They're afraid of immigration [officials]; they feel like"—and here she struggles for a word—"chickens."

When asked how such fear might be diffused in Brewster, Istebon Jiminez, who came to Brewster from Mexico about 10 years ago, gained citizenship and now runs a downtown Mexican restaurant, says "communication." Yet he admits to never having approached merchants just a few doors down the street, such as Jane Neri, to talk about dealing with what even he recognizes is a problem for local business people. One significant obstacle to such contact is obvious: Jiminez, a potentially powerful emissary to the local business community because of his background and his clear understanding of the roots of tension in town, speaks very little English. Given their level of interaction, Jiminez and Neri might as well be living in different towns.

The other factor that's impossible to ignore is color. As some in Brewster point out, the village has a long history of accepting and assimilating immigrants. In the early 1900s, Irish and Italians arrived in Brewster to work at the thriving Borden condensed milk plant at the east end of Main Street and the quarries outside of town. But Brewster's liaison to the day-labor community, Victor Padilla, thinks this wave of immigrants is having a harder time of assimilating for the simple reason that "they may be a little too brown."

Policy Failures

Whatever the roots of the problems, the clearest failure on the day-labor front is political and runs up and down the governmental food chain. Convoluted and complicated federal immigration laws inconsistently and sporadically applied haven't helped, nor has the fact that Congress is bitterly divided on immigration issues. States, meanwhile, are for the most part absent from the debate, as they neither have the authority to deal with immigration policy, nor suffer the consequences of local day-labor skirmishes. Counties have been a bit more involved. In fact, the Westchester County Legislature held the first of what will be a series of hearings on the day-labor issue in February, investigating how the county might step in to help. But in the final analysis, the day-laborer conflicts continue to fall squarely in the laps of city and town governments, and most seem to experience bitter fights before things improve.

The Village of Mount Kisco, a half-dozen stops south of Brewster on the same commuter rail line, is one of those places. Ten years ago, it was open warfare in the village. Mel Berger, a former local pharmacist, remembers fuming over the growing number of day laborers congregating around the village's downtown train station. "I even went as far as to call the U.S. Immigration and Naturalization Service in New York City," says Berger. "I said, 'Come up here and arrest these people!' The INS guy laughed and said, 'What are you kidding? I could walk out my door and go around the corner and arrest 100 people right here.'"

So Mount Kisco decided to take matters into its own hands. The town launched midnight housing raids looking for code violations in dwellings known to harbor day laborers, and also passed a law restricting public solicitation of work. The flurry of activity certainly got people's attention, but not the kind that the village wanted. The Westchester Hispanic Coalition brought a discrimination suit against the village. As part of the settlement, Mount Kisco agreed to stop openly harassing Latinos, to open up a local park to the day-laborer community and to be more bilingual in official postings and signage.

At the same time, a group led by a local Presbyterian church launched an effort to find a suitable site for a day-labor center as a further way to defuse community conflict. The search committee was led by, of all people, Mel Berger, who says his view began to shift as he got to know members of the Latino community and to understand what the day-laborer phenomenon was all about. While he says the search was an eye-opening exercise in NIMBYism, the center opened in 2000.

Located in a mini-industrial park, the center is spacious, with a front room lined on one wall with banks of computers. Volunteers teach everything from English to budgeting. Hiring is handled in two ways: Unskilled laborers are listed on a first-come, first-served basis on a board in the front room. Skilled laborers—painters or roofers, for example—are matched with employers looking for such skills. On busy days, as many as 60 to 80 laborers will circulate through the center.

Its $410,000 budget is covered entirely by private contributions. When it comes to the immigration status of those who use the center, "We never ask," says executive director Carola Otero Bracco. While the situation in Mount Kisco isn't perfect—there is still tension, and day laborers report that they continue to be hassled regularly by the police—the community has clearly made progress.

If Brewster has any advantage over the Mount Kisco of 10 years ago when it comes to working through the day-labor issue, it's that key political leaders understand what the village is up against by way of bringing together a divided community. Mayor John Degnan has no interest in touching off a Mount Kisco–like war as a prelude to working things out. "It is an evolution," says Degnan, "but we've seen the successes in other communities around us. The key is going to be community involvement. Even if you make progress with a brick-and-mortar day-labor center, you still have to do a lot better job of communication within the community."

22. Business and Labor Unite to Try to Alter Immigration Laws

Steven Greenhouse

After decades of friction over immigration, the nation's labor unions and the leading business association, the Chamber of Commerce, have formed an unusual alliance that is pushing hard to revamp American immigration laws.

These oft-feuding groups agree on the need to enact a way for the 11 million immigrants illegally in the United States to gain citizenship. And they are also nearing common ground on a critical issue—the number of guest workers allowed into the country—that has deeply divided business and labor for years and helped to sink President George W. Bush's push for an immigration overhaul in 2007.

In redefining what constitutes a guest worker and in revamping the method to determine how many should be allowed in, business and labor groups are sketching out new proposals that are distinct departures from earlier legislative approaches.

The issue has long been one of contention, with businesses like hotels and farmers saying they need a large supply of seasonal workers while unions complain that these workers are often exploited. To try to resolve their differences, they are discussing what they call a "data-driven system" that would determine how many "provisional workers" would be let in each year to work on farms, summer resorts and elsewhere.

One proposal labor is pushing would have Congress establish a panel that would use economic, industry and regional data (like unemployment rates) to determine how many provisional workers should be allowed in annually to work in industries, like farming, that have seasonal surges in their demand for laborers. But business groups say they worry that such a panel would be unwieldy and act too slowly to meet employers' needs.

Under the proposals, the number of provisional workers permitted might increase when America's unemployment rate was low and then shrink if the rate was high. In addition, many of these provisional visa holders, after working successfully in the United States for several years, might be given permanent residency that could lead to citizenship.

In another important step forward, many labor unions have joined with the Chamber of Commerce and other business groups in embracing E-Verify, a federal electronic system that uses Social Security numbers and other data to verify that newly hired workers are in the country legally. Union leaders have frequently denounced E-Verify as error-prone, a continuing concern. They said it often declared that immigrants with valid papers were not authorized to work.

When President Bush pushed for an immigration overhaul in 2007, many unions—long detesting the guest-worker program—helped to persuade the Senate to phase out that program within five years. Once that phaseout was approved, many business groups grew far less enthusiastic about the immigration effort. That encouraged many Republicans—already uneasy about what they viewed as "amnesty"—to vote against the plan.

Maria Elena Durazo, the chairwoman of the A.F.L.–C.I.O.'s immigration committee, said labor's opposition to the guest-worker program was longstanding. "Guest workers have no rights and no voice and no possibility of ever becoming legalized," she said. "If they protest about wages or unsafe conditions, they risk getting deported."

Many businesses have complaints with the current guest-worker program, disliking the frequent requirement to place advertisements to determine whether American workers are available before they can bring in guest workers.

"You have to go through four government agencies and often hire a lawyer and an agent," said Shawn McBurney, senior vice president of governmental affairs at the American Hotel and Lodging Association. "It's unbelievably complicated, cumbersome and expensive."

Labor unions have urged business to embrace a plan pushed by Ray Marshall, labor secretary under President Jimmy Carter. He suggests creating a commission of experts who would use economic data to determine, for instance, whether 20,000 or 40,000 immigrants should be granted provisional visas to do seasonal work nationwide at shellfish plants, restaurants or apple orchards.

"Instead of a system that works at the whim of any employer, it will be a data-driven system," said Richard Trumka, president of the A.F.L.–C.I.O. Under the current system, he noted, employers have applied repeatedly for new batches of guest workers. A data-driven system would ensure an adequate flow of immigrants to help employers meet seasonal needs, he said.

Mr. McBurney of the hotel association disagreed. "It will never work," he said. "There are no experts who will know exactly what the economy will need—this was proved by command and control economies. The bureaucracy will never be able to respond to the economy. The economy is a very dynamic thing. Bureaucracies aren't so dynamic."

Randel K. Johnson, senior vice president for labor policy at the United States Chamber of Commerce, agreed. "We oppose the commission because it would never be able to determine shortages in a timely manner that reflect the always-changing realities of the marketplace."

Angelo Amador, vice president for labor policy at the National Restaurant Association, serves on the business-labor group seeking a consensus approach. "I'm optimistic about reaching an agreement," on guest workers, he said. "The pressure on both sides is great. If we don't come up with something, someone else is going to be drafted by other people."

Demetrios G. Papademetriou, president of the Migration Policy Institute, a Washington research group, predicted that it would be "extremely difficult" for the two sides to reach agreement on guest workers. He warned that without a deal between business and labor, the whole push for immigration changes could fail.

"They could get very close on this issue but might not be able to build a bridge to the other side," he said. "One side starts from wanting zero guest workers and the other starts from unlimited. The unlimited side might move a lot, but the one that started with zero might not."

He said the stakes were high for the union movement because if it plays a major role in gaining legal status for illegal immigrants, labor's image will soar among immigrants, and that might help persuade many immigrants to push to join unions.

Eliseo Medina, secretary-treasurer of the Service Employees International Union, said labor unions were making a huge push for immigration changes.

"If we are going to make conditions better for all workers, we need to make sure that undocumented workers have the same rights as everybody else," he said. "Otherwise, they'll be used to lower labor standards."

23. Georgia Immigration Law: Many Agencies Fail to Comply

Jeremy Redmon

Many city and county government agencies across Georgia have failed to comply with a key part of the state's year-old anti-illegal immigration law, putting them at risk of losing access to state loans and grants, according to an *Atlanta Journal-Constitution* analysis of public records.

The funding—which includes state community development block grants—helps Georgia cities and counties maintain their jails, manage development, encourage commerce and boost employment.

At issue is the centerpiece of the Illegal Immigration Reform and Enforcement Act of 2011, which is aimed at blocking illegal immigrants from taking jobs from U.S. citizens and stopping taxpayer support for government contractors who hire illegal immigrants.

That provision requires all but the smallest private employers and government agencies and contractors to use a federal work authorization program called E-Verify. The program helps employers ensure that newly hired employees are authorized to work in the United States.

An *Atlanta Journal-Constitution* investigation has found that numerous city and county agencies—including Chamblee, Sandy Springs and the DeKalb County Housing Authority—did not file required reports on time to confirm that they and their contractors are using E-Verify.

So many agencies have failed to submit the reports that the state is preparing to send out a mass mailing this week to remind them that their state funding could be in jeopardy if they don't comply.

The lapses highlight the complexities of enforcing a law that will eventually touch tens of thousands of employers throughout the state, especially in a time when state and local governments face budget and staff cutbacks. The newspaper's investigation also found that:

"It is impossible to confirm that all private employers required to use E-Verify are doing so, because of the way state and federal records are kept."

Beyond keeping tabs on the paperwork filed by government agencies, the state has no way to check their compliance, because there is no money for performance audits.

Some local governments, which bear much of the burden for enforcing the law, are confused about how to follow it. Sandy Springs, for example, sent a letter this year to 6,700 businesses that included erroneous information about the E-Verify requirement.

The Barnesville Housing Authority signed up to use E-Verify Tuesday, after The *Atlanta Journal-Constitution* asked why it was not registered.

State lawmakers approved the sweeping law in April of last year, saying it would help block illegal immigrants from taking jobs from legal U.S. residents.

Parts of the law—also called HB 87—started to take effect on July 1 of last year. Other parts are tied up in a federal appeals court in Atlanta by a legal challenge brought by civil and immigrant rights groups.

The fate of one key provision, authorizing state and local police to investigate the immigration status of certain suspects, could be determined within days. The U.S. Supreme Court is expected to rule by the end of this month on the constitutionality of a similar Arizona law.

Proponents of Georgia's statute often cite a Pew Hispanic Center estimate that 325,000 illegal immigrants held jobs in Georgia in 2010. They say that is unacceptable, particularly since many citizens and legal residents are struggling in vain to find work. Georgia's unemployment rate stands at 8.9 percent, well above the national rate of 8.2 percent.

State Rep. Matt Ramsey, R–Peachtree City, the author of HB 87, said he and others are monitoring the law's implementation and "will take legislative action if necessary to carry out our intent, which is to protect Georgia's taxpayers from the social and economic consequences of illegal immigration."

"I don't think anyone that worked on HB 87 believed there would be universal compliance in the relatively short time it has been in effect, given how sweeping and comprehensive the changes are in that law," Ramsey said.

Critics said state lawmakers sowed confusion by legislating around complex areas of federal immigration law. They argue those matters are best left to the federal government.

"The problems and confusion experienced by municipalities underscore the many problems with the new law: no training for municipalities, no funding for such training, no specificity within the law, and no clear goals or the will to achieve them," said Carolina Antonini, a local immigration attorney who teaches at Georgia State University.

Governments employ about 16 percent of Georgia's workers, meaning that the law's greatest impact will be achieved through compliance by private companies.

In all, more than 18,800 public and private employers in Georgia are enrolled to use? E-Verify, according to U.S. Citizenship and Immigration Services records.

However, state Labor Department officials said they can't confirm that all businesses in Georgia are complying, because the state and federal government databases include different information, making cross-checking impossible.

For private companies, the law takes effect in stages. As of Jan. 1, businesses with 500 or more employees were supposed to start using E-Verify. On July 1, the requirement will extend to employers with 100 or more employees but fewer than 500. More than 5,600 such businesses are operating in Georgia, Labor Department records show.

Companies that have more than 10 workers and fewer than 100 must start using E-Verify by July 1 of next year. Smaller companies are exempt.

To be licensed to operate in a city or county, companies that are subject to the law must file sworn affidavits, saying that they are in compliance.

Some government officials are confused by the requirements. Sandy Springs, for example, sent a letter to 6,700 businesses this year, telling those with 10 or more employees they must provide the city with their E-Verify identification number. (Even after July 2013, companies with 10 workers will be exempt.) City officials said they would send a revised letter out in November.

"It is a new law," said Sharon Kraun, the city's spokeswoman, "and as with anything new, there is learning you gain as you move forward."

When it comes to governments, the law requires all agencies with more than one employee to file annual reports certifying that they use E-Verify.

Agencies must also certify that contractors they hire use the system to check workers employed on building and road projects and "any other performance of labor for a public employer within this state under a contract or other bidding process."

Of the 2,324 local and state government agencies tracked by the state, 1,176 did not file reports by the Dec. 31 deadline, according to records obtained from the state Department of Audits and Accounts. There is no way to know how many of those who failed to file are exempt, but the results did not please state officials.

"I certainly would have hoped for a better response," said Russell Hinton, the state auditor. City and county officials blamed the missing reports on unfamiliarity with the law, heavy workloads, staff turnover and other problems.

Among those that missed the reporting deadline is Sandy Springs, one of the state's largest cities with about 94,000 residents. The city filed its report this month after The *Atlanta Journal-Constitution* contacted officials there about it. Sandy Springs is enrolled to use? E-Verify, federal records show. When organizations enroll with E-Verify, they sign a document promising to use it to check newly hired employees.

"As a matter of practice, the city requires all contractors, and all companies submitting a bid for doing business with the city, to complete E-Verify documentation," Kraun, the city spokeswoman, told The *Atlanta Journal-Constitution*.

Stewart County, home of the state's largest detention center for illegal immigrants, also did not file its report as required. A county official blamed the problem on staff turnover and said the report would be filed this week. The county is enrolled to use E-Verify.

Forty other local and state government organizations started the process of filing their reports but did not finish, including Chamblee and the DeKalb housing authority.

Chamblee City Manager Niles Ford said the city's report would be filed this month. The Chamblee Police Department is registered to use E-Verify.

An official at the DeKalb housing authority—which is also enrolled to use E-Verify—said her agency was looking into the matter.

Also, 620 agencies reported they had no public works contracts to report for the period of July 1 to Nov. 30.

Among the 488 agencies that did report using contractors, the thoroughness of the reports differed widely. For example, while Cobb officials reported doing business with more than 120 contractors, Fulton—the state's most populous county—identified just one. The county said it would submit a revised report.

"After re-reviewing the law and the report submitted to the state in December 2011," the county said in a prepared statement, "it appears that our initial interpretation of [the law] may not have been fully comprehensive of all types of services addressed in the law."

Georgia's law tasks the Department of Audits and Accounts and the Labor Department with doing audits to test whether government agencies and their contractors are actually using E-Verify—but only if they receive funding to do the work. This month, officials at those agencies told the AJC they have not received any money. Mark Krikorian, executive director of the Center for Immigration Studies, bemoaned the lack of audits.

"Obviously, they ought to be doing spot checks, audits, something," said Krikorian, whose Washington-based organization advocates for tighter immigration controls. "This is why a federal [nationwide] E-Verify requirement is necessary. The state measures just aren't going to be enough."

Illegal Immigration Hard to Measure

Identifying the precise impact of Georgia's year-old anti-illegal immigration law is impossible, partly because there are only estimates and no official counts of illegal immigrants living in the state. Further, no estimates exist yet for this year. Some points to consider:

The U.S. Homeland Security Department's most recent estimates of Georgia's illegal immigrant population (for 2010 and 2011) are based on census data gathered 10 years apart (in 2000 and 2010, respectively). That makes a year-to-year comparison invalid. The estimate for 2011 was 440,000.

Last year, the Pew Hispanic Center released a report estimating that Georgia was home to 425,000 illegal immigrants in 2010. The center has not yet released estimates for 2011.

Georgia school officials don't track the immigration status of their students. The number of Hispanic students statewide rose by 4,310 from last March to this March. That was about half of all enrollment growth.

For fiscal year 2011, Georgia's state prison system and local jails together received about $3 million from a federal program that partially reimburses states and counties for jailing illegal immigrants. No such information is available for 2012.

24. Immigrant Investors: A New Source of Real Estate Capital
Alex Hutchinson

When the Athia family arrived in Washington, D.C., during the 1990s, they gained entrée to the local motel industry through connections from their native India. What began for them as front desk check-ins and the cleaning of motel rooms in suburban Maryland has grown into Baywood Hotels, a successful family-run hospitality development firm that has completed more than 70 hotels nationwide. The Athias' experience represents immigrants' traditional American dream story—the ethos that hard work at one's business can pay off in prosperity.

Baywood's latest project is a dual-branded Hilton hotel—the U.S. Capitol Hotel Complex, Hampton Inn & Homewood Suites—and is a redevelopment of the family's first hotel, where they once lived. Not only does the project represent the dreams of the Baywood hotel team, but $39 million of financing also represents the dreams and investments of 78 foreign investors who have contributed to the project in exchange for two-year conditional green cards, with the possibility of becoming permanent green-card holders.

The Baywood investors are participating in the employment-based Immigrant Investor Program, also known as EB-5, which is administered by the U.S. Department of Homeland Security (DHS). The program is quickly becoming a household name in the immigration law, real estate, and economic development industries.

The financing for the Baywood project came from a regional center, a federally approved private company that pools the foreign investment.

Originally published as Alex Hutchinson, "Immigrant Investors: A New Source of Real Estate Capital," http://urbanland.uli.org/capital-markets/immigrant-investors-new-source-real-estate-capital/, May 23, 2014. Reprinted with permission of the publisher.

Interest in the EB-5 program has led to the exponential growth of the regional center industry over the past five years.

Yet, critics argue the EB-5 program is an abuse of the immigration system that allows wealthy foreigners to buy their way into the United States. Detractors assert that the DHS lacks the necessary personnel trained in economics, business, and securities to properly oversee the system.

Regulators have struggled to keep pace with the increasing number of foreign investors and regional centers applying to participate in the EB-5 program. As a result, a number of high-profile cases in which regional centers attempted to defraud foreign investors have occurred. The rapid growth in the EB-5 program has raised concerns among critics and industry leaders who seek ways to improve this effective economic development program while safeguarding investors from fraud.

How It Works

Congress established EB-5 as a program that allows foreign individuals who invest at least $500,000 in eligible projects to receive temporary visas. To qualify, their investment must create or preserve ten full-time jobs in new or existing businesses. After two years, if the project has directly or indirectly created ten full-time jobs, the investors are eligible for permanent residency for themselves and their dependents. Typically, investors have no involvement with the project other than providing financing.

The EB-5 program was modeled after successful programs that have existed in Canada and Australia since the early 1980s. These immigrant-investor programs had received significant attention from Hong Kong investors in the early 1990s who were uncertain about their country's future due to the impending takeover by China.

The EB-5 program averaged only 450 applications per year in its first few years, but interest has surged since 2008. This coincided with the global recession, when many real estate developers lost funding and looked to alternative sources for investment. In 2013, a record 6,434 individuals applied for visas.

In 2012, the EB-5 program created 42,000 jobs and contributed $3.39 billion to the U.S. gross domestic product (GDP), according to a study commissioned by Invest in the USA (IIUSA), a trade association for regional centers. The same study found that spending from investors accounted for $447 million in federal tax revenue and $265 million in state and local tax revenues. The impact on the real estate industry was substantial. According to the IIUSA study, 38 percent of all jobs and 31 percent of GDP contribution created through the EB-5 program were in the real estate industry.

Regional Centers

Approximately 90 to 95 percent of EB-5 investments occur through regional centers, which are private companies designed to pool investments to fund larger projects and create employment opportunities. To operate as a private enterprise, a regional center must apply to the U.S. Citizenship and Immigration Services (USCIS), a division of DHS.

Regional centers have emerged alongside the EB-5 program. According to USCIS, these federally approved private investment companies expanded from 11 in 2007 to 442 in 2013. The centers have been instrumental in raising capital for office buildings, mixed-use developments, affordable and seniors' housing, health care facilities, shopping centers, infrastructure, and construction projects. In 2012, California, New York, and Pennsylvania witnessed the most EB-5 investment.

Regional centers have become a formidable industry in their own right: they typically charge foreign investors $45,000 to $50,000 in fees in addition to the initial $500,000 project investment. These fees go to immigration lawyers, business plan writers, economists, securities lawyers, investor agents, and other consultants required to execute a complex EB-5 deal.

A major reason for the spike in the number of regional centers is that private developers, looking to cut out the middleman from their transaction costs, have established their own regional centers to reduce the cost of capital. Most regional center investments are made in targeted employment areas (TEAs), zones designated by state economic development officials that have at least 150 percent of the national unemployment average. In TEAs and rural areas with fewer than 20,000 residents, investors have to put only $500,000 toward a project, compared with $1 million in non–TEAs. At present, there is not much of a market for non–TEA projects, since EB-5 deals typically have only a 0.5 percent to 3 percent return for the investor.

"Realistically, investors are perfectly happy having 0.5 percent to 1 percent, because the main return they are getting is their green card," says H. Ronald Klasko, an immigration lawyer and chairman of the EB-5 Committee of the American Immigration Lawyers Association. "They would rather have a green card than a few more percentage points." Regional centers are able to lower lending rates to partners, and value of this cheaper cost of capital is not lost on developers.

"Regional center projects are premised on the fact that if you build a hotel or an office building, it's not only a question of how many people will be employed in the office building, but the construction process as well," says Klasko. "There are many spinoffs of indirect and induced employment." Regional centers include both direct and indirect job creation statistics in visa applications.

Regional centers are tasked with documenting and tracking the employment gains from an EB-5 project. The centers hire economists who use sophisticated employment models to calculate job growth over the evaluation period. These employment numbers are reported to USCIS to help determine eligible visa applicants. USCIS does not maintain an active database categorized by regional center, project, industry, or other information, which could help improve transparency and the program's progress.

As the program grew after the recession, USCIS officials began to understand the limitations of immigration adjudication officers. These officers, while trained in immigration law, lacked the business acumen required to administer the growing program.

In 2011, President Obama instructed federal agencies to examine the program's rules, processes, and regulations to see if they prohibited economic growth. To deal with the growing interest in the program, USCIS has begun establishing a command center to review EB-5 visa applications in the immigrant-investor office based in Washington, D.C.

Yet the growing interest in the program has also brought increased criticism. In 2011, David North, a fellow of the Center for Immigration Studies and a prominent critic of the EB-5 visa system, testified before Congress about its flaws. It is "a program troubled with too many cooks, too many complications," he said, "and too many scandals [with] the basic question: should the U.S. be selling visas to people who cannot otherwise qualify for green cards?"

The program currently has a 10,000-visa capacity annually. Although this number has never been met, proponents of the program expect there to be a backlog of applications in the next few years, especially from China, where the majority of the investors are from.

How Funding Works

In 2008, the city of Dallas was looking at new ways to foster economic development and to promote foreign investment in the city. Civitas Capital

Group, a private investment company, learned of the city's intent to set up a regional center and approached the city.

Civitas now operates the City of Dallas Regional Center (CDRC) on behalf of the city, making it one of the few public/private partnership regional centers in the country. CDRC differs from most regional centers in that the majority are privately run companies that may have goals that differ from those of the public sector. "We go out in the city of Dallas and look for opportunities that are a good fit for the EB-5 program," explains Gabriel Hidalgo, managing director of Civitas Capital Group.

Regional centers' roles also include finding investors, managing the investments on behalf of clients, and ensuring that customers comply with EB-5 visa requirements to ultimately obtain their residency.

"Operating a regional center is a level of responsibility and type of risk a city shouldn't expose itself to," says Hidalgo. The risk for cities is that raising millions in capital, managing dozens of foreign private investors, understanding the intricacies of the EB-5 process, and ensuring a successful visa application for clients all fall outside of the expertise of local economic development officials.

"We keep a tight rein on our quality-control process," says Angelique Brunner, president and founder of EB5 Capital, a Washington, D.C.–based regional center operator involved with the Baywood hotel project. EB5 gives investors a list of well-vetted partners they will need for the immigration procedure. "If I get a check from them, and nothing else works, then I have failed the client," she adds.

Since banks were less inclined to underwrite risky projects following the 2008 credit crunch, developers and economic development agencies became interested in EB-5 as a tool to reignite stalled projects. One such project is the Alexan Trinity Apartments, a 166-unit apartment building in the North Oak Cliffs neighborhood of Dallas, which began construction in February 2013. The project includes 34 affordable units, defined as annual rent being less than 30 percent of the median income in the area.

Alexan Trinity needed EB-5 capital to make the project feasible. Twenty percent of the development's funding came from tax increment financing (TIF), which was used to pay for pedestrian linkages, public infrastructure, and overall project feasibility. The project will also be served by Dallas's future streetcar line.

Alexan Trinity, a Trammell Crow multifamily joint venture, is exceeding its pro forma and achieving rents above $1 per square foot in the area. The project was also successful from an EB-5 perspective; 180 direct and indirect jobs were created, and ten investors are awaiting permanent residency.

Now that leaders in the public and private sectors have seen a variety of successful projects across multiple industries, interest in and comfort using the program are growing. In 2012, the Washington State Regional Center established a company to buy bonds to replace an aging bridge, bringing $48 million worth of EB-5 investment to the project from 95 investors, mostly from China.

The project initially met with difficulty with USCIS because buying bonds did not satisfy the "at risk" condition (a requirement of the EB-5 program is that regional centers cannot guarantee return), but the project was ultimately approved.

"The EB-5 program has now become a tangible capital market, so there is a diversification in industries that are now benefiting from it," says Peter Joseph, executive director of IIUSA. Joseph notes that EB-5 can induce regional economic development through the creation of public/private partnerships.

The Baywood Hotel Experience

In 2012, when institutional investors had little interest in hospitality projects, Baywood found EB-5, which began to be an attractive financing option. "EB-5 funds do not carry the same covenants or constraints one might get from a typical lender, so they were perceived as more flexible dollars. There was a lot of interest in the industry," says Beau Athia, who is vice president of strategic development for the firm. As a number of high-profile brand-name hotels including Hilton, Marriott, and Hyatt began using EB-5 financing, comfort levels among developers increased.

The $59 million project in Washington, D.C., will be 67 percent financed by 78 individual EB-5 investors, mostly from China, who brought $39 million to the project. The investors will make a five-year loan to finance the project's construction. The project is expected to create approximately 800 jobs.

EB5 Capital, based in D.C. and San Francisco, has clients from more than 40 countries and claims a 100 percent approval rate for I-526 Petitions, which are a conditional green card, and I-829 Petitions, a permanent green card. The company relies on word of mouth in an increasingly competitive industry. "We do not advertise; we do not hold events; [an investor] can barely call our office and get a person to talk to unless [he or she has] been referred. Our client [investors] really call us for our track record," says Brunner.

Athia says one constraint of the program is timing. "If I wanted to put a shovel in the ground and start construction, there is a small amount of lag time between starting a project and how quickly EB-5 funds can be raised," he says.

Promotion Outside the United States

Economic development officials and regional center representatives from across the country travel internationally to develop relationships with potential EB-5 investors.

On these trade missions, local officials bring developers, regional center leaders, and other economic development officials to help promote interest in regional center projects. Most EB-5 investment missions take place in China, and for good reason: at present, 81 percent of all program participants are Chinese investors. Other major origin countries for EB-5 investors include South Korea, India, Canada, and Brazil.

The Chinese are the most frequent participants in the program for a number of reasons. "You are looking for a country with a lot of new millionaires, a lot of wealth, who value education, but who currently live in a less-than-ideal environment," says Brian Ostar of EB5 Capital. While China has been the most heavily recruited nation in recent years, as other emerging countries grow wealthier they become prime candidates for the program as well.

EB-5 projects with government support and subsidy as part of the capital stack are more palatable for foreign investors. The higher the level of government, the more appealing the project. Debt financing is more typical than equity in EB-5 projects since investors want to get their visas and have little, if anything, to do with the project.

Growth and Fraud

As the program has grown, a number of high-profile cases of fraud have been exposed. In February 2013, the U.S. Securities and Exchange Commission (SEC) uncovered a Chicago regional center owner who fraudulently sold $145 million in securities and took $11 million in fees from more than 250 investors. The SEC froze the assets of the would-be developer, and all of the investment funds were returned to investors. Nonetheless, the case has been a cautionary tale for the EB-5 community. In response to the Chicago case and other cases of fraud, IIUSA has responded by creating tools to help self-police and create trust with the public sector.

Other critics argue that cases of fraud are a symptom of DHS's inability to properly administer the program. The Brookings Institute released a report in February that finds that despite efforts to ramp up USCIS staff with a business background, DHS is the wrong institutional home for such a complex program. The report recommends creation of an oversight role for the U.S. Department of Commerce; creation of incentives for partnerships with local economic development authorities, much like the CDRC; and generation of a public database that can help investors and officials evaluate regional center projects. At present, USCIS offers limited benchmarking on regional center statistics.

Yet the popularity of the program is representative of the deficiencies in U.S. immigration policy, says Angelique Brunner of EB5 Capital. "We have clients who are PhDs who received their education from American schools, who weren't able to find jobs to stay in the U.S.," she says. "They met their wives here, had their children here, and then had to leave the country, and the only way to get back was to use EB-5." EB-5 visa applications fast-track the immigration process. EB-5 investors typically are granted temporary status within 12 to 18 months and permanent residency in just 2.5 to three years as opposed to six to ten years in traditional visa applications.

The EB-5 program is clearly gaining interest from the real estate and construction industry. The growth of regional centers and foreign investors has brought about changes in federal regulation and innovative public/private partnerships at the local level. As more developers decide to go it alone, there are more opportunities to gain access to capital at a reduced price through the program. However, the program's steep learning curve and the dependence on federal approvals for visas should serve as a caution for developers simply looking to the program as an opportunity for easy money. As foreign investors become savvier and expect more from deals, project promoters may have to look harder and farther for willing investors in the future.

25. City of Bellevue Recognized as Immigration Trend-Setter

International City/County Management Association

With a large, skilled, Asian immigrant population that contributes to its success as a high-tech center, Bellevue is apparently at the vanguard of a national trend. The latest evidence is a new report that shows Asians are now the fastest growing immigrant group in the U.S.

In "The Rise of Asian Americans," a study released June 19, the nonpartisan Pew Research Center reported that the influx of Asians—the most educated and highest-earning population in the U.S.—is helping the country's economy.

In Bellevue, Asians account for 28 percent of the city's population, the highest share of any city in the state. A significant number work for tech companies downtown, including Microsoft and Expedia. From 2000 to 2010, the number of Asians in Bellevue increased by 77 percent, to 33,659, making it the city's fastest-growing racial group.

Bellevue's diverse, high-powered workforce, will continue to attract international businesses here. Mayor Conrad Lee, who was born in China, hailed the Pew study for acknowledging the positive impact the country's growing immigrant population has.

"There is no doubt that our diversity makes our city stronger," Lee said, noting that businesses from India and China, the world's economic

Reprinted with permission from the July 11, 2012, issue of *Public Management (PM) Magazine*, published and copyrighted by ICMA (International City/County Management Association), Washington, D.C.

juggernauts, are coming to Bellevue because a network of skilled workers and compatriot CEOs is already here.

A Wall Street Journal article about the Pew study cited Maria Zhang, a Chinese national who launched a mobile technology company in Bellevue in late 2010. Nearly all of the employees at her small firm are from Asia. She told the paper that finding quality engineers is difficult.

According to the Pew report, the bulk of Asians in the U.S. come from China, India, Japan, Korea, the Philippines and Vietnam. Chinese residents make up the largest portion of the Asian population in Bellevue, but over the past decade Indians have been the fastest-growing group.

Fifteen percent of the state's Indian population lives in Bellevue. In Bellevue, Indians are a distinct presence. In 2009, the government of India gave Bellevue a statue of Mahatma Gandhi, which stands outside the Bellevue Regional Library, to honor the people of the city where many Indian nationals have settled and found success.

The Pew study reported that Asians recently nudged Hispanics from the top spot for immigration. In 2010, about 36 percent of new immigrants were Asian, compared to 31 percent who were Hispanic.

Consistent with the scenario in Bellevue, the study noted, "Recent Asian immigrants are about three times as likely as recent immigrants from other parts of the world to receive their green cards—or permanent resident status—on the basis of employer rather than family sponsorship."

For the Rise of Asian Americans report, the Washington, D.C.–based Pew Research Center surveyed a nationally representative sample of 3,511 Asian Americans by telephone over the first three months of this year, in English and seven Asian languages.

26. Bilingual Vocational Education for Immigrants

Cheryl Harrison

Between 3.5 and 6.5 million adults in America are limited English-proficient (LEP). Most are immigrants; many understand virtually no English. Eighty percent of the "new" immigrants (those arriving since 1970) are from developing countries and have limited job skills.

Such limitations make the immigrant's earliest tasks difficult. Housing and food are pressing needs, but limited English proficiency and no job prospects make food shopping difficult and apartment hunting nearly impossible. Then, the children must be enrolled in school and utilities must be contracted. The individual has to learn to read a bus schedule, to shop for goods and services, and to sign a check (which may require learning a new alphabet).

To finance this new way of life, the individual needs a job. Most immigrants face major obstacles in obtaining employment. Lopez-Valadez and others (1985) have identified four such obstacles.

—Lack of English skills is possibly the greatest single barrier to employment success faced by LEP adults.
—Cultural differences, which can cause symptoms from slight confusion and homesickness to a total "shut down" of functioning, impede the individual in all phases of the employment process.
—Few immigrants have skills directly transferable to the American workplace.

Originally published as Cheryl Harrison, "Bilingual Vocational Education for Immigrants," *ERIC Digest* No. 49. http://www.ericdigests.org/pre-923/immigrants.htm, 1986. Reprinted from public domain.

—Many employers and the general public resist the hiring of immigrants, fearing that there will be communication difficulties or that "American" jobs will be taken.

What Methods Can Be Used to Teach English for Employability?

A major obstacle for immigrant Hispanic workers is the lack of English skills (National Commission for Employment Policy 1982). It is indeed likely that language problems are the strongest single barrier to success for all LEP workers in the United States. Thus, the adult immigrant must set learning English as a second language (ESL) as a high priority.

Vocational ESL (VESL) provides adult immigrants with English skills on an "as-needed" basis in cooperation with a program of vocational training. The ESL teacher and the trainer coordinate their efforts. VESL has been shown to be an effective approach for teaching English to adult immigrants. Since students can see the connection between their needs and the lessons in English, they are motivated to stay in class and to learn their lessons. Under ideal conditions, VESL students can finish their training as quickly as their English-speaking peers. However, it must be noted that the English taught in VESL classes is far from comprehensive.

Friedenberg (in Lopez-Valadez and others 1985) says that the successful VESL program has three characteristics: VESL instruction must be job specific; VESL instruction and job training should occur simultaneously and be closely coordinated by the instructors; and when necessary, job training should use the student's native language.

After the trainer and the VESL instructor have discussed priorities and the various tasks to be taught, the VESL instructor creates a lesson plan for each unit that includes the vocational topic, vocabulary, relevant grammatical structures, language skills needed (listening, speaking, and so forth), and relevant cultural information. VESL instructors usually balance structured activities (drills, puzzles, and close-ended responses) with communicative activities (role playing, completing forms, and open-ended questions).

What Strategies Are Used to Overcome Cultural Differences?

Cultural adjustment may be more difficult for many LEP individuals than learning English because cultural laws have not been codified and are not formally taught.

The American workplace has a subculture all its own, characterized by acceptable and unacceptable behaviors and unwritten laws. The American job interview requires such cultural behaviors as directness, clear and confident responses, and eye contact. These behaviors are difficult for many Americans to master and are even harder for immigrants who have very different values and a weak command of the English language.

Awareness of and sensitivity to cultural obstacles by the educational service provider are the first steps toward helping the immigrant adjust to American life. Talking with a culturally sensitive person, the immigrant can get the right answers about what is expected and what is considered wrong.

Lucas (in Lopez-Valadez and others 1985) lists the following activities that may facilitate cultural adjustment.

—Role play job interviews and on-the-job situations.
—Set aside Job Interview Dress Day.
—Listen to or read a job interview or on-the-job conversation and discuss.
—Tour vocational training centers and local industries.
—Develop slides or videotapes of appropriate and inappropriate employability behaviors for discussion.

These activities allow students to experience "real world" situations in a nonthreatening environment. This experience is followed by discussion of findings with peers and with a culturally sensitized American. The activities build cultural self-confidence and facilitate cultural adjustment.

What Methods Are Useful in Teaching Vocational Skills?

Immigrant clients have varying backgrounds, and thus, their training needs are very different. The amount and type of assistance required by a trainee are determined by an analysis of employment background, educational background, English language proficiency, experience with United States culture, and the individual's personal goals.

Adult immigrants need to enter the job market quickly. Short-term (less than 1 year) intensive training is usually appropriate, although some will opt for longer term or part-time programs. Those who lack English or other basic skills may need to spend some time in a preentry training preparation program that will extend the total time needed for training.

Typically, employment-related training for immigrant adults can be delivered through vocational programs, work experience programs, ESL classrooms (discussed earlier), and the workplace (Kremer and Savage 1985). In Lopez-Valadez and others (1985), Kremer focuses on the vocational classroom approach that prepares adult immmigrants for specific occupations. Students may either be mainstreamed into regular vocational classes with English-speaking vocational students or be placed in special classes. In either case, the student needs extensive support services to be successful. Support may range from peer tutoring to providing a personal translator for exams and quizzes.

Since training will usually occur in English, some adaptation is required. Adaptation of instruction for LEP students includes adjustments in the curriculum, materials, and approaches. The following techniques are suggested.

—Introduce one concept at a time.
—Use a slower pace in introducing information.
—Use shorter lectures and more demonstrations.
—Explain key concepts in the native language.
—Provide bilingual glossaries.
—Check readability and adapt materials if necessary.
—Summarize or outline long, difficult readings.
—Check comprehension frequently.
—Use visual support materials.
—Modify tests to evaluate mastery of content, not of English.

Two other approaches are also used to teach employability skills. The work experience approach combines classroom learning with unpaid experience in a work setting. Another option, the workplace training approach, emphasizes training at the work site. The individuals who take part in this training are already employed: the purpose of training is to make them better, more promotable employees. Often, this special training is supported by the employer.

At the completion of a training program, most immigrants will need help finding jobs. The job developer may provide the link between the trained immigrant and the American employer. There are two methods of job development: crisis placement and investment. The former views the client's need for employment as critical. The investment approach, on the other hand, does not guarantee immediate placement but builds for the future. In this approach, the job developer researches employers' needs and provides a product (the client) that addresses them. The agency runs less risk of dissatisfied employers and may actually receive other job offers because of a good first placement.

References

Kremer, N., and Savage, K. Lynn, eds. (1985). *Approaches to Employment Related Training for Adults Who are Limited-English Proficient.* Burlingame, CA: Association of California School Administrators.

Lopez-Valadez, J., Friedenberg, J., Lucas, N.L., Kremer, N. and Reed, T. (1985). *Immigrant Workers and the American Workplace: The Role of Voc Ed.* Information Series no. 302. Columbus: ERIC Clearinghouse on Adult, Career, and Vocational Education. The Ohio State University.

National Commission for Employment Policy (1982). *Hispanics and Jobs: Barriers to Progress.* Washington, DC: National Commission for Employment Policy.

27. The Case for Structured English Immersion

Kevin Clark

When Arizona voters passed a ballot initiative in 2000 that required all English language learners to be educated through structured English immersion (SEI), the idea seemed simple enough: Teach students the English language quickly so they can do better in school. But as other states, districts, and schools that have contemplated an SEI program have learned, the devil is in the details. As it turns out, the simple goal to "teach English quickly" frequently evokes legal wrangling, emotion, and plain old demagoguery.

Few people would disagree that English language proficiency is necessary for academic success in U.S. schools. Less clear, however, is the optimal pathway for helping language-minority students master English. Conflicting ideologies, competing academic theories, and multiple metrics for comparing different approaches have rendered many schools, districts, and educators paralyzed by confusion. Bill Holden, principal of a California elementary school in which ELLs are three-fourths of the student population, told me, "At a certain point there were just so many mixed messages and contradictory directives and policies that we didn't really know what to do."

Despite the controversy, however, many schools in Arizona and other states have implemented structured English immersion or are in the process of doing so. As I have worked with educators, school boards, and the Arizona English Language Learners Task Force to explore, design, and imple-

Originally published as Kevin Clark, "The Case for Structured English Immersion," *Educational Leadership*, April 2009. Reprinted with permission of the author.

ment structured programs, a common theme emerges: These programs have the potential to accelerate ELLs' English language development and linguistic preparation for grade-level academic content.

Why Do Schools Implement Structured English Immersion?

Several factors usually account for school and district leaders' decisions to opt for structured English immersion. In three states (California, Arizona, and Massachusetts), the reason is straightforward: Laws passed through voter initiatives now require structured English immersion and restrict bilingual education.

Another factor is that most state student performance assessments are conducted in English, and schools or districts that miss targets face increased scrutiny and possible sanctions. This provides added incentive for schools to get students' English proficiency up to speed as soon as possible.

A third factor is the burgeoning subpopulation of ELL students who reach an intermediate level of English competence after a few years—and then stop making progress. These students (more than 60 percent of all ELLs in some districts, according to analyses I conducted for 15 districts) possess conversational English competence. But they lag in their ability to apply the rules, structures, and specialized vocabularies of English necessary for grade-level academic coursework; and their writing typically features an array of structural errors. My analyses showed that the typical intermediate-level ELL scores well below proficient on state-level tests in English language arts.

Some educators have acknowledged, in fact, that intermediate English competence is the logical outcome of their current practices and program designs. "Once we really analyzed our program for ELL students," one district superintendent told me, "we saw that we really didn't teach English to our students. We were teaching in English, but not really teaching English."

Confusion About Structured English Immersion

Keith Baker and Adriana de Kanter (1983) first coined the term structured English immersion (SEI) in a recommendation to schools to teach English to non-native speakers by using program characteristics from the successful French immersion programs in Canada. In 1991, J. David Ramirez and his colleagues conducted a voluminous study of ELL instructional programs and found that SEI programs shared two basic components: (1) teachers maximize instruction in English and (2) teachers use and teach English at a level appropriate to the abilities of the ELLs in the class (Ramirez, Yuen, and Ramey 1991).

Since then, many people have taken a crack at defining structured English immersion. The definition presented to voters in Massachusetts was similar to those used in election materials in California and Arizona: "Nearly all classroom instruction is in English but with the curriculum and presentation designed for children who are learning the language" (Massachusetts Department of Education 2003, p. 7).

But when Arizona's English Language Learner Task Force began meeting in late 2006, it found that few people seemed to know what SEI should look like. Many teachers, academics, and school administrators who testified before the task force had a negative view of the state-mandated approach. Presenters frequently confused SEI with submersion, the process of placing ELLs in regular classrooms that feature little or no instructional modifications and minimal instruction in the actual mechanics of English. Others viewed SEI as synonymous with specially designed academic instruction in English (SDAIE), also known as sheltered instruction, which features an array of strategies designed to help students of intermediate or higher proficiency access grade-level subject matter (Aha! 2007).

Experience Fills in the Details

Notwithstanding the hodgepodge of definitions, mixed messages, and underlying emotions, educators have implemented structured English immersion programs at both the elementary and secondary levels. A framework for effective SEI is emerging that includes the following elements.

Significant amounts of the school day are dedicated to the explicit teaching of the English language, and students are grouped for this instruction according to their level of English proficiency. In Arizona, all ELLs must receive four hours of daily English language development. Other states and districts also provide large amounts of explicit instruction in English. For example, in Massachusetts, students at the lowest levels of English competence receive a minimum of two and one-half hours of daily English language development.

Grouping students for English-language instruction according to their English language ability is an important component of SEI because it enables teachers to effectively design language lessons. True beginners, for example, can benefit greatly from a direct lesson on common nouns, whereas intermediate students need to understand how subordinating conjunctions are used in academic writing.

The English language is the main content of SEI instruction. Academic content plays a supporting, but subordinate, role. The dominant focus is language itself: its rules, uses, forms, and application to daily school and nonschool situations and topics. The operant principle is that students must have a strong understanding of the English language before they can be expected to learn grade-level content.

Massachusetts, for example, tightly defines English language development instruction as "explicit, direct instruction about the English language intended to promote English language acquisition by LEP students and to help them 'catch up' to their student peers who are proficient in English" (Massachusetts Department of Education 2006, p. 2).

Martin Ramirez, principal of a Yuba City, California, high school that has gained national attention for its SEI program, puts the language-content issue this way: *"We are charged with giving our ELLs a rigorous core content curriculum that is comparable to their English-speaking peers. But just putting them in a science course does not make it a rigorous curriculum. They will get access when they possess the language skills to be able to understand the content, and that is the role of our SEI program."*

English is the language of instruction; students and teachers are expected to speak, read, and write in English. Accelerated language programs like SEI are based, in part, on the comprehensible output theory (Swain, 1985). This means that we cannot expect students to advance their language competence mainly through oral comprehension; instead, students get more proficient in English when they actually try to produce increasingly complex English language sentences. All materials and instruction in SEI programs are in English. For this reason, teachers and instructional support staff are not required to be able to speak a language other than English.

Although controversial, the limit on use of students' home languages keeps the goal of SEI programs clear. One administrator in an Idaho district summarized the rationale: "Unfortunately, our ELD classrooms in the past sometimes featured as much Spanish as English. It was just sending a very confusing message to students and staff."

Teachers use instructional methods that treat English as a foreign language. Structured English immersion programs reject the notion that teaching in English is the same as teaching English and that complex language skills can be learned through osmosis. SEI's foreign-language orientation calls for active, direct, and explicit instructional methods. Students have abundant opportunities to learn and produce new and more complex English language structures.

Students learn discrete English grammar skills. In SEI classrooms, teachers try to accelerate students' natural tendency to acquire language by providing grammatically focused lessons that raise students' conscious awareness of how English works while engaging them in relevant, age-appropriate learning tasks. Students are overtly taught English pronunciation and listening skills; word building; word-order rules; a wide range of vocabulary (synonyms, antonyms, survival vocabulary, academic word groups); and formulaic expressions not easily explained by grammar analysis ("There you go again"; "What's up with that?"). The overt teaching of verb tenses—almost nonexistent in most traditional public school English language development programs—is typically the anchor of many of these programs, accounting for up to one-fourth of the total instructional time.

Rigorous time lines are established for students to exit from the program. English language learners have little time to waste. While they are learning English, their English-proficient classmates continue to move ahead. For that reason, most SEI programs are designed to last one academic year. An SEI graduate should possess a foundational understanding of the mechanics, structure, and vocabulary of English that enables him or her to meaningfully access core content.

These SEI program graduates, however, are not finished learning English. Indeed, until students are reclassified as fluent English proficient, they are entitled to support services. In Yuba City, for example, when students exit the SEI program, they are enrolled in a mixture of sheltered and mainstream courses, including one period of advanced English language development. Federal law requires that students who have been reclassified be monitored for a two-year period.

Charting New Territory

Each of these program elements in some way runs counter to the assumptions and beliefs that have guided ELL program development throughout the last 30 years. In Arizona and elsewhere, advocates of structured English immersion face strong criticism from detractors who argue, among other things, that these programs are segregatory, experimental, not based on research, nonculturally affirming, damaging to students' self-esteem, and perhaps even illegal (Adams 2005; Combs, Evans, Fletcher, Parra, and Jimenez 2005; Krashen, Rolstad, and MacSwan 2007).

Proponents of SEI maintain that students can learn English faster than many theories suggest, that grouping students by language ability level is necessary for successful lesson design, and that the research support for immersion language-teaching methods and program design principles is solid (Arizona English Language Learners Task Force 2007; Baker 1998; Judson & Garcia-Dugan 2004). As for the question of self-esteem, SEI advocates point out that ELLs are motivated by measurable success in learning the fundamentals of English, as well as by the improved reading comprehension, enhanced writing skills, and higher levels of achievement in core subjects that come from these enhanced language skills.

On the legal front, ballot initiatives requiring SEI programs have been found to comport with federal law. Under the federal framework, as articulated in *Castañeda v. Pickard* (1981), immersion programs are viewed as "sequential," in that their goal is to provide foundational English skills before students participate in a full range of academic content courses.

SEI Programs in Action

George Washington Elementary School in Madera, California, enrolls more than 500 English language learners in grades K-6. Located in the middle of a Spanish-dominant portion of a town in central California, the school was a magnet bilingual education site for decades—and unfortunately one of the lowest-achieving schools in the district. The school missed state and federal academic performance targets for years, and fewer than 3 percent of ELLs annually were reclassified as fully English proficient.

District data analyses showed that after the first full year of SEI program implementation, the school gained almost 30 points on state test metrics, and English language growth rates tripled in all grades, easily exceeding district and federal targets. The reclassification rate last year quadrupled to 12 percent. Perhaps most significant, almost 50 percent of the school's intermediate students advanced to the next level of proficiency or met the criteria for being fully English proficient. Before the SEI program, 70 percent of the school's ELL population regularly showed no English language growth—or even regressed—on the state's yearly English assessment.

Here's what an average day looks like for an ELL student at George Washington Elementary School:

Pronunciation and listening skills, 20 minutes.
Vocabulary, 30 minutes.
Verb tense instruction, 20 minutes.
Sentence structure, 20 minutes.
Integrated grammar skills application, 20 minutes.
English reading and writing, 60 minutes.
Math (specially designed academic instruction in English), 40 minutes.
Science, social science, P.E., 40 minutes.

At Yuba City High School in Northern California, almost half of the school's 450 ELLs test at intermediate or below on the state's language assessment. These students are enrolled in four periods of daily English language development courses: Conversational English and Content Area Vocabulary, English Grammar, English Reading, and English Writing. The school offers three levels for each course; students take an assessment every six weeks that could qualify them to move to the next level. Some students move so quickly that they exit the SEI program in less than a year. After the first year of Yuba City's SEI program, the proportion of students reclassified as fully English proficient tripled to 15 percent, nearly twice the state average.

Rethinking Assumptions and Beliefs

Not surprisingly, the decision to implement a structured English immersion program—whether by law or by choice—frequently brings about conflicts over ideology, pedagogy, and the very role of schooling for English language learners in a culturally and linguistically diverse society. Notwithstanding these challenges, an increasing number of schools, districts, and states across the country have seen that structured English immersion can help students gain the English language skills that are crucial for academic success and opportunities beyond school. As Adela Santa Cruz, director of the Office of English Language Acquisition Services for the Arizona Department of Education, said, *"We understand that implementing an SEI program requires some new ways of thinking and teaching, but once teachers and administrators come to understand SEI, they see it as a positive and effective vehicle for helping ELLs learn English much faster than we thought."*

Few people would disagree that English language proficiency is necessary for academic success in U.S. schools.

Structured English immersion programs reject the notion that complex language skills can be learned through osmosis.

"We were teaching in English, but not really teaching English."

REFERENCES

Adams, M. (2005). *Unmasking the myths of structured English immersion.* Cambridge, MA: Center for Critical Education.

Aha! (2007). *Report of state-wide district survey to the Arizona English Language Learners Task Force.* Tempe, AZ: Author.

Arizona English Language Learners Task Force. (2007). *Research summary and bibliography for structured English immersion programs.* www.asu.edu/educ/sceed/azell/model%5fcomponent%5fresearch.pdf.

Baker, K. (1998). *Structured English immersion breakthrough in teaching limited-English-proficient students.* Phi Delta Kappan, 80(3), 199–204. pdkintl.org/kappan/kbak9811.htm.

_____, and de Kanter, A. (Eds.). (1983). *Bilingual education: A reappraisal of federal policy.* Lexington, MA: Lexington Books.

Castañeda v. Pickard. 648 F. 2d 989 (5th Cir. 1981).

Combs, C. , Evans, C. , Fletcher, T., Parra, E., and Jimenez, A. (2005). "Bilingualism for the children: Implementing a dual-language program in an English-only state." *Educational Policy,* 19(5), 701–728.

Judson, E., and Garcia-Dugan, M. (2004). *The effects of bilingual education programs and structured English immersion programs on student achievement.* Phoenix, AZ: Arizona Department of Education.

Krashen, S., Rolstad, K., and MacSwan, J. (2007). *Review of "Research Summary and Bibliography for Structured English Immersion Programs" of the Arizona English Language Learners Task Force.* Takoma Park, MD: Institute for Language and Education Policy.

Massachusetts Department of Education. (2003). *Questions and answers regarding Chapter 71A: English language education in public schools.* Maiden, MA: Author.

_____. (2006). *Designing and implementing sheltered English immersion (SEI) programs in low incidence districts.* Maiden, MA: Author.

Ramirez, J. D., Yuen, S. D., and Ramey, D. R. (1991). *Final report: Longitudinal study of structured immersion strategy, early-exit, and late-exit transitional bilingual education programs for language-minority children.* San Mateo, CA: Aguirre International.

Swain, M. (1985). "Communicative competence: Some roles of comprehensible input and comprehensible output in its development." In S. Gass & C. Madden (Eds.), *Input in second language acquisition.* New York: Newbury House.

28. New Immigrant Populations Recreating Community

Thomas C. Reynolds

MML's convention workshop on integrating new immigrants into your community took place just as the U.S. Congress was in its final days of deliberation regarding its latest effort to pass comprehensive immigration legislation. However, as workshop speaker Laureen Laglagaron of the National Center on Immigrant Integration Policy at the Migration Policy Institute observed, "In all the debate, nobody's talking about how to integrate that population."

To the extent that such a conversation is happening, the dialogue is occurring principally at the local level. Here in Maryland, where an estimated 641,000 residents are foreignborn, the discussion is taking place in municipalities large and small as evidenced by presentations from Rockville Assistant to the City Manager Maty Lou Berg and Berwyn Heights Mayor Cheye Calvo.

Ms. Berg established the extent of the immigrant challenge in noting that one-third of Rockville's population is now foreign born, and 40 percent of those residents speak languages other than English in their homes. Rather than allowing these populations to become isolated the city has undertaken several initiatives to better connect with newcomers and inform them of their rights and responsibilities as residents of the City of Rockville. Berwyn Heights, located in northern Prince George's County, has seen its foreign-born population increase from 8.2 percent in 2000 to roughly 30 percent.

One of the true keys to Rockville's success in this effort, according to

Originally published as Thomas C. Reynolds, "New Immigrant Populations Recreating Community," *Municipal Maryland*, November 2007. Reprinted with permission of the publisher.

Ms. Berg, has been an ability to recruit and retain bilingual staff. Thirty-seven Rockville employees currently speak languages in addition to English, and they've collectively helped translate in nearly 200 instances within the space of one year. These employees might be called in to translate whether a resident needs assistance in applying for a permit, understanding a water bill, correcting a code violation, or providing the police with information to help solve a neighborhood crime.

Mayor Calvo seconded the inherent value in having employees on staff with the ability to communicate in other languages. He lamented, for example, the recent loss of a part-time code enforcement officer who was fluent in Spanish. This individual's skills were used not only on a day-to-day code enforcement basis. The Town also supplied her with a cell phone so that she could be reached during off hours should a language barrier issue arise. Several workshop attendees found the loss of this employee to be emblematic of the recruitment and retention challenges facing cities and towns as they try to bridge the communication gap that frequently exists between governments and their burgeoning immigrant populations.

Bridging the communication gap ultimately cuts both ways according to each of these speakers. While it is important for municipalities to provide critical information to their constituents in a form they can understand—for without it, code compliance and public safety awareness become a greater challenge—the presenters found a parallel need to assist newcomers in learning English and generally assimilating.

Accordingly, the City of Rockville provides funding to a local non-profit that offers English language courses to residents and partners with the community college to offer citizenship classes. For smaller towns like Berwyn Heights, Mayor Calvo suggested collaborating through existing programs such as those offered by the county and the school system. Berwyn Heights, for example, has helped to advertise and promote adult English as a Second Language (ESL) classes at the local elementary school. Ms. Laglagaron pointed out that the demand for these types of programs continues to outstrip their availability throughout the state.

To take it one step further, Mayor Calvo stressed the need to "not just assimilate immigrants into our communities, but to make it their community as well." A great way to do this, he suggested, was through the children of immigrants, especially in conjunction with neighborhood schools. This too can be a collaborative effort by working with organizations such as the PTA and the Boys & Girls Club.

Ms. Berg offered Rockville's Senior Center as a place where this type of community-building effort has paid substantial dividends. There, seniors of diverse backgrounds take advantage of information available in English, Spanish, and Chinese encouraging them to participate in a range of activities including computer literacy and health and wellness programs. They've also been booking multi-cultural acts at the city's fairs and festivals.

In conclusion, Mayor Calvo emphasized that our demographics are changing and that "we're all changing together." The important thing to remember, however, is that we can have an impact on how things change. With immigration politics so explosive at the moment, "negative change usually happens loudly," he observed. "Positive change, on the other hand, happens quietly." And, while the definition will vary from community to community, it's at the "middle ground" where that positive change is most likely to take hold.

29. Linking to Prior Learning
Yu Ren Dong

Several easy-to-implement strategies can help teachers support language learners in all content areas.

Julieta, an English language learner from Argentina who came to the United States at the beginning of the year, sat in her 9th grade world history class, reading the following passage: *"Rome Begins: While Athens and Sparta were at the height of power, another great early civilization was starting. In another part of the Mediterranean Sea area, Rome was born. About 1500 BC, a tribe called the Latinos crossed the Alp Mountains into what we now call Italy. They settled along the Tiber River. The land was good. It was easy for the people to raise their cattle and crops. These people were the first Romans."*

From the outset, Julieta had difficulty with the phrase height of power in the handout. She quickly punched the words into her electronic translator. It didn't help. She soldiered on, bogged down by more unknown words: civilization, Mediterranean, tribe, settled. The teacher initiated questions to check for students' understanding of the passage, but Julieta was so busy searching for word meanings that she heard little of what the teacher said and how her classmates responded.

After class, Julieta explained, sighing, "Sometimes even the words that the teachers say in class are new and hard for me to understand. I get confused. 1 don't have time to look up everything in my electronic translator." Julieta felt that it wasn't typical of her to get so lost; she had been a straight-A student in her school in Argentina.

Originally published as Yu Ren Dong, "Linking to Prior Learning," *Educational Leadership*, April 2009, Vol. 66, Issue 7. Reprinted with permission of the author.

Language Overload

Like Julieta, many English language learners find themselves sitting in mainstream subject-matter classes confronted with an overwhelming vocabulary load in both the assigned reading and class discussions. The language overload is compounded by the need to learn challenging disciplinary-specific knowledge and skills, meet rigorous graduation requirements, and pass standardized tests.

To reduce the vocabulary overload that English language learners experience, some mainstream subject-matter teachers use such strategies as referring the students to the textbook glossary and encouraging them to use a dictionary or an electronic translator. But as Julieta pointed out, it's often difficult for students to consult the dictionary while engaging in class discussion, reading the textbook, and copying notes from the board. In addition, textbook glossaries and dictionaries are not always helpful because the definitions themselves may contain unfamiliar words.

One support strategy that mainstream subject-matter teachers can use is activating English language learners' native languages and prior knowledge (Cummins et al. 2005). Some teachers have concerns in this area, however. Students' prior knowledge is encoded in their native languages and acquired through schooling in their native countries and sometimes may not be the appropriate prior knowledge that the teacher anticipates. For example, some English language learners may have different prior knowledge concerning the word propaganda. The word for propaganda in Chinese means passing on information in a good sense. This is not congruent with the prior knowledge that the teacher has in mind when she discusses the propaganda that the Nazis used in World War II.

Also, some subject-matter teachers may not be convinced about the merits of introducing students' home languages in the classroom. Some teachers may fear that students will use their native languages as a crutch that will ultimately impede their learning of English. Other teachers may fear that their own lack of understanding of the students' native languages may impede their ability to support student learning of the subject matter in English.

Second-language research has repeatedly shown, however, that English language learners' native languages and prior knowledge play important roles in learning subject-matter knowledge in English (August, Carol, Dressier, and Snow 2005; Meyer 2000; Rubinstein-Avila 2006). According to Cummins (1979), the linguistic and cognitive interdependence between the first and second languages facilitates rather than impedes students' learning of English in general and of academic English in particular. This interdependence becomes even stronger as the student moves into higher grade levels (August et al. 2005).

What Teachers Need to Know

Over the years, in a teacher education class I've taught for secondary preservice teachers, I've worked with my students to develop effective language support for English language learners in subject-matter classes. As part of the course, the teachers must observe an English as a second language class to develop sensitivity to and awareness of learners' needs and to learn effective teaching strategies. Students also keep a journal to document their growing knowledge.

Working in their subject-matter groups, the preservice teachers examine the teaching materials used in mainstream secondary subject-matter classes, ranging from textbooks to extracted passages, from novels to laboratory manuals. The teachers learn to think from the perspective of English language learners, identify prior knowledge that students might bring to the lesson, and highlight difficult words and cultural concepts. In their observations, they also have identified helpful teaching strategies, two of which have proven most effective: using cognates to help students understand challenging English academic vocabulary and activating prior knowledge.

Cracking the Code with Cognates

Those of us who have learned a second language can remember when we first encountered an unknown word in the new language. Our brain automatically searched for patterns or similarities between the new language and our native language to help us understand the new concept or word (Cummins 1979; Dong 2004; Short and Echevarria 2004/2005). This mapping of a new word in the second language to a cognate or translational equivalent in our native languages has been proven to be a successful strategy (Freeman and Freeman 2009; Kieffer and Lesaux 2007; Rubinstein-Avila 2006).

Despite the occasional mismatches, such as false cognates, the benefits of using cognates to learn far outweigh the drawbacks. Researchers have noted a tremendous possibility for cross-language transfer through cognates, especially for native Romance language speakers learning academic English vocabulary (August et al. 2005; Freeman and Freeman 2009; Kieffer and Lesaux 2007; Rodriguez 2001). A large number of academic English words are similar in both spelling and meaning to Spanish words, and Spanish-speaking English language learners can use these words as a rich resource in their acquisition of English vocabulary.

Many of my preservice teachers who are French and Spanish native speakers have mentioned that this is how they learned academic English. To illustrate how students' native languages can help them learn English, John, a native-Spanish-speaking preservice teacher, modified a reading passage on hibernation from a science textbook (Brockway 1985, p. 128) by highlighting Spanish-English cognates:

> **Hibernation (Hibernación)** In the fall, mammals (mamíferos), such as mice and squirrels, gather and store food. Woodchucks and skunks develop thick layers of fat. These adaptations (adaptations), and others (otros), help many animals (animales) survive the cold winter months when food is scarce. Some birds and insects (insectos) migrate (emigran) from the forest to warmer climates (climas) where food is abundant (abundante). Small animals, such as snakes and chipmunks, spend the winter in burrows in a sleeplike state called hibernation (hibernación). During hibernation an animal's body temperature (temperatura) is lower and its heartbeat and breathing rates decrease. Hibernation allows an animal (animal) to survive the winter on very little energy (energía). In the spring the animal "wakes up."

English language learners see that they have an extra tool to help them crack the code of daunting academic vocabulary words in English.

Teachers who have no knowledge of Spanish can ask their Spanish-speaking students to identify cognates and include them in the lesson for language support. Vincent, a preservice mathematics teacher, was planning a lesson on the angle bisector theorem for a group of five 10th grade students in a beginners' class in English as a second language. With a visual glossary that he prepared beforehand, Vincent began the lesson by asking his students about the English equivalent of such words as triangle, vertex, congruent angle, and theorem. He was delighted to discover that his students recognized many of the cognates and understood their meanings because they had learned these concepts previously. All five students' knowledge in mathematics was more advanced than that of their grade-equivalent U.S. peers. Teachers can expand Vincent's glossary to include equivalents in other languages.

By shifting English words to students' native-language equivalents, teachers direct students' attention toward something they already know. Teachers can ask students to translate key words in their native languages and discuss them along with the English definitions. Comparisons between languages also lead to a discussion of academic vocabulary at a higher level.

Activating Prior Knowledge

Most secondary English language learners begin learning English with an already developed ability to think, speak, read, and write in their native languages. Although some students may have disrupted schooling or limited native-language literacy, others may have more advanced knowledge and skills in certain academic subjects than their native English-speaking peers.

Although activating prior knowledge before learning new knowledge is an important teaching practice for all students, it is especially important for language learners. Language learners often don't connect their prior knowledge to the content matter they are learning in English. They may assume that their native languages and prior knowledge are too different to be relevant.

Writing About Their Literacy Experiences

One way to draw on English language learners' prior knowledge to is to invite these students to talk and write about their previous literacy experiences (Dong 2004). Many of the preservice subject-matter teachers have noticed that students will respond enthusiastically when the teacher demonstrates a sincere interest in their previous learning.

To familiarize themselves with their students' literacy backgrounds, English teachers might ask the students to write answers to some of the following questions:

- What is your native language?
- When and how did you learn to read and write in your native language?
- Which book or writing assignment do you remember in your native language and why?
- How did your teacher back home teach you to read and write in your native language?

- Do you read or write in your native language now? If so, what do you read or write about?
- What are the similarities and differences between schools in the United States and schools in your native country?

Teachers can encourage students who have difficulty writing in English to write their answers in their native language. Either native-language peers or a bilingual teacher can translate their comments into English. Other subject-matter teachers can use this writing exercise to learn about their students' previous learning experiences, whether they be in science, mathematics, social studies, or another content area.

For example, John, a Chinese 8th grade student, wrote about the kind of books he loved reading as a child:

> The first book I ever read is a Chinese book called Funny Master. It's about an old man who is very funny, and he tells jokes in the book. I like his jokes. I love to write stories about myself in those funny books. Now I am in the 8th grade, and I don't read those funny books any more.

Maria, a 10th grader, wrote about her extensive background in reading in her native China:

> When I was in China, I loved reading books. I always started reading as soon as I got home and usually forgot to do my school homework. Because of this, my dad yelled at me a million times.... He felt that math was more important than literature.... I still read and write in my native language. I read a Chinese newspaper called World Journal every day, usually about half an hour to an hour. I also write my daily journal in Chinese, not so often though, maybe I should call it a weekly journal, and sometimes even a monthly journal.

Kim, a 9th grader from Korea, described how she became more confident in her writing:

> The most influential book I read was a book about a Korean emperor. I got it for Christmas. In Korea, teachers check your journal entries every day. I wrote about my trip to a mountain, and I received a certificate for it. That was the first piece of writing that I received a certificate for, and I was proud of it. In the 3rd grade, my teacher congratulated me on my writing because I copied down the whole book. That made me more confident as a writer.

Some students, such as an 11th grader named Sam from Colombia, explain the differences in schooling between their native countries and the United States:

> In Colombia ... we have the same teacher for all classes or sometimes we have a different teacher, but we stay in the same room. But here [in the

United States] we have different rooms and different teachers. Another difference is that the teacher in my country speaks Spanish and teaches in Spanish. But here many teachers can speak Spanish, but they don't teach in Spanish. The textbooks we use here for social studies talk about America and Colombia, not like the books we had back in Colombia, it was all about Colombia. But in math they teach the same as it is here.

These students' writings offer a window into their previous education and can help teachers modify instruction according to students' strengths, weaknesses, and interests. For example, after reading about John's interest in Chinese funny books, his English teacher might want to include comic book reading and writing to sustain John's interest and facilitate his language learning.

Connecting with Students' Historical Knowledge

Many English language learners have already studied history in their native countries. Numerous topics in the world geography and history curriculum provide social studies teachers with opportunities to connect to their students' prior historical knowledge (Salinas, Franquiz, and Guberman 2006; Salinas, Franquiz, and Reidel 2008; Short and Echevarria 2004/2005). Teachers can invite students to share their perspectives on historical events or important figures in world history with the rest of the class.

For example, in teaching the Korean War, the social studies teacher can engage the class in reading not only U.S. texts but also a Korean companion text see Lindaman and Ward (2004) for a side-by-side comparison.

Students from Korea can play a cultural insider's role by sharing their views and understandings of the war in either their native language or English. The teacher might ask such questions as, How are the two accounts of the Korean War similar and different? and Which account do you think is more accurate and why? In so doing, the teacher not only creates a comprehensible and meaningful learning environment in which to teach the new concepts, but also encourages a more in-depth discussion of the Korean War and related concepts. This will also lead to an exploration of the perspectives and possible biases of history textbooks, thus facilitating students' development of critical-thinking skills. Students come to view the writing of history as a dynamic process, which often reveals multiple views of the past (DeRose 2007).

Making the Connection

English language learners' previous cultural, language, and literacy experiences influence their ways of learning both English and subject-matter knowledge. Their native languages and prior knowledge are rich resources to tap into. When teachers invite English language learners to link new knowledge to what they have already learned, learning becomes more comprehensible, meaningful, and exciting.

References

August, D., Carol, M., Dressier, C., and Snow, C. (2005). "The critical role of vocabulary development for English language learners." *Learning Disabilities Research and Practice*, 20(1), 50–57.

Brockway, C. (1985). *Allyn and Bacon general science*. Newton, MA: Allyn and Bacon.

Cummins, J. (1979). "Linguistic interdependence and the educational development of bilingual children." *Review of Educational Research*, 49(2), 222–251.

Cummins, J., Bismilla, V., Chow, P., Cohen, S., Giampapa, F., Leoni, L., et al. (2005). "Affirming identity in multilingual classrooms." *Educational Leadership*, 63(1), 38–43.

DeRose, J. (2007). "Comparing international textbooks to develop historical thinking." *Social Education*, 71(1), 36–39.

Dong, Y. R. (2004). *Teaching language and content to linguistically and culturally diverse students: Principles, ideas, and materials*. Greenwich, CT: Information Age Publishing.

Freeman, Y., and Freeman, D. (2009). *Academic language for English language learners and struggling readers*. Portsmouth, NH: Heinemann.

Kieffer, M., and Lesaux, N. K. (2007). "Breaking down words to build meaning: Morphology, vocabulary, and reading comprehension in the urban classroom." *The Reading Teacher*, 61(20), 134–144.

Lindaman, D., and Ward, H. (2004). *History lessons: How textbooks from around the world portray U.S. history*. New York: The New Press.

Meyer, L. M. (2000). "Barriers to meaningful instruction for English learners." *Theory and Practice*, 39(4), 228–236.

Rodriguez, T. A. (2001). "From the known to the unknown: Using cognates to teach English to Spanish-speaking literates." *The Reading Teacher*, 54(8), 744–746.

Rubinstein-Avila, E. (2006). "Connecting with Latino learners." *Educational Leadership*, 63(5), 38–43.

Salinas, C., Franquiz, M. E., and Guberman, S. (2006). "Introducing historical thinking to second language learners: Exploring what students know and what they want to know." *The Social Studies*, 97(5), 203–207.

Salinas, C, Franquiz, M. E., and Reidel, M. (2008). "Teaching world geography to late-arrival immigrant students: Highlighting practice and content." *The Social Studies*, 99(1), 71–76.

Short, D., and Echevarria, J. (2004/2005). "Teacher skills to support English language learners." *Educational Leadership*, 62(4), 8–13.

30. Keeping the Dream Alive
Julie Bell

Alfredo is going to graduate from Colorado College, but he never would have believed that when he entered Denver's South High School. The son of immigrants, his family did not have the experience, information or money to support his dream. But thanks to help from a local foundation and a committed school counselor, Alfredo ended his senior year with a 4.5 grade point average and a full scholarship to the prestigious private school.

The resources—both financial and personal—that helped Alfredo succeed are rare. State legislators have been creating programs to help first generation and immigrant students get into and succeed in college. These students and their families, however, often are unaware of the programs and don't believe college is a possibility.

Now, as legislators face tight budgets in the years ahead, experiences such as Alfredo's could become the exception. Many lowincome, first generation and minority students may have fewer places to turn for help in going to college. Tuition has gone up and, until enactment of the economic recovery package, the federal government's share had not. Many states have decided to put money into merit programs rather than need-based programs. School counselors, who provide critical information and support to such students, are often among the first to lose their jobs. The growing income gap between those who are successful in the education system and those who are not may widen even more without programs to help these kids.

"Improving the numbers of students gaining access to higher education

Original published as Julie Bell, "Keeping the Dream Alive," *State Legislatures*, May 2009. Reprinted with permission of the publisher, National Conference of State Legislatures.

and successfully earning their degrees is a pressing and urgent issue for state legislators," says Connecticut Representative Denise Merrill. "The challenges are particularly acute for traditionally underserved students."

The Value of College

The same severe economic decline affecting state budgets also makes it hard for families and students to afford college. A college education, however, is more important than ever in determining future earnings. The annual income of an employee with a bachelor's degree is about 80 percent higher than for a person with a high school diploma—or more than $1 million over a lifetime, according to the College Board. College graduates are more involved in community and philanthropic affairs, are healthier, and require fewer state services than those without a degree.

The high school achievement gap between whites and minorities is prevalent and alarming. Nationally, while 80 percent of white students graduate from high school, the figures are only 72 percent for Hispanics and 69 percent for African Americans. And the picture of college enrollment is bleak: 73 percent of white high school graduates enroll, compared to 58 percent of Hispanic students and 56 percent of African American students.

Texas recently studied changing demographics and the lack of success of lowincome and minority students in its higher education system. "We faced a grave realization of where our state would be in 10 years if we did not figure out a way to improve college success for these students and families," says Representative Geanie Morrison.

Minority and first-generation students account for all the current growth in our nation's public education system, according to the Western Interstate Commission for Higher Education. The 2007–08 school year will boast the highest number of high school graduates ever—more than 3.34 million. The commission projects that, between 2004 and 2014, Hispanic public high school graduates will increase by 54 percent, Asians by 32 percent, American Indians and Alaskans by 7 percent, and African Americans by 3 percent. The number of white graduates will decline by 1 1 percent.

Meanwhile, tuition and fees have risen an average of 4.2 percent each year at public four-year institutions over the past decade, according to the College Board, to an average of $6,585 for in-state students. Add in room and board and you're at a hefty $14,333–nearly 6 percent higher than last year. For out-of-state students, the figure is $17,452 for tuition, and for private institutions, tuition and fees are $25,143 or more. Public community colleges that have traditionally served a large number of low-income students are a bargain at $2,402.

Students borrowed about $19 billion from state and private sources to help finance their education in 2007–08, according to the College Board. Two of three college students graduate with debt, and the average borrower who graduates from a public college owes about $17,000 in student loans, according to the American Association of State Colleges and Universities.

Getting the Word Out

Letting low-income, first-generation and minority students know that college is possible is as important to success as counseling and ongoing support through college.

Private foundations can help. Yessica Holguin is the counselor at Denver's South High School who helped Alfredo. Her position is supported by the Denver Scholarship Foundation, which helps low-income students attend college. The foundation is an example of a local fund that provides scholarships, but first requires students to seek federal money and other financial aid. There are many similar programs in other states, but they operate at a relatively small local or community level.

These local efforts cannot reach all the kids who need help, however.

Federal Role

Providing support for low-income students in higher education traditionally has been a role of the federal government. Until passage of the economic recovery act, Pell grants for low-income students had increased little over the last decade, and the federal government was moving away from grants toward loans and tax credits, which largely do not help low-income families.

Low-income students are receiving more assistance in the Obama administration. The economic recovery package includes $17 billion to increase the maximum Pell grant by $500 to $5,350 in school year 2009 and 2010 and to $5,550 in school year 2010 and 201 1. In addition, the package includes $14 billion in expanded higher education tax credits that would, for the first time, be available to students from low-income families that do not pay taxes. Another $200 million is included for increased college work-study, which has been a particularly valuable program for helping students work and earn rather than take out loans.

Low-income students, however, need more help than the federal government can provide. Students also are looking to states, communities and the private/philanthropic sector. Money for college and ongoing support for students once they are there are critical to college success.

In recent years, states have begun to invest in a new generation of financial aid programs that let students and families know about resources to attend college and encourage students to take a rigorous high school curriculum and graduate. These programs acknowledge the growing population of lowincome and minority students; account for the diminished role of the federal government; recognize limited resources at the state level; simplify the process of applying for and receiving financial aid; reduce the reliance on loans; and are flexible for adult and part-time students.

The Rethinking Student Aid Study Group—an independent team of policy experts, researchers and higher education professionals convened by the College Board is calling for a policy shift that would change how students and their families think about and prepare for futures with college. The recommendations will likely help spark the national dialogue over financial aid reform.

What Works

"Early commitment financial aid programs" guarantee college tuition to qualified students, serve low-income students and sign kids up in middle school. They help those most in need, reach out early and offer incentives for kids to graduate. Students earn the money for college by taking tough courses, staying out of trouble and maintaining a good grade point average.

The Indiana 21st Century Scholars Program increased the percentage of kids who completed a college prep curriculum from 12 percent in 1994 to 68 percent 14 years later.

Minnesota and Oregon have developed a new "Shared Responsibility Model" of financial assistance that outlines various responsibilities—of the student and family, the public and the philanthropic partners, and the university—to make college more affordable. It assumes that all students have a responsibility in investing in post-secondary education, but that low- and moderate-income families need public help to reduce a disproportionate burden of the price of a college education. At the same time, students can choose to attend the institutions that will best meet their needs.

Requiring students to complete the free application for federal student aid form, called FAFSA, allows states to target federal money first. Oregon's program takes full advantage of all federal aid available to a student and his or her family before calculating the share to be paid by the state.

The programs range from in-school programs that start as early as elementary school, to college-based programs that start in the senior year of high school. Some programs focus on increasing academic readiness, while others specialize in college admissions or financial aid. Some involve families and mentors, and others incorporate service learning or recreational activities. A major role is to help students with the financial aid process—critical assistance because current federal forms are extremely difficult to complete, and many students who are eligible for federal aid never apply for it.

Expanding need-based aid is difficult during an economic crisis. But changing demographics, grim high school graduation rates and rising college costs make delaying the decision until the economy betters risky. All of this adds up to another tough decision facing legislators in the challenging days ahead.

States Craft Demanding Programs for College-Bound Students

States are experimenting with programs to reward low-income students who succeed in high school with grants to attend college.

Indiana's 21st Century Scholars program provides academic and college preparation assistance through high school to low-income middle school students who sign a pledge to complete high school and avoid illegal activities. If a student graduates from high school with a "Core 40" (a rigorous curriculum) diploma and at least a 2.0 grade point average and has stayed out of trouble, he or she is guaranteed four years of financial aid covering all tuition and fees at an in-state public college or university, or an equivalent amount at an in-state private institution.

"The goal is to create a pipeline of low-income and first-generation students going to college," says Indiana Representative Greg Porter.

The "Core 40" high school diploma requires four years of English, three years of math through at least algebra II, and three years of science. There's also an honors diploma that includes more credits in math, foreign language and fine arts.

The program receives substantial state support–$25.4 million in FY 2007. Forty-nine percent of scholars come from single-parent families, and 32 percent are members of racial and ethnic minorities whose families have a median income of $29,000.

The results have been promising. In 2006, 68 percent of Indiana students completed a college prep curriculum in high school, compared with 12 percent in 1994. In 1992, Indiana ranked 34th in the nation in the percentage of high school graduates who enrolled in college the following fall. By 2004, Indiana was 10tn in the nation, and enrollment continues to grow.

Another concern is that kids drop out of college and never finish. In response, Indiana is providing these college students with special supports. Programs elsewhere include:

* Oklahoma's Promise Scholarship targets low-income students in middle school. They agree to take a rigorous high school curriculum, maintain a 2.5 GPA, sign a contract for good behavior, and complete the federal financial aid form. The state provides $54 million in funding for about 19,000 students.
* Wisconsin's Covenant program focuses on getting information to students about the resources to help them get into and attend college. The Legislature is considering a budget of about $25 million to help pay for the program.
* The Washington State Achievers program is in 16 high schools. It targets low income students who can receive up to $5,000 per year for college.

Endowments Victim of Market Collapse

As if state budget cuts weren't bad enough, college and university endowments also are taking a significant hit because of the dramatic drop in financial markets. This has left many schools less willing or able to draw money from their endowments to cover expenses.

Endowments showed an average rate of return of -3 percent for FY

2008, according to a survey by the National Association of College and University Business Officers and TIAA-CREF Asset Management. A follow up survey of the first five months of FY 2009 showed an additional average decrease of a whopping 23 percent, or an estimated $94.5 billion loss. The extraordinary speed and size of the losses are putting many institutions in a tough position. And market volatility is making future spending decisions extremely uncertain.

But it is not all bad news. The survey shows that endowments have realized a 6.5 percent average 10-year rate of return, outperforming all market indices.

"This year's results remind us of the importance of taking a long-term view in assessing endowment performance," says John Walda, president and CEO of the business officers group. "Past reports show that endowments fell 3.5 percent in FY 2001 and 6.3 percent in FY 2002, before enjoying several years of double-digit average returns prior to FY 2008."

In addition, legislation enacted in 26 states and under consideration in at least nine others should help endowment managers by increasing their flexibility to spend funds that have fallen below a specific point—and otherwise would be off limits—on critical needs. Called the Uniform Prudent Management of Institutional Funds Act, the legislation updates the laws governing the investment and expenditure of funds held by charitable institutions.

Even with greater spending flexibility, college endowments will continue to be strained as declines in state funding and private donations compete with increasing demands for student financial aid. And to think it was only last year when many of the policy discussions in state capitals and Washington, D.C., revolved around encouraging institutions to spend more from their flush endowments to help decrease student costs. What a difference a year makes.

31. In-State Tuition and Unauthorized Immigrant Students

Ann Morse

In 2013, four states—Colorado, Minnesota, New Jersey and Oregon— enacted in-state tuition for unauthorized immigrant students, bringing to 15 the number of states that offer this benefit through legislation.

In 1996, the illegal immigration reform law instituted a restriction on states' residency requirements and in-state tuition benefits for higher education, affecting an estimated 50,000–65,000 unauthorized immigrant students annually.

Seventeen states subsequently enacted legislation to allow long-term unauthorized immigrant students to become eligible for in-state tuition if they meet certain requirements: California, Colorado, Connecticut, Illinois, Kansas, Maryland, Minnesota, Nebraska, New Jersey, New Mexico, New York, Oklahoma, Oregon, Texas, Utah, Washington and Wisconsin. In 2008, Oklahoma ended its support for in-state tuition for students without lawful presence. In 2011, Wisconsin ended its support in the 2011–2013 budget law. In addition, several state university systems established policy to offer instate tuition rates to unauthorized immigrant students, such as the Hawaii Board of Regents (2013), Michigan Board of Regents (2013) and Rhode Island Board of Governors (2011). Three states currently offer state financial assistance to unauthorized students: California (A130, 2011), New Mexico (S582, 2005) and Texas (H1403, 2001). On Feb. 18, 2014, the Washington legislature approved legislation to expand the state need grants for certain unautho-

Original published as Ann Morse, "In State Tuition and Unauthorized Immigrant Students," http://www.ncsl.org/research/immigration/in-state-tuition-and-unauthorized-immigrants.aspx, February 2014. Reprinted with permission of the publisher, National Conference of State Legislatures.

rized immigrant students. The governor is expected to sign the legislation (S6523).

Since 2001, Congress has been considering bipartisan legislation to repeal this provision and help certain immigrant students gain legal status. In the 113th Congress, legislation in both the House and Senate was introduced with bipartisan cosponsorship. The U.S. Senate passed S744 which includes provisions repealing Sec. 505 of the 1996 illegal immigration law addressing instate tuition and offering an expedited path to citizenship for young unauthorized immigrant students. In the House, HR15, which largely mirrors the Senate bill, was introduced with 193 cosponsors.

Federal Background

The Illegal Immigration Reform and Immigrant Responsibility Act (IIRIRA) of 1996 (Sec. 505) sought to prohibit states from providing a postsecondary education benefit to an alien not lawfully present in the United States on the basis of residence unless any U.S. citizen or national is eligible for the same benefit (P.L. 104–208). The Congressional Research Service noted that there is disagreement about the meaning of the provision. There is no guidance in congressional report language or in federal regulations.

The Development, Relief and Education for Alien Minors Act of 2011 (the DREAM Act) would restore the state option to determine residency for purposes of higher education benefits. It would provide conditional legal status to an individual who: was under the age of 15 when he or she entered the country; has been physically present in the United States for at least five years; has earned a high school diploma or GED; is a person of good moral character; is not inadmissible or deportable under criminal or security grounds of the Immigration and Nationality Act; and was younger than 32 years of age when the law is enacted. Applicants must submit biometric and biographic data; undergo security and law enforcement background checks; undergo a medical exam; and register for military selective service. These students would be able to obtain permanent resident status after two years of college or military service.

Proponents of these bills argue that unauthorized immigrant children had no choice in entering the United States illegally, have grown up in the United States, and can make economic and social contributions if allowed to continue their studies. Opponents believe the bills would reward lawbreakers, that only lawful resident students should qualify for resident tuition, and that it could result in added cost to taxpayers.

Any child, regardless of immigration status, is eligible for free primary and secondary education under a 1982 Supreme Court decision (*Plyler v. Doe*). The Supreme Court feared that denying children an education might create a permanent underclass of illegal immigrants who would probably remain in the United States the rest of their lives. Discrimination against the children would punish them for the acts of their parents, since the children had no choice in entering the United States. The denial of an education to these children would stamp them with an "enduring disability" that would harm both them and the State all their lives.

When students without legal residency apply for college they are asked for a social security number and citizenship status. While they may still be allowed to attend, they are not eligible for federal aid until they gain legal immigration status. Legal status can sometimes be obtained through family or work-based petitions (e.g., U.S. citizen can apply for their spouse or an employer can apply for their employee), or through the Diversity Lottery Program.

State Actions

Fifteen states currently have statutes that condition eligibility for instate tuition on attendance and graduation from a state high school and acceptable college admission applications. In June 2001, Texas (HB1403) was the first state to pass legislation allowing in-state tuition for immigrant students, followed by California (AB540), Utah (HB144), and New York (SB7784) in 2001–2002; Washington (HB1079), Illinois (HB60) in 2003; Kansas (HB2145) in 2004; New Mexico (SB582) in 2005; Nebraska (LB239) in 2006; Wisconsin (A75) in 2009; Maryland (S167/H470); Connecticut (H6390) in 2011 and Colorado (S33), Minnesota (S1236), New Jersey (S2479) and Oregon (H2787) in 2013. The state laws permit these students to become eligible for in-state tuition if they graduate from state high schools, have two to three years residence in the state, and apply to a state college or university. The student may be required to sign an affidavit promising to seek legal immigration status. These requirements for unauthorized immigrant students are stricter than the residency requirements for out-of-state students to gain in-state tuition.

In 2003, Oklahoma passed SB 596 allowing instate tuition, but in 2008,

HB 1804 was enacted, which ended its in-state tuition benefit, including financial aid, for students without lawful presence in the United States. HB1804 allowed the Oklahoma State Regents to enroll a student in higher education institutions permitted that they meet special requirements.

In 2009, Wisconsin added instate tuition for unauthorized immigrants in the 2009–2011 budget law; it was ended in the 2011–2013 budget law.

In 2011, Maryland enacted legislation allowing instate tuition for unauthorized immigrant students provided they meet certain conditions, including the completion of 60 credit hours or graduation from a community college in Maryland. The law was put on the 2012 ballot and on November 6, Maryland voters approved the ballot measure 59 to 41 percent.

In July 2011, California enacted legislation permitting unauthorized immigrant students to receive state financial aid and scholarships (A130), joining New Mexico (S582, 2005) and Texas (H1403, 2001). On Feb. 18, 2014, the Washington legislature approved legislation to expand the state need grants for certain unauthorized immigrant students. The governor is expected to sign the legislation (S6523).

In addition, several state university systems established policy to offer instate tuition rates to unauthorized immigrant students, such as the Hawai'i Board of Regents (2013), Michigan Board of Regents (2013) and Rhode Island Board of Governors (2011).

States that have barred unauthorized immigrant students from in-state tuition benefits include Alabama (HB56, 2011), Arizona (Proposition 300, 2006), Colorado (HB 1023, 2006), Georgia (SB 492, 2008), South Carolina (HB4400, 2008), and Indiana (H 1402, 2011).

Court Cases

California: Students paying out-of-state tuition attending California schools filed a lawsuit in the Yolo County State Superior Court (*Martinez v. Regents*, No. CV 05–2064), claiming that education officials violated the IIRIRA by offering in-state tuition to unauthorized immigrant students while continuing to charge U.S. citizens out-of-state tuition rates. The complaint was filed against the University of California, California State University, and state community college systems, who offered in-state tuition to unauthorized immigrant students following Assembly Bill 540, enacted in October 2001. On October 6, 2006, Judge Thomas E. Warriner upheld the schools' decision to grant eligibility to unauthorized immigrant students for in-state tuition. In September 2008, a California appeals court reinstated the lawsuit and returned it for consideration in Yolo County Superior Court. In November 2010, the California Supreme Court upheld the state's method for providing in-state tuition to unauthorized immigrant students and ruled it did not conflict with federal law. An appeal was filed with the U.S. Supreme Court. On June 6, 2011, the Supreme Court declined to review the ruling.

Kansas: A claim was brought to the Kansas District Court by a Missouri resident denied in-state tuition while unauthorized immigrant students were granted in-state tuition benefits, arguing that this violated IIRIRA (*Day v. Sibelius*, No. 04–4085/*Day v. Bond*, No. 07–1193). The Kansas District Court dismissed the claim for lack of standing. The decision was upheld in the U.S. Court of Appeals for the Tenth Circuit. On June 23, 2008, the U.S. Supreme Court declined to review the federal review court's ruling.

32. Financial Literacy Programs for Immigrants

Jamie Durana

The Challenge

New immigrants face several obstacles to using the U.S. banking system, including a distrust of banks, a language barrier, lack of knowledge about banking and lack of documentation. As a result of these barriers, new immigrants—and even more established immigrants—pay excessive fees for check cashing and services to send money to their home countries. Consequently, immigrants routinely become targets for thieves because of large amounts of cash kept at home. Local leaders can help encourage increased financial literacy among immigrants by supporting the types of programs described in this guide.

Initiatives that encourage immigrants to build wealth and take part in the formal financial system—banking the "unbanked"—must overcome language and cultural barriers to reach sometimes insular communities. Financial literacy programs can help immigrants develop the confidence to effectively use the banking system and even get on the path to homeownership. Local efforts to help immigrants save and become financially literate promote stable neighborhoods and contribute to the economic vitality of the community.

Original published as Jamie Durana, "Financial Literacy Programs for Immigrants," *Municipal Action Guild*, Washington, D.C.: National League of Cities, Winter 2010. Reprinted with permission of the publisher.

Strategies

PROGRAM TYPES

1. Remittance-based Programs

Immigrants are a large, growing and relatively untapped market for financial institutions. Many immigrants send remittances—money sent to one's home country, usually by wire transfer—and many banks are able to attract new customers through targeted advertising of money-transferring services. Using targeted advertising of an already existing bank service, banks can then market other products to their new customers. Wells Fargo, which operates a remittance transfer service called InterCuenta Express, has found that remittance program customers use more of Wells Fargo's products than non-remittance customers on average. Remittance-based programs are an improvement over traditional money wiring services because they promote positive financial habits by requiring customers to utilize other banking services, such as savings accounts.

Remittance transfer programs can be established at the community level at individual bank branches. Typically, remittance program customers are required to open a bank account and gain awareness of other banking services in the process. These programs are often advertised via word-of-mouth and therefore do not require large advertising campaigns.

Although remittance transfer programs have been successful, they require a significant investment in preparation. In addition to identifying the target group and hiring bilingual staff, banks must compete with money wiring services traditionally used by immigrants. Banks generally offer significantly lower wire transfer fees than traditional money wiring services, but companies like Western Union are known quantities in immigrant communities.

2. Non-remittance-based Programs

Financial literacy programs are designed to acquaint newcomers with the American banking system. These programs can be as simple as a financial planner from the immigrant community answering questions on a radio show or as comprehensive as a multi-week course covering a broad range of personal and small-business financial topics. Although financial literacy programs are provided by a variety of entities, they are typically the domain of community-based or immigrant organizations and commercial banks. Community-based and immigrant organizations develop financial literacy programs to encourage immigrants to use the banking system in order to build wealth and protect their earnings.

The Semillas Program, developed by the International Migrant's Development Fund in Washington, D.C., includes seven workshops to educate students about financial options and services. Commercial banks often support these kinds of programs. Bank of America provides funding to the Banking on Our Future program operated by Operation Hope in Los Angeles. Recognizing the demand for financial literacy training, many immigrant organizations have added a personal finance component to existing activities like English as a Second Language or citizenship programs. Rather than funding outside programs, some banks have developed their own. First National Bank in Rogers, Arkansas, developed a financial literacy seminar series as part of its effort to reach out to new Latino immigrants in the town. This program grew to include a partnership with a major employer of immigrants living in the town. Like remittance programs, banks can broaden their customer base by providing financial literacy services.

Action Steps

Financial literacy programs for immigrants are operated by a variety of providers, including cities (e.g. public libraries and public schools), community-based organizations (CBOs), and immigrant service organizations. All of these programs were developed in part by answering several key questions:

- **Who is the target audience?** Who are the immigrants living in the community? From what country did they arrive? What is their native language?
- **What are the banking goals of the audience?** Is this immigrant group primarily seeking to send money to their home country? Are they interested in purchasing homes or starting small businesses?
- **What is the audience's previous experience with banking?** What are mainstream financial institutions like in their home country? Are they mistrustful of banks?
- **How can the audience be encouraged to participate in a financial literacy program?** Are there opportunities to work with major employers of immigrant residents? Can advertising be tailored to reach potential immigrant customers? What local organizations and businesses can provide input and assistance in developing a program?

The answers to these questions provide the details necessary to tailor financial literacy programs to immigrant communities. Having a solid knowledge base about the prospective students helps ensure that the program offered will be taken seriously and be a helpful tool for immigrant residents. Lack of knowledge about the community from which prospective students are drawn will be evident and can discourage those potential participants.

Many cities already operate financial literacy programs that are not geared toward the immigrant community. Therefore, the classes may be missing a large group of potential students. These existing programs are often developed to attract underserved communities in the city, including low-income residents. The curriculum and promotion of the programs can be modified to encourage immigrants to join by:

- Encouraging banks and city agencies to participate. Local bank branches can bring their experience identifying customer needs to participating in or supporting a financial literacy program for immigrants. Rogers' First National Bank went beyond drawing immigrant customers into the bank and provided financial education seminars. A Citizens Bank branch in Dorchester, Massachusetts, developed a remittance-based program.

  The program allowed the bank to reach the previously untapped market of Cape Verdean immigrants and provided the new customers with lower-cost remittance wire-transfer fees and an opportunity to learn good banking practices.
- Working with CBOs and immigrant service providers. Establishing connections with CBOs and other organizations that work with immigrants is an important step in developing and promoting a financial literacy program. Even if a CBO is unable to contribute resources, its experience can be invaluable. Effective promotion hinges on building trust with potential students. Through working directly with organizations that have a relationship with the local immigrant community, a new program will be more likely to attract students.

Resources

The following resources offer information and materials that can be used as part of developing a financial literacy program:

Money Smart Program Financial Education Program (Federal Deposit Insurance Corporation)

The Federal Deposit Insurance Corporation's Money Smart program is a financial education curriculum. The program provides basic lessons about banking and is geared toward those unfamiliar with mainstream financial institutions. The comprehensive program includes train-the-trainer, adult education and youth education materials. These materials are available in seven languages. http://www.fdic.gov/CONSUMERS/CONS UMER/moneysmart/

Appleseed's Financial Access Program

The Appleseed Network has developed several publications aimed at promoting financial access among immigrants. These publications include Banking Immigrant Communities, a toolkit that provides banks and credit unions with information for reaching "unbanked" immigrants, and a series of brochures available in English and Spanish. http://www.appleseednetwo rk.org/

Banking on the Future with Citi (U.S. Committee for Refugees and Immigrants) The U.S. Committee for Refugees and Immigrants provides a series of financial education brochures in six languages. The brochures cover basic banking topics, including credit and electronic banking.

National DOLLAR WI$E Campaign

The U.S. Conference of Mayors' Council for the New American City developed the National DOLLAR WI$E Campaign as a way for mayors to offer financial literacy programs the residents in their communities. Mayors that join the campaign establish the local financial literacy programs and the Council for the New American City provides materials for the programs. http://usmayors.org/dollarwise/about.asp

33. New Immigrant Center at the Austin Public Library

Diana Miranda-Murillo

Austin Public Library (APL) offers a variety of services through its New Immigrants Centers. In most cases, being an immigrant is not easy. An immigrant comes from a different country, speaks a different language, and has a different culture. While immigrants struggle to cover their basic economic needs, they must also work to understand a new culture and find a place for themselves and their families in a new country. To survive and prosper in a in a new society, they must navigate different social norms, civic institutions, transportation systems, and (often) a new language. APL's New Immigrants Centers provide fundamental tools to help new immigrants achieve these goals and facilitate their adaptation to a different way of life.

Austin Demographics

The City of Austin's demographic information illustrates the diversity of the city and helps understand the importance of the New Immigrants Centers for this community.

The 2000 Census shows interesting data about the area that includes Austin and San Marcos Texas. It reports that, of the total population of 1,249.763 habitants, 12.2 percent is foreign born and 10.5 percent of this population speaks English "less than very well." The Hispanic and Asian communities are projected to double in the next 20 years.

Original published as Diana Miranda-Murillo, "New Immigrants Center at the Austin Public Library," *Texas Library Journal*, No. 82 (Winter, 2006): 144–147. Reprinted with permission of the publisher and author.

This year, *Money Magazine* (2006) ranked Austin as the second best big city to live from a list of 10 cities in the United States. Invariably, this publicity helps attract people not only from across the country but also from abroad. Austin is also home for The University of Texas and big technology companies that makes this city attractive to foreigners to study and find employment. For these reasons and the changing demographics affecting most Texas cities and towns, the New Immigrants Centers represent an important investment in the city's future—one recognized by the city's leaders.

History of Austin's New Immigrants Centers

Austin City Council created the Austin Task Force on Immigration Issues in 1997 to inform the City Council about the situation of immigrants in Austin and their needs. The Task Force recommended the implementation the New Immigrants Project Centers in public libraries as a way to enhance services for the immigrant community.

The purpose of the centers is to provide resources in various formats for newcomers to the United States. Immigrants can utilize the centers to improve English language proficiency; study for the United States Citizenship Test; create documents in respective native languages; practice keyboarding skills; e-mail friends and relatives abroad; or download forms from the Immigration and Naturalization Services website (City of Austin, 2000).

The City elected three libraries to begin the program:

- Little Walnut Creek Branch to provide services for the Asian community growing nearby
- Terrazas Branch to offer services for the Latino community
- Faulk Central Library would offer services for a wider audience due to its location in Central Austin

The Ruiz and St. John branches joined the New Immigrants Center Project in 2004. In this year also, the name of the centers changed to New Immigrants Center to reflect better the nature of the service. Today, six branches located in areas with high number of foreign-born communities have a New Immigrants Center, and two more branches just started offering English conversation sessions and information for immigrants as a pilot to later adding their own a New Immigrant Centers. The city also increased the number of bilingual employees according to the communities that were surrounding the libraries.

The city allocates $1000 per fiscal year to improve their collection. Additional equipment and materials for some of the newer centers have been also funded by grants from the Texas State Library and Archives Commission, Friends of the Austin Public Library Austin Public Library Foundation, Rachael & Ben Vaughan Foundation, and the Texas Book Festival.

The Adult Literacy and Immigration Issues Committee manage the New Immigrants Centers. This committee is composed of the staff members from each of the New Immigrant Centers and from the library's administrative department. The committee seeks to enhance the materials and services offered in the centers and also promote literacy and English as Second Language (ESL) opportunities throughout the library system.

Immigrant Communities' Characteristics and Needs

The immigrant community has diverse needs and characteristics. It not only has people who come from different countries in the world, speak different languages, but it includes individuals of different levels of literacy and infinite reasons to migrate. One finds people with different legal status, people who came from rural or urban settings, and from diverse economic conditions.

Fear characterizes a large part of the immigrant community. Carmen Ospina (2005), senior editor of *Críticas* magazine wrote: "Many of you may have found that some Latinos are reluctant to get a library card or simply use the library because they fear being reported to the U.S. Citizen and Immigration Services." In some cases they fear deportation, but in some other cases they fear rejection or simply speaking.

Based on the report Library Services for Immigrants (2006) published by the U.S Citizenship and Immigration Services office, information about what other public libraries nationwide are doing to serve immigrants and the experience gathered at the Faulk Central Library, the main needs of this community are:

- English as a Second Language (ESL) classes
- English conversation classes
- Citizenship classes and preparation materials

- Literacy programs
- Employment and housing information
- Legal help
- Materials in their native language
- Computer literacy programs
- Health seminars.

What Are the New Immigrants Centers?

A New Immigrant Center combines a variety of different services and materials to provide needed support for new immigrants.

- **Study Centers**

Study centers have ESL books, videos, audio cassettes, compact disks, and DVDs which patrons can check out. If patrons don't have a library card or if they don't have the appropriate equipment, the centers also have VHS players, audio players for CDs, and audio cassette players that can be used in the library. Each center is also equipped with a brochure stand of information about non-profit organizations that offer services to the immigrant community in Austin. Centers also offer computer and Internet access that is made easier to use through the provision of resources such as Rosetta Stone, Oxford Picture Dictionary Interactive, Road to Citizenship, and Global Writer. Computer use statistics for study centers show that usage is increasing. In 2004, a total of 1266 patrons singed into these computers system wide and, for 2005, a total of 1994 patrons logged on. For 2006 (by September), a total of 1285 patrons used the centers' computers.

- **Talk Time**

Talk Time is an English conversation class hosted weekly at eight branches, six of them with New Immigrants Centers. Talk Time provides a safe and relaxed environment for non-native English speakers to practice their listening and oral language skills. Volunteers facilitate these sessions that are held in spring, summer, and fall.

- **English as a Second Language (ESL) Classes**

Some libraries with New Immigrant Centers host free ESL classes. Right now St. John partners with the Austin Independent School District, while the Little Walnut Creek and Cepeda branches partner with Austin

Community College. People interested in these classes have to contact the providers directly for information and to sign up with them.

- **Library Tours**
  The librarians in charge of the New Immigrants Centers in each branch offer special library tours of the centers. In these tours, librarians show patrons the equipment available to learn English and other materials the centers have available. These tours are offered to ESL schools or any organization working with immigrants in Austin. Occasionally, librarians will receive groups organized by other library employees that work with children in libraries with a large immigrant population.

- **Computer Classes**
  Faulk Central Library, Little Walnut Creek Branch, and Ruiz Branch offer free monthly computer classes in English, Spanish, and Vietnamese. Staff and volunteers teach these classes. The topics covered by these classes go from basic computer skills to building web pages. There is also a bilingual class (English–Spanish) on how to use Rosetta Stone, software installed on the centers computers to study English.

- **Multilingual Materials**
  Each New Immigrant Center has fiction and non fiction materials in multiple languages, including Chinese, French, German, Italian, Hebrew, Korean, Polish, Portuguese, Russian, Spanish, and Vietnamese. This collection may vary depending on the origin of the immigrant communities that live close by the branches. Little Walnut Creek Branch has more books in Asian Languages and Terrazas branch has more books in Spanish, for example.

- **Spanish Book Club**
  This is a project that two librarians recently started at University Hills Branch. Four to five patrons meet once a month with these librarians to discuss a book of their choice. Initially, librarians suggested reading titles. Now, participants select their own books and are expanding the program. They have recently read works by authors like Gabriel García Márquez, Carlos Cuautémoc Sánchez, Lois Lowry, Isabel Allende, and Miguel Ruiz.

- **Adult Literacy collection**
  The Adult Literacy combines ESL and easy-to-read books in English. This collection provides resources to patrons who are just beginning to learn

English. Topics include health, job searching, psychology, and communication as well as fiction materials.

Conclusion

The New Immigrants Centers of the Austin Public Library help immigrants living in Austin to improve their quality of life. The centers facilitate immigrants' adaptation to a new culture and also to a new language. When reviewing the history of the New Immigrant Centers and the materials and services they offer, one sees multiple efforts coming from all directions to make these centers possible. However, the work with the immigrant community is a continuum; products and services require constant maintenance and improvement. For that reason, librarians in charge of the centers plan to offer new services in the future like Spanish conversation classes, informative meetings for the immigrant community on topics like immigration law, housing, health, and literacy classes.

A patron from the Terrazas Branch wrote a letter to the staff saying how much the New Immigrant Center help her learn about the services and opportunities available for her as an immigrant. She also mentioned that the centers also changed the way she saw libraries and she is now a regular patron of this branch. The satisfaction about these centers however, does not only come from the community, but also from the libraries staff. One librarian from Little Walnut Creek Branch reported that he finds his work particularly fulfilling when he is able to help immigrants set up appointments for the Immigration Office using Internet or when he gives them information on organizations providing legal help or computer classes. It is, he commented, all about what libraries should be doing.

Through this project, the library has not only helped thousands of immigrants; it has moved the library closer to it, both figuratively and literally. The centers have helped libraries accomplish their mission of providing information to anyone in their communities and to address their information needs. And, the centers provide a crucial role in helping the city educate it community to provide a meaningful infrastructure for growth and quality of life.

References

Ashford, K., et al. (2006). "Best Places to Live." *Money*, 35 (8), 95–108.
City Demographer, Department of Planning, City of Austin (2001). *Ethnicity Shares:*

Central Texas, Counties and Cities, Census 2000. September 8th, 2006: www.ci.
austin.tx.us/census/downloads/ethnic_compare.xls
_____. (s.f). *Ethnicity Shares History and Forecast.* September 9th, 2006: www.ci.
austin.tx.us/census/downloads/ethnicity_forecast.pdf
Ospina, C. (2005). "Libraries and Immigration Reform. Críticas." September 8th,
2006:www.criticasmagazine.com/index.asp?layout=articlePrint&articleID=
CA6292734
United States Census Bureau (2000). *Profile of General Demographic Characteristics:
Census 2000.* September 9th, 2006: www.ci.austin.tx.us/census/downloads/city_
of_austin_profile.pdf

34. Librarian's Toolkit for Responding to Anti-Immigrant Sentiment

Robin Imperial

Many librarians across the United States are struggling to provide or continue to provide adequate library service to Latinos and other immigrants in the face of anti-immigrant sentiment that serves to dehumanize and criminalize family members and workers who seek a better life for themselves and their loved ones in the United States. REFORMA, the National Association to Promote Library and Information Services to Latinos and the Spanish-Speaking, strives to be at the forefront of the effort to educate the general public about the communities we serve and to advocate for and seek to protect Latinos' rights to decent library service. As librarians and library workers, we pride ourselves on access to relevant information.

In that vein, we offer these materials for use by library administrators, staff, and all other interested parties in an effort to enlighten, inform, and expand their knowledge of immigrants and their rights to free public library access. The American Library Association Council joined REFORMA in June 2005 in approving the RESOLUTION IN SUPPORT OF IMMIGRANTS' RIGHTS TO FREE PUBLIC LIBRARY ACCESS. Furthermore, in April 2006, REFORMA passed a resolution opposing H.R. 4437 (the Sensenbrenner Bill) due to its deleterious effect on the entire Latino community: RESOLUTION OPPOSING SENSENBRENNER BILL (H.R. 4437).

As an affiliate association of the American Library Association, we

Original published as Robin Imperial, "Librarian's Toolkit for Responding Effectively to Anti-Immigrant Sentiment," http://www.reforma.org/content.asp?contentid=67, May 2006. Reprinted with permission of the publisher and author.

reaffirm concepts from the Library Bill of Rights here: ... "that all libraries are forums for information and ideas, and that the following basic policies should guide their services."

"I. Books and other library resources should be provided for the interest, information, and enlightenment of all people of the community the library serves."

"V. A person's right to use a library should not be denied or abridged because of origin, age, background, or views."

> Recommendations to Enable, Encourage, and Increase Access to the Library by the Latino Community
> Make your priority to serve the community regardless of individuals' legal status
> Promote your library as a welcoming place where revealing or explaining one's legal status is neither expected or required
>
> Accept alternative forms of identification such as:
>
> Matrícula Consular (Mexico)
> Photo ID & proof of current local address
> Other forms of address verification including utility bills, printed checks, rent receipts, or other post-marked official mail Ensure that all library staff, both professionals and paraprofessionals, receive cultural competency training that includes current immigrant issues
> Hire staff who speak the language(s) of your immigrant communities
> Promote your library as a source of accurate information on all aspects and perspectives of the immigration issue, both currently and historically.
> Act as advocates for the education of undocumented immigrants about their human rights

In short, libraries should be working to expand access to their materials and services by accepting alternative forms of identification such as the Matricula Consular issued by the Mexican Consulate.

Reformistas reported the following policy details and sentiments in recent posts to the REFORMANet listserv:

> "...the County of Los Angeles Public Library ... used to send out postcards.... We would (1) fill out the postcard with the potential patron's con-

tact information, (2) I think we charged them for the postcard stamp, and (3) mail the postcard. They would receive it and then come back with another form of ID, such as a passport, out of state ID, etc." "...what I really like about that system is that it allows staff to emphasize to patrons that we want to be able to send you mail and make sure you receive it. This can take emphasis away from "where are you from" and put it on "where can we contact you"—which just seems so much more friendly."

... First of all, this is not an immigrant, illegal immigrant issue. As a library, we don't care about your immigrant status.

We just to need to make sure that you prove who you are (photo id) and that we can contact you (proof of address). Those items can be anything— passport, Matricula Consular, etc. For women who do not have anything "official" in their name, those postcards are great. Since we usually accepted anything with name and address and they could usually provide mail from family, postcards from the library were an option in rare cases when they were needed and probably not a big expense." Potential library patrons "not only included immigrants (illegal or legal) but others who might not have the documents more restrictive libraries require—children, teens, non-drivers, etc.

[One public library in Minnesota] has a policy that requires a picture ID and verification of address to get a library card. We prefer a state driver's license as the picture ID, but I have taken driver's licenses from other states, from Mexico, Matricula IDs, and more. The verification of address can be ... a printed check, lease form, any kind of bill, and even a piece of mail as long as it is postmarked and has the person's name with address on it. We prefer something formal, but there's some leeway there for personal judgement.

The schools issue picture IDs for middle school and high school students here, so we accept student IDs for those who don't have a driver's license yet.

[A number of other public libraries in Minnesota] have very similar policies.... If a potential patron does not have a picture ID ... we require only a letter delivered by the postal service to their address. If they do not have such a letter, a local ESL teacher has been willing to mail a post card to her students in order to verify mailing address. Our local police department, business community and school system also sponsored a visit from the new Mexican Consulate office in the Metro area so people would have a convenient opportunity to come and get a [Matrícula] ID issued by the Mexican government.

"...an increasing number of libraries do not require that users explain their legal status when registering for library cards. For example, Queens Library, [does] not ask for any user's legal status. The important thing is to serve the community no matter their legal status."

Best Practices for Issuing Library Cards to the Latino Community

Library staff may accept the following forms of identification & proof of residency:

List A:

Documents that Establish Identity and Place of Residency
Valid state-issued driver's license
Valid state-issued ID card

OR

List B:

Documents that Establish Identity
Passport from any country
Matrícula Consular
Employment ID with name & photo

AND

List C:

Documents that Establish Place of Residency
Utility bill with address on it
Lease agreement
Printed checks
Any POST-MARKED piece of business or personal mail

One thing to remember is that just because we have a law doesn't mean it's the right thing to do. Historically we have had many laws (Jim Crow, etc.) that have legislated the wrong thing. Protests and demonstrations are the way these "bad" laws get changed. This is the response we should be giving to those who are saying they aren't against immigrants, they're just against them breaking the law. We should remember that except for Native Americans, we are a nation of immigrants.

35. Immigrant-Friendly Cities Want What Arizona Doesn't
Dylan Scott

In the heart of Dayton, Ohio, three rivers come together to form the Great Miami River. That's the image that 62-year-old Sarvar Ispahi, an Ahiska Turk who moved here with his family in 2005, conjures to illustrate the sense of community that has developed in Dayton, this unexpected home for immigrants in the middle of the country. "If you're neighbors, you come to know all people. You can make one culture," says Ispahi, his broken English aided by his son Fergano. "If you are together, this is good. If you are separate, this is not good. But this is a good community."

Ispahi, his wife and their children are among the several thousand Ahiska Turks who have settled in Dayton after escaping persecution in Russia. The Ahiskans have a long history of oppression, which Ispahi vividly recounts on a blistery summer day in the cool comfort of his New York Pizzeria on East Fifth Street, wearing a shirt that reads: "Dayton, Ohio: My Kind of Town." In 1944, more than 90,000 Ahiska Turks were deported from Georgia into the Soviet satellites of Kazakhstan and Uzbekistan, where Ispahi was born. When the Soviet Union collapsed in 1991, his family moved to Russia, where they were granted safe harbor but no citizenship.

"Those were terrible years," Ispahi recalls. "We couldn't do anything." A new governor of the Russian state where they resided had launched a public relations campaign that painted Ahiska Turks as criminals and drug dealers. Given their lack of official status, the situation became untenable for Ispahi and his people. In 2004, the United States granted refugee status

---

Original published as Dylan Scott, "Immigrant-Friendly Cities Want What Arizona Doesn't," *Governing*, September 2012. Reprinted with permission of the publisher.

to Ahiska Turks. When Ispahi and his family decided to come to America in June 2005, they chose Dayton because an uncle had settled there and found the transition to be easy. Today, Ispahi owns his own business and employs four people, two of whom are his sons.

City officials estimate that 10 percent of the Ahiska Turks in the United States have established themselves here in Dayton. But they aren't alone. There are also immigrants from Mexico, Vietnam, Samoa and elsewhere.

Watching some of these residents' difficulty in adjusting to their new surroundings—some encountering language barriers and others struggling to secure housing—convinced city officials they needed to do more to help. Dayton's Human Relations Council, a city department that investigates discrimination complaints, started in 2010 by initiating a study into allegations from Hispanic residents regarding housing discrimination. Around the same time, City Manager Tim Riordan and City Commissioner Matt Joseph resolved to make public services more accessible for those who spoke English as a second language.

It didn't take long for Dayton's leaders to figure out that incremental steps wouldn't do, that the immigration issue needed a comprehensive solution and the involvement of the entire community. "It requires a huge partnership. There are only so many things we can do as the city," Joseph says. "And the big thing is an attitude change. We have to make sure we're encouraging people to be more welcoming and that the incentives are running the right way. That's our role."

For every government that's taking a tough line against immigrants, there are others that are embracing immigration-friendly policies. Though much attention has been paid to states like Alabama and Arizona, where laws viewed as anti-immigrant have sparked a political firestorm, a quieter undercurrent of immigrant-friendly policies is in motion. Major cities like New York, Chicago, Detroit and Houston—longstanding immigrant destinations—have begun to revisit their policies in an effort to become more welcoming. But the idea is also taking hold in Middle America, in places like Dayton and Boise, Idaho. It's not simply out of a sense of goodwill; many leaders see these policy changes as economic development tools. Dayton's approach has been hailed by pro-immigration groups as an important example of redefining public policy for those seeking better opportunities in this country.

To forge the partnership imagined by Dayton's leaders, a workgroup of more than 125 stakeholders convened regularly for five months and developed what became the Welcome Dayton Plan. The city commission approved it in October 2011 as its framework for making the city immigrant-friendly.

The plan's goals are expansive, covering everything from health care to public safety. To encourage economic development, Dayton is setting aside one section of its downtown as an international marketplace for immigrant entrepreneurs. City officials plan to authorize new grants to help business owners set up shop and to coordinate with local realtors to market the area so that companies will see the advantage of locating there.

The city itself has pledged to improve government services in particular ways that will make them more accessible for newly migrated residents, such as revamping public notices and adding staff members who speak foreign languages.

Welcome Dayton is also about changing the city's culture. One of the plan's first successes was the sale in April of a former city building to the Ahiska Turk community, which is turning it into its own community center. Events like a Global Dayton Soccer Day are intended to bring disparate groups within the community together. The city is organizing a "cultural brokers" training program to assist volunteer groups outside the government's purview in working with different ethnicities. The initiative urges private businesses and citizens to embrace the city's goals and find their own ways to advance them. "If you don't assist them to gain a foothold or to have a positive and constructive experience, you marginalize them and it could stay that way for generations," says Tom Wahlrab of the Human Relations Council. "So you've got to quickly get them in the stream of things and help these folks get into play."

Dayton officials seized on a growing academic consensus that embracing immigrants is beneficial to the country as a whole and specifically the economy. A June 2011 Brookings Institution report concluded: "U.S. global competitiveness rests on the ability of immigrants and their children to thrive economically and to contribute to the nation's productivity." The U.S. Chamber of Commerce wrote last year that research shows "immigrants significantly benefit the U.S. economy." The Obama administration estimated in May 2011 that immigrant business owners generate more than 10 percent of business income.

And they continue to come. Some 13.1 million immigrants (legal and illegal) arrived in the United States between 2000 and 2010, according to the Census Bureau, trumping the record migration levels seen during the 1990s. While migration has slowed during the financial downturn, many analysts expect it will rebound as the national economy improves. That's one reason more localities are looking at the Welcome Dayton model and beginning to think about how they can become welcoming communities.

"We talk about how Alabama was trying out 'unwelcome Arizona,' whereas we're interested in a dynamic where cities are actually competing to be seen as the most welcoming," says David Lubell, founder and executive director of Welcoming America, a grassroots organization on immigration. "Dayton is a model that's held up, and the fact that they came out and said it's in their best interest to be welcoming is a huge step in a different direction."

But there are skeptics. Welcome Dayton was opposed by various groups who warned of a detrimental effect on the city's job market and social services. Some drove across the state to speak out against an initiative that they viewed as placing outsiders ahead of those who already live here. Generally, though, city officials say the public has embraced the plan. While the political discourse about immigration sometimes descends into posturing and hyperbole, cities like Dayton have resolved to welcome newcomers and integrate them into their new communities.

The Welcome Dayton Plan has given the city a long-term vision for what it means to be accommodating to immigrants. While it's too soon to gauge what the ultimate impact of the initiative will be on migration patterns or population, early signs suggest it's been effective. Since January 2011, more than 1,000 individuals from 113 countries took an oath to become U.S. citizens. City Manager Riordan says he's received emails from individuals in China and South Africa who have heard of the plan and are interested in what it would take to come to Dayton.

The plan could also provide population gains for a city that lost nearly 15 percent of its residents from 2000 to 2010. In that respect, Dayton shares many similarities with Detroit. Both are former manufacturing centers that have been hit hard by the shifting economic landscape, and both have been losing population (Detroit's dropped by 25 percent over the last decade). A group of business and government leaders in 2010 began developing what would become the Global Detroit plan; after they heard about the work being done in Dayton, they asked Wahlrab to come and share his city's experience. The Global Detroit initiative has so far secured more than $4 million in private money to fund various efforts, including retaining international students and providing resources for immigrant business owners to establish themselves.

"I believe there is a certain elegance and opportunity in the plan that Dayton has put together," Steve Tobocman, a former state legislator and director of Global Detroit, said in an interview with WBEZ Chicago. "They've done certain things so profoundly right that I think we have a lot to learn from it."

Many major cities, including Chicago, Houston, New York and Philadelphia, have been integrating immigrants into their communities for most of their existence. But that hasn't stopped their public officials from taking proactive steps to be more welcoming. Chicago Mayor Rahm Emanuel and Philadelphia Mayor Michael Nutter both have pledged to make their cities the most immigrant-friendly in the country.

A recent Rice University study concluded that Houston is the most diverse city in the United States, and city officials have developed a plan to connect with these new residents. Mayor Annise Parker established the Office of International Communities in November 2011 to lead these efforts. "We're trying to brand Houston as a welcoming city," says Terence O'Neill, whom Parker pegged to head the office. "We want the one thing you remember about Houston to be that it's welcoming to all people. Texas friendliness transcends any barriers."

As in Dayton, Houston officials believe a holistic approach is the best way to handle the immigrant issue. O'Neill's office serves as a clearinghouse of information for other agencies, such as health and public safety. The office has conducted needs assessments, consulting immigrants on what would improve their experience in Houston. One of the early successes of the effort is the New Americans Employment Initiative, which offers interview training to incoming immigrants and connects them with jobs. A Citizenship Week provided informational sessions, with up to 30 people in attendance, explaining the process for gaining American citizenship.

Despite being seated in a deeply red state that is often perceived as having a political culture not unlike Arizona and Alabama, O'Neill says Houston has seen great buy-in from its native citizens during his office's early work. Businesses and community groups have become active participants, taking the lead in projects like the employment initiative. The key, he explains, is demonstrating to residents that integrating new people into the city is beneficial to the community as a whole.

"Success is when every single person in Houston says it's great to have all these people from all over the world," O'Neill says. "Success is when the average person will realize that this is a really good thing for us."

Projecting the long-term momentum of immigration-friendly policies is difficult. But recent national events suggest such a shift might be under way. President Obama announced this summer that his administration

186 **Part II—Practices and Experiences**   SECTION I: CIVICS

would cease the deportation of some undocumented immigrants, such as the young and educated. It has been a controversial move but one seen by many as an olive branch to a substantial portion of the U.S. population (estimates place their number at 10 million or more) that has otherwise felt unwelcome. Iterations of the DREAM Act, which would aid children of undocumented immigrants in obtaining a college education, continue to resurface in Congress and statehouses nationwide.

With these forces in motion, cities like Dayton may be well ahead of the curve.

"Those that are the most forward-looking, that have the most pragmatic view on immigrants, are the ones that are reaching out and creating environments that immigrants can not only survive in but thrive in," says Audrey Singer, a senior fellow at the Brookings Institution who studies demography and migration. "I think that is definitely the future of this country."

It seems to be the future for Dayton. A drive down East Third Street, slotted as the future international business corridor, already reveals advertisements written in Spanish. A Mexican family that runs one of the city's authentic ethnic restaurants is buying up storefronts along the street, planning to open an organic foods market and clothing store for other members of the community. A Vietnamese woman owns an international foods market up the road, replete with Buddha statues and foreign foods branded in different languages, and converses with her customers in their native tongue. Like the three rivers that Ispahi, the Ahiska Turk, describes, people from across the globe meet and mingle in downtown Dayton.

The welcoming atmosphere that Dayton has tried to foster is already having a trickle-down effect.

Ispahi and his sons have founded a nonprofit organization called International Ahiska Human Rights, which they hope will be instrumental in bringing more of their people to the United States—and Dayton. "We found a way out of [our oppression], and we want to give this way to other people," Ispahi says. "Now we can try to help them."

36. Serving Diverse Communities—Best Practices

Julie C.T. Hernandez, John C. Brown
and *Christine C. Tien*

Across the nation, local communities are experiencing rapid growth of diverse ethnic populations. This is happening in both traditionally ethnically diverse states such as Arizona, California, and Texas as well as in states that are less traditionally diverse such as Arkansas, Georgia, and North Carolina. Along with this growth comes an inevitable clash of cultures.

Local governments are called on to provide services to residents without a full understanding of the unique practices and expectations of diverse populations who are new to their areas. What is the best way to provide services to growing diverse populations? What practices are most effective?

This article is the first of two articles designed to address these questions. In this article, three best practices case studies (one in Woodburn, Oregon, and two in Stockton, California) and an introduction to a recently completed best practices study are presented, along with key learnings from the implementation of these best practices. In the second article, scheduled for publication in the July 2007 issue of *PM Magazine*, a more in-depth look at the findings from the International Hispanic Network's (IHN) best practices study, "Municipal Best Practices for the Hispanic Community," will be presented.

Reprinted with permission from the June 2007 issue of *Public Management (PM) Magazine*, published and copyrighted by ICMA (International City/County Management Association), Washington, D.C.

187

Interest in an article on the topic of best practices for serving diverse communities was generated by a telephone coaching panel called "Serving Diverse Communities—Best Practices" held in October 2006, which was organized by Cal-ICMA's Preparing the Next Generation Committee (cochaired by Frank Benest, city manager, Palo Alto, California, and Tim O'Donnell, city manager, Brea, California).

The telephone coaching panel was presented to highlight the best practices study completed by IHN, and it was presented as one of several telephone coaching panels held throughout the year to train the next generation of local government managers and new public agency executives about key leadership topics.

The coaching session was moderated by Don Maruska of Don Maruska & Company, who also serves as director of the Cal-ICMA coaching program. Serving on the telephone coaching panel were two practitioners and a college professor. Dr. Abraham Benavides, assistant professor, Department of Public Administration, University of North Texas, reported on the IHN's recently completed best practices study for serving Hispanic communities.

Authors John C. Brown, city administrator, Woodburn, Oregon, and Christine C. Tien, deputy city manager, Stockton, California, shared concrete examples of best practices and strategies from their own cities that other local government agencies can follow to reach out to diverse communities and also bring diversity into their workplaces. Their stories are presented here.

Study Results: Municipal Best Practices for the Hispanic Community

IHN is a nonprofit organization whose purpose is to encourage professional excellence among Hispanic local government administrators; improve the management of local government; provide unique resources to Hispanic local government executives and public managers; and advance the goals of professional, effective, and ethical local government administration. One of the organization's objectives is to improve the management of local government and, in particular, target the management of communities with Hispanic populations.

To further this objective, IHN commissioned the University of North Texas to survey cities across the nation to determine the best practices of local governments in Hispanic communities. The survey also investigated information regarding the effects of Hispanics on local government services, including housing, family services, personal safety, and the needs of lower-income families. Additional information was also sought to scrutinize immigrant services and the best practices conducted by differing local govern-ments. The study was funded by the Annie E. Casey Foundation.

The survey was conducted during January and February of 2005, and it was sent to Hispanic city managers and to non–Hispanic city managers who manage cities with populations that are at least 12 percent Hispanic. The survey received a 31 percent response rate, with responses from 31 states.

Responses include the identification of 29 best practices programs conducted in Hispanic communities, with an additional 16 best practices programs in police services identified through a review of the literature. A more in-depth description of the results of this study will be presented in the July 2007 *PM*.

Best Practices Case Studies

Woodburn, Oregon. Woodburn has 22,000 residents and a unique cultural composition. Natives of Woodburn are joined by immigrants (Latinos and "Old Believer" Russians), seniors, and commuters. Immigrants come for work, for affordable housing, and to join family. The effect of migration is so pronounced that fewer than one-fifth of Woodburn residents are natives, more than one-third are foreign born, and 30 percent lack U.S. citizenship.

In 2000, Latinos accounted for 50.1 percent of the population, making Woodburn Oregon's largest city with a Hispanic majority. This number is likely higher than reported because of undercounting by the U.S. Census Bureau. Enrollments in Woodburn's schools, where nearly 70 percent of all students are Latino and 66 percent are monolingual Spanish speakers or English-language learners, may be a more accurate measure.

Woodburn's cultural change has been gradual. Beginning in the 1950s, immigration has continued unabated to the present day as migrants from Texas, Russia, Mexico, and Central America have come to harvest crops. Many recent arrivals speak Spanish or one of 19 indigenous dialects as their primary language.

Civic leaders have long recognized Woodburn's cultural change. They also recognize the barriers limiting equal access to services by all residents.

Language is an obvious barrier, but barriers also include lack of knowledge of regulations and procedures and distrust of government, especially law enforcement. Efforts to increase the number of Spanish-speaking employees were undertaken in the 1990s, but they fell short of addressing the other barriers.

The 2000 census accelerated discussions about the city's responsiveness to all of its residents and Latino involvement in civic affairs. In 2001, the city council directed staff to improve outreach and provide translation at council meetings. The council also sought to concentrate efforts on informing, communicating with, and engaging the city's Latino residents. The city council hoped to increase civic participation, improve the responsiveness of city services to the needs of the Latino community, and reduce negative contacts between law enforcement personnel and residents.

The city relies on its community relations officer (CRO) to meet these objectives. It also altered incentive structures and recruitment strategies to increase the numbers of culturally competent, bicultural, and bilingual employees. More than one-quarter of the police force is now bicultural, and every department in city hall has Spanish-speaking employees greeting the public.

The CRO position was created in 2002 and is responsible for specific activities:

- Providing oral and written translation.
- Providing ombudsman services.
- Producing a bilingual quarterly newsletter.
- Coordinating with merchants and other agencies to produce events.
- Promoting city services and activities in multiple media.

For this position, Woodburn hired an individual who could provide translation services in flawless Spanish, build relationships and trust, understand and explain government, and exhibit cultural competency. The CRO is a naturalized citizen with a legal and administrative background in the Mexican government and family ties to Woodburn.

Strategic placement of this office in the entry to city hall assures accessibility for those who cannot ask for its location. technical qualifications, the CRO brings to the job an ability to educate and develop community-wide cultural appreciation. Woodburn uses Spanish-language movies, live theater, and celebrations honoring holidays such as September 16, which is Mexican Independence Day, to build goodwill and knowledge of Latino culture.

Radio and television also help the city connect with Latino residents. The CRO develops public service announcements and audio and video broadcasts. Beyond local radio and public access television, the CRO also partners with a regional Spanish-language channel. The CRO is producing and hosting a new show, *City Life*, on FM radio. It will be broadcast in English, Spanish, and indigenous languages to inform, advise, and discuss city issues for residents of the community.

The CRO has assisted more than 2,500 individuals, businesses, and organizations since 2002. Issues span the range of services, although business licenses, utility billing, and traffic citations are frequent topics. Not surprisingly, when afforded the opportunity to communicate, non–English speakers voice the need for the same services and have the same concerns as English speakers.

The CRO has also translated hundreds of printed city materials, most of which are used to invite public participation or to provide notice. Long-range projects include translations of ordinances, applications, forms, and the city's Web site.

Finally, the CRO produces a fully bilingual, quarterly newsletter, distributed to more than 5,000 homes. Each issue includes typical newsletter fare, plus an installment of "How It Works," a civics lesson, and cultural infor-mation about the holidays, customs, and historic individuals and events of the city's diverse populations.

The newsletter is an important tool for developing cross-cultural appreciation. Merchant advertising subsidizes newsletter costs and has had unexpected relationship-building benefits with Latino-owned businesses. A downtown business watch, ongoing sponsorships for events and festivals, and user-friendly code enforcement are all products of this relationship.

Although Woodburn has a long way to go before it realizes the goal of inclusivity, the community relations officer provides an effective communication tool for those who are underrepresented in the community. Factors beyond the control of the CRO, such as immigration and citizenship status, can limit effectiveness on some issues. But through this position, Woodburn has a way to explain civic activities to all its residents, a way to invite them to participate, and a way to ensure their voices are heard regardless of language barriers or voting rights.

Stockton, California. Stockton is a diverse urban community with a rapidly growing population of 286,000. Stockton is 37 percent Latino; 23 percent Asian; 11 percent African American; 1 percent Native American, Hawaiian, Alaskan Native, and Pacific Islander; and 4 percent multiracial. The majority of Stockton's residents are U.S. born, but Stockton also has a large number of residents who are recent immigrants and who are not fluent English speakers.

Three years ago, Stockton was ranked number 17 nationwide for a city with the most residents born outside of the United States—almost 25 percent. These numbers have made city officials aware of the importance and value of outreach efforts to the group of people who are not native English speakers. Stockton provides two different best practices programs that directly target services to its diverse communities.

Lao Khmu Community Liaison Program. On October 8, 2002, the city entered into a partnership with Lao Khmu Association, a local community organization, to provide outreach services to the Southeast Asian refugee community to promote a greater understanding of local government and to enhance the job skills of those in the program. This program was funded by a grant received by the Lao Khmu Association from the Office of Refugee Resettlement (part of the U.S. Department of Health and Human Services) to enhance the job skills of residents with refugee status. In Stockton, the majority of residents with refugee status are from Southeast Asia.

Stockton became the first city in California and the second in the nation to establish a fully grant-funded refugee job placement program, with job placement occurring within a local government agency. From December 4, 2004, through October 31, 2006, a total of 18 participants or "Lao Khmu community liaisons" have participated in this program. These liaisons were mainly of Cambodian and Hmong descent. Each started with a six-month contract. Most received an additional six months of employment. Each liaison also received full job-related benefits.

The liaisons worked in a total of five city departments—the city clerk's office, the city manager's office, the fire department, parks and recreation, and the library. In the library, the liaisons were successful in their outreach efforts to the Southeast Asian community by using the library's bookmobile program. A few also assisted with translating and labeling Hmong videos and books. In the parks and recreation department, one liaison taught art at one of the city's after-school programs and eventually became an art instructor. Several liaisons were retained by city departments after the completion of their contracts.

Although funding for this program ended, the city benefited tremendously from the liaisons' work by tapping into their language skills to help with outreach to their respective communities. The participants also benefited tremendously by gaining a better understanding of local government and enhancing their job skills.

LEALES Program. A few years ago, the city began to hear complaints from Latino business owners about crime in the East Main corridor, a business district that is primarily Latino owned and serves the Latino community. Under the leadership of Gary Giovanetti, Stockton's vice mayor at that time, the city encouraged the businesses to form the East Main Business Alliance. The city envisioned a business watch group similar to the existing neighborhood watch groups.

After several months of meetings with the alliance, the Stockton police department noticed a pattern of crime that targeted Latino migrant farmworkers. The police department began to track and investigate each incident. The city found two primary reasons why Spanish-speaking migrant workers were vulnerable victims: they carried large amounts of cash, and they feared deportation.

In April 2005, the city enlisted the help of local trusted community and business organizations to create a new program called the Latino Education About Law Enforcement Services (LEALES). The goal of LEALES is to prevent and reduce crimes targeted at Latino community members who work on farms.

The name LEALES was created because it sounds like the Spanish word *lealtad*, which means "loyalty." LEALES members include a city council-member and representatives from the city manager's office, the police department, the San Joaquin County Hispanic Chamber of Commerce, Hispanic media outlets, El Concilio (a local nonprofit organization), and the Diocese of Stockton.

To address the fears of the Latino farmworker community about deportation, the Stockton police department developed a policy that states that police officers will not ask about the immigration status of crime victims. LEALES coordinated several successful media campaigns in both Spanish and English to inform the local Latino community about the police department's new policy and to provide tips on how not to be a victim.

Staff handed out flyers at hot spots, fairs, and venues frequented by the Spanish-speaking population. To help pay for brochures, the city received sponsorships from businesses that included the Community Trust Credit Union, the San Joaquin County Hispanic Chamber of Commerce, Food for Less, and Anheuser Busch.

There was coverage in the local media. The city also assigned a police officer to provide interviews on local Spanish-language radio and television shows. Segments on "How Not to Be a Victim" continue to be played on local Hispanic television stations. LEALES has been a great success. Since the inception of LEALES almost two years ago, there has been a 16 percent increase in the reporting of crimes, including robberies and aggravated assaults, over a one-year period. LEALES is now working on alternative ways to help prevent farmworkers from being targets of robbers.

Many farmworkers do not have bank accounts and therefore carry large amounts of cash. LEALES is beginning a new push to encourage farmworkers to sign up for bank accounts and to let farmworkers know that check-cashing venues often take a large amount of their paychecks for administrative processing fees.

To set up a bank account, most banks require two forms of identification. For noncitizens of Mexican descent, a *matrícula consular*, a form of identification issued by the Mexican consulate, and a tax identification number are usually adequate forms of documentation. Large banks like Bank of America, Wells Fargo, and Washington Mutual accept *matrículas consulares* as a form of identification.

LEALES is working on convincing other banks to accept matrículas consulares as forms of identification. LEALES has also assisted with efforts to encourage Latinos to sign up for matrículas consulares by inviting the Mexican consulate to fairs and events.

Implementation of Best Practices: Lessons Learned

At the end of the telephone coaching panel, panelists identified these key learnings from implementation of their communities' best practices programs:

1. Support from the top is important to success.
2. Start with a needs assessment that includes input from diverse communities.
3. Don't focus on immigration status; services will not be utilized with-out trust.
4. Provide extensive outreach and make drop-in services easily accessible.
5. Analyze contacts to identify common issues, themes, and problems for follow up.
6. Translate written materials, city Web site information, and

newsletters into the languages and dialects of diverse communities. Present not just the "what" but also the "why." Use these materials to educate about government.

7. Use radio and television; some members of diverse and immigrant communities are not literate.
8. Cultivate local minority-owned businesses as partners in serving diverse communities.
9. Coordinate with other agencies that provide services to diverse and immigrant communities. The local Mexican consulate and farm labor unions are good examples that may be overlooked.
10. Understand the cultural differences in how meetings are conducted: meetings should be neighborhood based; start with meet-and-greet time to establish trust; provide child care; and solidify trust by "breaking bread" together—have food or snacks available.
11. Implement best practices in two phases: short term for demonstrated successes; then longer-term programs.
12. Evaluate regularly the effectiveness of new best practices programs for serving diverse communities.

The changing demographics and ethnic diversification of local communities are occurring rapidly, sometimes quicker than local governments are prepared to handle effectively. The results can be fear, anger, and frustration in the community; but these results can be avoided. Tools are available to support local government efforts to cope effectively with this change, and they are available through several professional organizations.

37. Courting the Filipino American Immigrant Vote

Joaquin Jay Gonzalez III

Official demographic data point to a "Filipino American voting bloc" that has solidified incrementally during the past century from hundreds to present-day millions. The bloc's existence in the U.S. Census Bureau's statistics began with a mere 160 respondents in 1910, while the 2010 Census revealed that Filipinos numbered 3,416,840, a million more Filipino residents than in the 2000 Census, which is a 44.5 percent jump in a decade. Except for the 1930s, when their population rose by 0.8 percent, the decade-by-decade increases have been notable

Because of their increasing numbers, Filipino American (a.k.a., FilAm) influence on the ballot box has gained considerable attention from political parties and individual candidates. Political parties are aware that FilAms have the third highest naturalization rate behind Mexico and India—as reported in the U.S. Department of Homeland Security's *Yearbook of Immigration Statistics* (2012). Filipinos have led all immigrants from Asia in citizenship rates since the 1990s (Lien 2004). This is notable considering there are 52 possible U.S. immigrant-originating countries in Asia.

Thus, at naturalization ceremonies in major U.S. cities, many political parties jockey to attract new Filipino voters. They know that the Filipino voter registration rate is higher than the national average and they parallel the U.S. average in going to the polls. Their registration and voting rates are second to the Japanese as the highest among Asian Americans (Taylor 2014). As new U.S. citizens, Filipinos are also easier to "inform and register"

Original published as Joaquin Jay Gonzalez III, "Filipino American Voting," in Thomas Baldino and Kyle Kreider (Eds.), *Minority Voting in the United States* (Santa Barbara, CA: ABC-CLIO, 2015). Reprinted with permission of the publisher and editors.

because of their relatively higher English proficiency, political awareness, and educational attainment.

The Filipino Americans' primary source of political information and outreach derives from a mix of mainstream and ethnic FilAm media. Besides their local news channels, many also view FOX News and CNN, while some also watch MSNBC, Al Jazeera, or the BBC. However, a large segment also supplements its cable TV subscriptions with The Filipino Channel (TFC) and wouldn't want to miss the popular "Balitang America" show. The more tech savvy 1.5th generation (i.e., those who arrived before adolescence) and second generation FilAms gravitate to their internet and social media sources. At Manilatowns or Asiatowns, FilAm newspapers are readily available at Asian or Filipino restaurants and food outlets, convenience stores and supermarkets, and other commercial places in the community where people gather. The languages are English, Filipino (Tagalog), and Taglish (mix of Tagalog and English).

The stock of eligible FilAm voters is only expected to increase given that they are currently the fourth largest, legal, permanent residence-receiving ("green card") group. Adding to this stock annually are immigrant visa recipients from the 10–15 year backlog waiting in the Philippines. They are lined up to join their American families who have petitioned for them under the "family reunification" provisions of the U.S. Immigration and Nationality Act of 1965. Hence, the Filipino bloc will continue to surge into the future at a rate of one hundred thousand annually or one million new Filipino Americans every 10 years.

Given these demographic shifts, Filipinos have established themselves as the second ranked Asian American political bloc after the Chinese. The Filipino population is followed closely by Asian Indians, Vietnamese, Koreans, and Japanese with each group also numbering more than one million. As Asian American numbers grow, so too will their political, economic, and social influences.

From a regional perspective, Filipino Americans are the largest group of Asian Americans in ten of the 13 western states: Alaska, Arizona, California, Hawaii, Idaho, Montana, Nevada, New Mexico, Washington, Wyoming, as well as the territory of Guam. FilAms are also the largest group of Asian Americans in South Dakota (Lott 2006).

Examining the Census data, it appears that Filipino Americans will have their largest impact in California because the state has 1.5 million FilAms, the most among the 50 states. Following California, the battle to sway FilAm voters is in Hawaii, with more than three hundred thousand, followed by Illinois, Texas, Washington, New Jersey, New York, Nevada, and Florida with more than one hundred thousand FilAms each. The 10th state is Virginia with close to a hundred thousand FilAms.

In terms of proportion, however, the greatest political influence of FilAms at the municipal and state level will be in Hawaii, which reported that more than one-quarter of its population is ethnically Filipino. In the last decade, FilAms have overtaken Japanese Americans as the largest Asian American group in the state.

The effects have already been felt with Filipinos and Filipinas in Hawaii achieving political firsts. In 1994, Benjamin Cayetano was elected Hawaii's fifth Governor and the first Filipino American Governor in the United States. Previously, he was elected the first Filipino American Lieutenant Governor in the U.S. Most recently, in January 2013, long-time state House Representative and State Senator Donna Mercado Kim made history as the first Filipina American State Senate President.

Thus, it has become common to see Hawaiians of Filipino descent elected to state and municipal positions. For instance, in the 2012 statewide contests, a record 11 first and second generation FilAms easily won seats in the State's House of Representatives. Many ran unopposed. For some districts it was a choice between two FilAms. As a side note, the high FilAm population proportion in Hawaii is equaled by the U.S. territory of Guam. Hence, as in Hawaii, Guam FilAms are becoming more visible in both elected and appointed public offices.

Nevada, a crucial swing state, is an interesting case for the FilAm bloc. From 2000 to 2010, the state's Filipino population soared 142 percent. Like Hawaii, Filipinos have become the largest Asian American group in the state, comprising 4.59 percent of the total population. Close to 124,000 reside in metropolitan Las Vegas, Clark County, where their votes were critical in tightly contested statewide and local elections. In 2010, when Senate Majority Leader Harry Reid was seriously challenged by Republican Sharron Angle, he turned to the popularity of Philippine Congressman Manny Pacquiao to assure him the Filipino vote, particularly in Clark County. Pacquiao not only helped solidify his Democratic FilAm vote, while also charming undecideds, Independents, and even FilAm Republicans.

Nevertheless, the idea of FilAms running for Nevada public office remains novel. There are no elected FilAms in municipal and state positions. Very few second generation FilAms are interested in working for Nevada politicians. New FilAm organizations, including the recently established non-partisan Filipino-American Political Organization With Equal Representation (POWER), intend to change things. They already have a FilAm milestone: in the November 2012 elections, Clark County issued ballots and election materials in Filipino (Tagalog).

California is where the Filipino voting bloc has the greatest potential to influence electoral contests at the national level, especially during Presidential elections, while its influence at the state and municipal levels is strongest in Hawaii. Forty-three percent of FilAms live in California. All of the state's 58 counties experienced an increase in the number of Filipino residents since the 1960s. Interestingly, the only exemption to the trend is San Francisco County, whose Asian population has increased significantly but the number of Filipinos has declined from a peak of 42,652 in 1990 to 36,347 in 2010.

FilAm constituents have increased significantly, specifically in Santa Clara, Alameda, San Mateo, Contra Costa, and Solano counties. Daly City, in San Mateo County, has the highest concentration of FilAms in any municipal jurisdiction in the U.S., more than 30 percent of 101,123 residents.

Southern California contains the highest density, nationally, of FilAms. Approximately ten percent of Filipinos in the U.S. and more than 20 percent of Filipinos in California live in Los Angeles County. The Westlake section of the Los Angeles City hosts one of the country's oldest Filipinotowns. The largest jumps are in the vote rich counties of Los Angeles, San Diego, Orange, Riverside, and San Bernardino. Ranked second, after Los Angeles County in FilAms, is San Diego County, which has also seen a marked increase in its FilAm population from 121,147 to 146,618 between 2000 and 2010. But the most notable increase during this ten-year period is in Riverside County, which saw more than 30,000 additional FilAm residents in a traditionally Republican jurisdiction.

Thus, FilAm voting blocs are slowly electing FilAm mayors, vice-mayors, councilmembers, school board members, and college board members in the San Francisco, Los Angeles, and San Diego regions. But FilAm voters in California have not had similar results as FilAms in Hawaii in electing one of their own to the state legislature. The first major breakthrough occurred recently when Alameda Vice Mayor Rob Bonta won a seat in the State Assembly during the 2012 elections. Two other Northern California FilAm candidates lost.

In Southern California, no FilAm ran for any elective position from community college board to city council member that was open in 2012.

Nonetheless, despite not having sufficient ethnic elected and appointed representation in state and local executive and legislative offices, FilAm community leaders and organizations have successfully influenced policies and pressured politicos through aggressive advocacy, lobbying, and activism.

The Filipino American voting bloc is not all about numbers. Wealth is power. According to the 2010 American Community Survey (ACS), Filipinos possess the capacity to transform their reported economic strength to political muscle, because the median annual individual earnings for FilAm full-time, year-round workers are $43,000, higher than for all U.S. adults overall ($40,000) but lower than for all Asian Americans in general ($48,000). But among U.S. households, the median annual income for Filipinos is $75,000, higher than for all Asians ($66,000) and significantly higher than all U.S. households ($49,800). FilAms are far less likely to live in poverty than other immigrant groups. Although it is important to add that FilAms reported larger households of 3.4 persons compared to the average American household, which is at 2.6 persons. Larger households also mean more potential voters (Takei, Sakamoto, and Kim 2013).

Based on ACS data, more than six-in-ten Filipino Americans (62 percent) own a home, compared with 58 percent of all Asian Americans and 65 percent of the U.S. population overall. Their very low poverty rate, at 6.2 percent, is remarkable, since this is only half of both the U.S. (12.8 percent) and Asian (11.9 percent) averages. In the eyes of politicians and parties, they are more than just voters and constituents but important taxpayers and campaign contributors as well.

Democrat or Republican?

Answering the question of whether Filipino Americans lean Democrat or Republican is difficult. Because while past anecdotal evidence and media reports seem to indicate that they support Democrats, recent independent surveys indicate mixed results.

If we rely on the question "If you had to choose, would you rather have a smaller government providing fewer services or a bigger government providing more services?" from the Pew Research Center 2012 survey, then the answer is Filipinos lean Democrat. This is because 58 percent of the Filipinos surveyed responded "bigger government, more services." Their response aligns with most Asian Americans, particularly the Chinese (50), Korean (68), and Vietnamese communities (69). Not surprisingly, this trend runs counter to the U.S. national average of 39 percent supporting this statement.

Moreover, if we examine the record of past and present elected officials of Filipino descent an overwhelming majority ran as Democrats.

But how does one explain the findings of both the Pew Survey and a 2012 National Asian American Survey that among Asian Americans only 50 percent of Filipinos voted for candidate Barack Obama in 2008, the lowest among major Asian American groups? Comparatively, both the Pew and NAAS polls indicated that Indian, Chinese, Japanese, and Korean American voters enthusiastically supported Obama. In addition, the NAAS study reported that only 45 percent of Filipino respondents perceived President Obama doing a good job, again, the lowest among Asian American respondents. While in the Pew research, 61 percent expressed "dissatisfaction with the way the U.S. is run."

Do these results suggest that Filipino Americans are Republicans? There seems to be some empirical evidence in support of an affirmative answer. It is accurate to infer from the two current and several past studies that Filipinos are one of the largest source of Asian American Republican Party votes. There is a segment of the Filipino voting bloc that sympathizes with the views of conservative Filipina blogger Michelle Malkin and relies on Fox News for information. In predominantly Democratic San Francisco, successful business owner, Juanita Nimfa Yamsuan Gamez, and community activist, Rudy Asercion, go against the grain by touting GOP views and interests. This conservative cluster probably explains why many Filipino Democratic political candidates lose during elections, especially if they rely primarily on the Filipino voting bloc to support them.

The major influence on Filipino views and ballot decisions may not be a political party and its platform but an entrenched social institution that upholds conservative teachings: the Church. The role of religion and faith are quite strong among Filipino Americans, particularly Christianity. This is documented in many studies including some written by the author (Gonzalez 2009 and Gonzalez 2012).

The largest beneficiary of the Filipino bloc's church-based conservatism is the Republican Party (Ramakrishnan et al. 2008 and 2012). Filipino Americans who grew up in the Philippines are swayed by the power of the pulpit, pastoral letters, and the religious views that were passed down to them in their other homeland. A majority of FilAms are Catholics. They are influenced politically by the pronouncements of the Vatican and the conservative interpretations of their pastors. Some Filipino Americans are followers of homegrown independent Philippine churches like the Iglesia ni Cristo (Church of Christ) and charismatic preachers like Brother Mike Velarde of El Shaddai. Still others are affiliated with the multitude of American evangelical churches. There are also networks of nationwide church-related organizations which may sway their ballot decisions like the Couples for Christ (including Youth for Christ) and Bukas Loob sa Diyos.

In the Philippines, Catholic and Christian Churches' influence is codified through specific provisions in the fundamental laws of the land. For instance, Article XV, Section 2 of the Philippine Constitution provides: "Marriage, as an inviolable social institution, is the foundation of the family and shall be protected by the State." Hence, divorce is not a comfortable topic to many churchgoers. Neither is abortion as proclaimed in Article II, Section 12, "The State shall equally protect the life of the mother and the life of the unborn from conception."

Perhaps an even more important political affiliation question is: Are Filipino Americans "independents?" This is an important question since, nationally, there is a trend toward registering independent among mainstream and minority voters (Hajnal and Lee 2012). As reported by the National Asian American Surveys, Filipino Americans seem to be following the trend. There is a growing segment of Filipinos who are unhappy with the party choices and so opt to be "independent minded," "have no party," or "be aligned with other parties," like the Libertarian or Green. Many state that they would like to place the candidate's stand on issues above party loyalty. This is not surprising to those who study politics in the Philippines, where there are multiple parties to choose from and personal connection with a candidate, or patronage, transcends party loyalty.

FilAm Democratic and Republican Clubs exist throughout the United States. The most active ones are in California, New York, and Hawaii. They are seen organizing strategic activities year-round, not just Get Out the Vote (GOTV) campaigns, canvassing, and membership drives. These groups also sponsor FilAm social, cultural, and economic events to project visibility. Members also appear on The Filipino Channel and write opinion pieces and blogs in the many FilAm newspapers and blog sites. Leaders and representatives of the parties are regular commentators after State of the Nation addresses and November elections. They participate in community and city hall town hall meetings. Most FilAm Democrats and Republicans are more active in the Asian and Pacific Islander Clubs, as opposed to the FilAm Club.

In California, the most active political clubs are in the San Francisco

Bay Area. There are numerous chartered FilAm Democratic clubs representing the various cities and towns in the area. For instance, the Filipino American Democratic Club is one of 26 chartered clubs in the City of San Francisco. The various FilAm Democratic clubs from around the state are networked together under the banner of the Filipino American Democratic Caucus of California or FADC. The FADC affiliates directly with California and County Democratic Central Committees. The FilAm Democratic clubs endorse candidates and ballot initiatives during elections. Filipino American Republicans are represented nationally by National Organization of Filipino American Republicans. Only a handful of FilAm Democrats and FilAm Republicans are members of their respective Central Committees. An even smaller number have made it to their party's national convention.

The most effective venue to reach out, build networks, and disseminate information to FilAms is through their hometown associations. This may be true in the cities and counties where there are large concentrations of Filipinos, like Los Angeles, San Diego, Honolulu, or Guam.

As of 2008, there are more than four hundred Philippine hometown associations in the San Francisco Bay Area. These hometown associations represent the regions, provinces, cities or towns, or linguistic group where the FilAm came from. They mainly organize dances, language classes, beauty pageants, or neighborhood cleanups. But they also organize fundraisers for local and international causes. They are at the core of annual city-wide FilAm events. Every June, it's the Philippine Independence Day celebration and parade on downtown Market Street. Every October, it's Filipino American History Month or Filipino American Heritage throughout the United States. Every December, there is a Parol (Christmas lantern) stroll and contest on Mission Street. FilAm Quezonians, that is, from the Quezon Province, make time for a Pahiyas harvest festival every May. FilAm Cebuanos, that is, from Cebu City and Province, look forward to feast of the Sinulog religious festival praising the Santo Niño de Cebu every January, the most popular Philippine icon. FilAm Bicolanos, from the Bicol region, create an American version of the Peñafrancia thanksgiving festival every September.

In the aftermath of the super typhoon Haiyan, Filipino America hometown associations, particularly from provinces directed affected, raised millions of dollars and sent thousands of care boxes for the relief and rehabilitation efforts. Recognition and support of these hometown association activities are keys to getting the political sympathy and respect of the FilAm voting bloc.

Important Issues

The single most important political issue for the Filipino American voting bloc is immigration. As mentioned in the previous section, the waiting period for a family member from the Philippines to come to the United States is too long. For instance, the U.S. Embassy in Manila is currently processing the immigrant visas of petitions filed in Aug 8, 1990, for F4 category, Brothers and Sisters of Adult U.S. Citizens, a 24-year wait!

Hence, the Washington politician, Democratic or Republican, who is able to pass legislation addressing this backlog will certainly gain the FilAm voting bloc's debt of gratitude (*utang na loob*) for many elections to come.

Most in the FilAm bloc are concerned about the lawful and legal immigration of their relations. They believe that comprehensive immigration reform should prioritize this issue over amnesty to unauthorized immigrants.

The Office of Immigration Statistics has estimated that 270,000, or two percent, of the approximately 10.8 million unauthorized immigrants in 2009 are Philippine-born. This is a 33 percent increase from the 200,000 estimate in 2000. Comparatively, this figure is still much smaller than the estimated seven million unauthorized immigrations from Mexico. TNT, for Tago Nang Tago, is the Filipino slang term for the unauthorized, which literally means "in perpetual hiding." A majority of TNTs came to the U.S. on non-immigrant visas, for example, tourist, student, and working, and decided to stay after their visa expired. Some were brought to the U.S. before adolescence and hence have no connection to the Philippines.

The FilAm voting bloc was divided on whether to support their TNT brothers and sisters until unauthorized immigrant and Pulitzer prize winning FilAm author Jose Antonio Vargas made the cover story of *Time* magazine. He was one of those brought to the U.S. by a relation as a child. When Vargas' revelation that he was unauthorized went viral in the mainstream and social media, the FilAm bloc's sympathy for a path to legalization for the unauthorized, especially those who were brought to the country at a young age, somewhat shifted.

The second issue lingering within the FilAm voting bloc is the veteran's benefits equalization issue for the aging and dwindling Filipino World War II veterans and their families. During the height of war preparations, General Douglas MacArthur and President Franklin D. Roosevelt issued a call for volunteers in the Philippines to enlarge the United States Armed Forces of the Far East (USAFFE). 22,532 young Filipino men heeded the call which included a promise of U.S. citizenship and veteran benefits.

But their expectations were dashed when Congress passed two Rescission Acts after the conflict essentially invalidating MacArthur and Roosevelt's promises. It partially corrected in 1990 when U.S. President George H. Bush signed the Immigration and Naturalization Act granting Filipino World War II veterans U.S. citizenship. Many finally arrived in the country for which they fought and risked their lives. However, most were elderly and suffering from physical and mental wounds. Although these gallant warriors were given citizenship, they were not granted much deserved veteran's benefits. In effect, they languished in their new homeland, relying on welfare and social security benefits. For many, being a citizen welfare recipient was tough to swallow.

On January 17th, 2009, 60 years after the 1946 Rescission Acts, President Barack Obama signed the American Recovery and Reinvestment, also known as the "Stimulus Package," which included a $198 million earmark for the remaining FilAm World War II veterans and their families. Under the law, each veteran was entitled to receive $15,000. However, they still were not provided full G.I. bill benefits, meaning the battle continues for many.

The economy, jobs and health care are political issues that align Filipino Americans with mainstream American society. Many FilAms were affected by the economic downturn that began in 2008 when their mortgage investments suffered, because like many Asian Americans, a large segment of the FilAm population invested in real estate and fell victim to easy-to-secure loans, which they were unable to afford long term. Some lost their jobs. Some FilAm engineers and medical professionals, who thought themselves in safe occupations, received pink slips.

The implementation of the Affordable Care Act was watched closely by FilAm Democrats and Republicans. Despite the fact that Filipinos have one of the lowest rates of noninsurance among minorities (around 2–3 percent), there are still at-risk sub groups in the population who needed to be reached and enrolled, especially in states like California and New York. The at-risk population includes the elderly, adult Pinays, who are susceptible to breast cancer and heart disease, adult Pinoys, who are prone to lung and prostate cancer, as well as children, who are prone to obesity.

Conclusion

This chapter sketched in broad strokes the relative size, magnitude, and key issues associated with Filipino American voting. The demographic and historical trend is clear: there is a FilAm bloc and it will continue to grow for decades to come. The bloc is comprised of FilAms who report themselves as Republican, Democratic, or Independent, but who may vote outside of party affiliation depending on the issue and their various community and socialization influences. In Hawaii, the large FilAm voter population has allowed them to gain many elective posts in municipal and state elections. In California, they are an important swing vote. Immigration policy and politics is of utmost importance to this FilAm bloc.

References

Gonzalez, J. Jay (2009). *Filipino American Faith in Action: Immigration, Religion, and Civic Engagement.* New York: New York University Press.

_____. (2012). *Diaspora Diplomacy: Philippine Migration and its Soft Power Influences.* Minneapolis, MN and Manila, Philippines: Mill City Press and De La Salle University Publishing-Anvil Press.

Hajnal, Z. and Lee, T. (2011). *Why Americans Don't Join The Party: Race, Immigration, And The Failure (Of Political Parties) To Engage The Electorate.* Princeton, NJ: Princeton University Press.

Lien, P. (2004). "Asian Americans and Voting Participation: Comparing Racial and Ethnic Differences in Recent U.S. Elections." *International Migration Review* 38, 2: 493–517.

Lott, J. Tamayo (2006). *Common Destiny: Filipino American Generations.* New York: Rowman and Littlefield.

Ramakrishnan, K. and Lee, T. (2012). *Public Opinion of a Growing Electorate: Asian Americans and Pacific Islanders in 2012.* Los Angeles, California: National Asian American Survey.

Ramakrishnan, K. , Junn, J., Lee, T., and Wong, J. (2008). *National Asian American Survey, 2008.* Ann Arbor, MI: Inter-university Consortium for Political and Social Research.

Takei, I., Sakamoto, A., and Kim, C. (2013). "The Socioeconomic Attainments of Non-immigrant Cambodian, Filipino, Hmong, Laotian, Thai, and Vietnamese Americans." *Race and Social Problems,* 5: 198–212.

Taylor, P., ed., (2013). *The Rise of Asian Americans.* Washington, DC: Pew Research Center.

U.S. Department of Homeland Security (2012). *Yearbook of Immigration Statistics.* Washington, DC: Department of Homeland Security.

38. Community Policing in the Delray Beach Haitian Community

Anthony Strianese

Prior to 1996, the city of Delray Beach became a support community for immigrants from Haiti. Newly arrived immigrants found it easy to assimilate into the already established Haitian communities within the city. As such, many illegal immigrants also made their home in Delray Beach. This created a problem whereby both the legal and illegal immigrants were being victimized by not only the American criminal element, but also by the Haitian criminal element that preyed on the new arrivals through intimidation. Having a natural tendency to distrust the police, born from years of abuse at the hands of the Haitian police, victims were reluctant to come forth and report crimes to the police. The police department knew that there was a problem in the Haitian community, but without the cooperation of victims and witnesses alike, little could be done to stop the problem.

Then in 1996, things began to change. The Police Department, under Chief Richard Overman, theorized that if we could create the huge success that we realized from our Police Volunteer Patrols in the other areas of our city, by mirroring this program in the Haitian community as well, we could help curb the victimization. But before we could recruit a Haitian Volunteer Patrol, we had to educate the Haitian community as to how the U.S. criminal justice system works. We needed to make the Haitian residents feel comfortable talking with the police and interacting with the police instead of being afraid and avoiding the police at all costs. The idea was to hold a Cit-

Reprinted from *Police Chief* Vol. 78, No. 3, pages 32–33, 2011. Copyright held by the International Association of Chiefs of Police, Inc., 44 Canal Center Plaza, Ste 200, Alexandria, VA 22314. Further reproduction without express permission from IACP is strictly prohibited.

izens Police Academy, the same one that we had conducted in English for years, translated into Creole and geared specifically for Haitian residents.

After a rocky start, what is believed to have been the first ever Citizens Police Academy conducted in Creole began. After weeks of encouraging Haitian residents to attend the academy, what should have been a packed first night of class, turned out to be a bust—or more accurately, a proposed bust. It seemed that the criminal element was so intent on not allowing the Haitian population to interact with the police, that a rumor was spread throughout the Haitian community that the Delray Beach Police Department was planning a "Trojan horse" trick. U.S. Immigration was going to be at the police station waiting for the class attendees and checking their immigration status! A clever trick, yes; and unexpected. But with the support of a few key Haitian residents, several attendees were convinced to attend the second night of the academy. Once others saw that there was no trick, attendance snowballed into the maximum room capacity of 40 by graduation night! This was truly a success in breaking down the barrier of mistrust between the Haitian community and the police department! With so many requests coming in now to attend the next Haitian Citizens Police Academy, the decision was made to change our yearly plan and conduct a second Haitian Citizens Police Academy immediately. With 43 attendees in the standing-room-only training class, our follow up class now gave us over 80 Haitian residents from which to recruit our first Haitian-American Roving Patrol.

Since its inception in 1996, the Haitian-American Roving Patrol, or HARP, has done much more than bridge a gap between the Haitian community and the police department. Whereas in the past, Haitian victims of crime were afraid to speak to the police, now they come running into the police station—without any hesitation—if someone pulls into a parking space ahead of them! There is no fear of the police like before. Haitian residents now bring items of concern to the police department before they become a big problem for the community. An example is the change in renewing a Florida Drivers License following the 2001 terrorist attacks. Prior to the law changing, once a drivers license was issued, one only needed to renew it by mail or on-line. There was no verification that a person who obtained a drivers license legally while on an immigration status was still legal at the time of renewal. Now all renewals for non–U.S. citizens had to be done in person, with supporting immigration documentation. It wasn't until our HARP members brought it to our attention, that this new law was causing a problem in the Haitian Community. Those who were "out-of-status," or illegal now, could not renew their license. But, already having jobs and family commitments such as school, they were being forced to drive illegally with no license. When involved in minor traffic crashes, or sometimes even major crashes, the drivers would flee knowing that they would be in trouble for driving without a license. Without realizing that hit-and-run crashes were increasing, we now had an answer to a problem that we hadn't even identified yet! Suggestions were made about carpooling and utilizing the church buses from our many small churches in the city, as shuttles on the weekdays when they weren't being used. Through creative dialogue, and with the proactive approach of bringing the problem to us before it became a huge problem, our HARP members were able to stop a potentially costly problem of hit-and-run crashes where the victim driver was forced to pay repairs for damage caused by the other driver.

The success of our Haitian Citizens Police Academy and our Haitian-American Roving Patrol cannot be measured in any tangible fashion. It is impossible to estimate the number of potential victims who were not victimized because they took a community education class such as RAD (Rape Aggression Defense) or a school program such as GREAT (Gang Resistance Education And Training). Or, how many Haitian citizens came to the police to file complaints after having attended one of our other 10 Haitian Citizens Police Academies and were no longer victimized, whereas before they would have coward in fear of both the criminal AND the police! The success of our program can be measured in the way that a Haitian resident tells of having been afraid to walk alone two or three blocks from the police station, for fear of being robbed or beat up—only because he or she was Haitian. But now he or she feels safe enough in their own community to traverse the city at will and fully participate in the many wonderful activities that our city has to offer! The success can be measured by the way an officer on patrol makes eye contact with residents in the Haitian community and both give a friendly wave, whereas before the Haitian resident wouldn't dare look a police officer in the eye. There are countless ways to measure the success of our Haitian Citizens Police Academy and Haitian-American Roving Patrol, but success ultimately is due to the foresight and innovation of Chief Overman and our current Chief Larry Schroeder who continues to bring foresight and innovation. As was reported in the *Sun-Sentinel* newspaper after our 2nd Haitian Citizens Police Academy began, "Delray Beach Chief Richard Overman took the initiative to the Haitian community, rather than waiting for it to come to him. Other cities will do well to follow Delray's lead."

39. Local Authorities in Fight with Feds About Enforcement

Kate Linthicum

More than a dozen California counties have stopped honoring requests from immigration agents to hold potentially deportable inmates beyond the length of their jail terms, saying the practice may expose local sheriffs to liability.

In recent weeks, officials in counties including Los Angeles, San Diego, Riverside and San Bernardino have stopped complying with so-called ICE detainers, citing a federal court ruling in April that found an Oregon county liable for damages after it held an inmate beyond her release date so she could be transferred into Immigration and Customs Enforcement custody.

The California counties are among about 100 municipalities across the country that have stopped the practice since the ruling, according to the Immigrant Legal Resource Center, an advocacy group that is tracking the issue.

Analysts say the changes could impair President Obama's current immigration enforcement strategy, which relies on collaboration between local law enforcement authorities and federal agents. "It's very significant because it represents a reduction of the involvement of local police in federal immigration enforcement," said Hiroshi Motomura, an immigration law professor at UCLA. He said the Oregon court ruling had changed the long-running debate over ICE detainers.

"It's not just political anymore," Motomura said. "It's about liability."

He and others said the decision of the Los Angeles County Sheriff's Department to stop complying with the requests was especially noteworthy, given the large number of people apprehended via ICE detainers in L.A. County jails each day. The Los Angeles Police Department is reviewing the Oregon case in weighing similar changes to its detainer policy, said Assistant Chief Michel Moore, who oversees the city jails.

Jo Wideman, executive director of Californians for Population Stabilization, which advocates for stricter immigration policies, said her group plans to fight the changes. "Criminals who should not even be here to begin with should not be released onto our streets," Wideman said.

ICE spokeswoman Virginia Kice said the agency hopes local jurisdictions continue to comply with detainers, which she described as an essential tool in capturing immigrants who pose a public safety risk.

"When law enforcement agencies remand criminals to ICE custody rather than releasing them into the community, it helps contribute to public safety and the safety of law enforcement," Kice said. Federal statistics show that more than 33,000 people who were identified by immigration authorities while in custody in L.A. County have been deported since August 2009, when the county first signed on to a federal program known as Secure Communities.

Under the program, fingerprints of inmates booked by local law enforcement authorities are checked against federal immigration databases. ICE agents use the information to decide whether to ask police to hold the inmates for up to 48 hours to give ICE time to take them into custody.

Immigrant rights advocates have pushed back against detainers with protests and litigation in recent years, saying they are unconstitutional and have eroded trust in police among immigrant communities. Last fall, advocates won a major victory when Gov. Jerry Brown signed the Trust Act, which instructs local officials to honor ICE detainers only in cases when inmates have been charged with or convicted of a serious offense.

The recent changes go beyond that, with counties deciding to stop honoring ICE detainers altogether.

San Diego County Sheriff Bill Gore said he made the decision last week after consulting with county attorneys about the Oregon lawsuit.

In that case, an immigrant from Mexico named Maria Miranda Olivares completed a jail sentence for violating a restraining order but was kept behind bars for an additional 19 hours on a federal hold at the request of immigration agents, who eventually took her into custody.

Lawyers for the county argued in a lawsuit brought by Miranda that the sheriff was required to hold her. The judge disagreed, saying ICE detainers are not mandatory and did not demonstrate probable cause for Miranda to be held. The judge said the county was liable for damages.

Gore said his agency felt it was too risky to continue holding inmates for ICE. Instead he said his agency will notify federal agents when inmates who have been flagged for potential immigration violations are released.

"If they want them, they can come and get them," Gore said. "We don't have to hold them for 48 hours."

Sheriffs from several counties, including Orange and Kern, say they will not change their policies relating to ICE detainers.

Lt. Jeff Hallock, a spokesman for the Orange County Sheriff's Department, said officials in his agency reviewed the federal court decision and decided their current policy was appropriate. He said Orange County operates in compliance with the Trust Act.

40. New York Gives Legal Counsel to Undocumented Immigrants

Cindy Chang

Anderson Cadet arrived at the Varick Street courthouse in an orange jumpsuit, shackled at the wrists, prepared to fight his deportation without an attorney.

In immigration court, there is generally no right to free legal counsel. Many immigrants represent themselves. But on this cold February morning, Cadet was greeted by a public defender who took on his case for free.

The Haitian immigrant is a client in a yearlong pilot program, believed to be the first of its kind, that provides free legal counsel to low-income people facing deportation.

With $500,000 from the New York City Council, about 20 percent of immigrants in nearby detention centers this year will receive a public defender. Proponents are looking for $7.4 million in city and state funding to expand the program to all of the 900 or so city residents who end up in immigration detention each year.

Immigrant rights advocates in cities across the country, are hoping to start their own public defender programs.

"Day after day, people are getting deported who shouldn't be deported," said Peter Markowitz, a professor at the Cardozo School of Law and a co-founder of the legal counsel program, called the New York Immigrant Family Unity Project.

Cadet's initial hearing began a few hours after he met his attorney, Brittany Brown of Brooklyn Defender Services.

Brown argued that Cadet should be allowed to keep his green card because his convictions, for petty theft and turnstile jumping, are not "crimes involving moral turpitude." A government attorney countered that the convictions make Cadet deportable. Judge Thomas Mulligan cited a case from 1945, then asked Brown to submit a written brief.

Since the pilot program began in November, hearings proceed more efficiently because attorneys have already explained the basics to their clients, its proponents say. Some, like Cadet, have possible defenses that they are unlikely to have unearthed on their own.

Others are advised by their new lawyers that deportation is unavoidable.

"The thought that someone could go up against a trained government attorney, argue a complicated area of law without legal training and competently represent themselves is really a fiction. It will rarely happen," said Oren Root, director of the Center on Immigration and Justice at the Vera Institute of Justice, which administers the program.

Prior to the pilot program, more than two-thirds of New Yorkers in immigration detention centers represented themselves, with a success rate of 3 percent, compared with 18 percent for detainees with attorneys, according to a study by backers of the program.

In Los Angeles, many immigrants also appear without attorneys, though exact figures are not available. On a recent morning at the federal building on Los Angeles Street, five of the 13 detainees on Judge Lorraine Munoz's docket had private attorneys. The others were navigating the byzantine immigration system alone.

"I have seen plenty of people who had defenses of various kinds and clearly did not understand that that was true," said Ahilan Arulanantham, deputy legal director at the ACLU of Southern California, who recently won a case requiring the government to provide attorneys for mentally disabled immigrants.

By allowing breadwinners to stay in the country and support their families, and by reducing the time that clients spend in detention, the New York program could save millions of dollars, more than paying for itself, its backers have calculated.

But Mark Krikorian, executive director of the Center for Immigration Studies, said the program is a misuse of public money. "The question is, should taxpayers be funding the defense of people, many of whom shouldn't even be in this country?" said Krikorian, who advocates for a more restrictive immigration system.

"The answer is no. It's absurd on its face."

As a federal appeals court judge, Robert Katzmann saw case after case in which immigrants missed legal arguments that could have saved them from deportation.

Katzmann convened a study group, which produced the 56-page report detailing the much lower odds for immigrants without legal counsel.

Advocates used the data to persuade City Council members to fund New York's pilot program.

"I had this view that justice should not depend on the income level of the immigrant, and that if we could improve the lawyering, we would have better confidence that justice was being done thoroughly and efficiently," said Katzmann, chief judge for the 2nd U.S. Circuit Court of Appeals.

In Los Angeles, the public interest law firm Public Counsel represents several hundred immigrants each year, mostly using pro bono attorneys from private firms.

Catholic Charities' Esperanza Immigrant Rights Project also represents people facing deportation. But many still go without, especially those held in detention centers in distant locations. "It's staggering that we don't have that, considering our needs here are as great or greater than New York's," said Judy London, head of Public Counsel's Immigrants' Rights Project. "Hopefully, this will put the fire under people's feet and be a real motivator for government and the philanthropic community to fashion something like this."

41. Obama Faces Growing Rebellion Against Secure Communities

Elise Foley

WASHINGTON—Last Wednesday, Philadelphia Mayor Michael Nutter (D) announced a significant change to the city's law enforcement policies. Going forward, Philadelphia officials would no longer acquiesce to the federal government's requests that they hold certain undocumented immigrants for extra time solely for deportation purposes.

The change in policy is among the latest acts of rebellion against the euphemistically-titled Secure Communities, a federally-run program launched in 2008 that allows U.S. Immigrations and Customs Enforcement to find and pick up immigrants it will eventually deport. The program has played a central role in deportations over the past six years, and, in the process, has raised the ire of immigration reform advocates who argue that not only is it a blunt and costly instrument that forces police officers to play the role of ICE agents, it also tramples on civil liberties. Nutter isn't the only one to grow tired with the program.

On Friday, Maryland Gov. Martin O'Malley (D) said the Baltimore City Detention Center would stop automatically honoring requests from ICE to hold people it would otherwise release. Meanwhile, more than a dozen counties in Oregon have announced after a court ruling on April 11 that they will no longer comply with ICE requests to hold individuals except under certain circumstances.

The revolt against Secure Communities—a significant part of the government's interior enforcement mechanism—is growing. And it's compli-

Original published as Elise Foley, "Obama Faces Growing Rebellion Against the Secure Communities Deportation Program," www.huffingtonpost.com/2014/04/24/secure-communities_n_5182876.html, April 24, 2014. Reprinted with permission of the author.

cating the Obama administration's already delicate attempt to recalibrate its immigration policies. Amid damage control with immigration reform advocates for its deportation numbers, the White House increasingly faces pushback from law enforcement and local officials who are frustrated with their role in funneling people into the deportation pipeline.

The Department of Homeland Security is currently reviewing its deportation policies to make them, in the administration's words, more humane. Lawmakers in the Congressional Hispanic Caucus urged the White House earlier this month to eliminate Secure Communities entirely. Activists also view eliminating the program as the ultimate goal. But short of that, they have called for the Obama administration to take a page from the states, counties and cities that are putting limits on who they detain for ICE purposes. Recent reports indicate the administration may be doing so.

DHS spokesman Peter Boogaard cautioned that it's too early in the process to predict the final result. Opponents of Secure Communities, however, are hopeful that the government will try to match their efforts to protect immigrants without serious criminal records, including those who have been previously deported or have other immigration violations.

"The tide has turned against the program, and I think there is now consensus that the program needs to be shut down completely, and I do think it will be shut down completely," said Chris Newman, who has fought against Secure Communities in his work with the National Day Laborer Organizing Network. "Before the program is scrapped completely, I think the administration will continue to do as they've done for some time, which is to roll out incremental reforms to try to put cold water on the growing pressure."

Secure Communities works as a relatively simple information-sharing program between the FBI and ICE. When an individual is arrested, his or her fingerprints are taken and sent to the FBI to screen for fugitives and ex-convicts. Under the program, that routine fingerprint process can lead to immigrants being picked up by ICE, detained and deported. ICE requests holds under other circumstances as well, but Secure Communities has made the process more common.

The program may seem sound in principle—after all, who wouldn't want their communities to be more secure? And those caught by Secure Communities and deported from the country by the Obama administration do include convicted sex offenders, murderers and thieves. But it's not just hardened criminals who are affected by Secure Communities.

The program has ensnared parents driving without a license because they need to work and can't get authorization to drive in their state. It has caught young people arrested for small levels of drug possession. Many of those caught are people who have previously been deported but came back to the U.S. to work or be with their families—immigrants who could be aided by a policy that put less emphasis on deporting repeat immigration law violators.

Since fingerprints are shared with ICE at the point of arrest—not conviction—people who are never charged or eventually ruled innocent can be caught up in the system. Opponents of Secure Communities point out that domestic violence victims are in some cases fingerprinted along with their abusers while the police sort out the details.

"The whole machinery is just so flawed," Fred Tsao, policy director at the Illinois Coalition for Immigrant and Refugee Rights, said of Secure Communities. "If the focus really is on people who have committed serious crimes and have been convicted of those offenses, then you don't try to catch people when they've first been arrested, in many cases before they've even had a bond set for them."

Secure Communities was originally touted as optional—law enforcement could, to officials' understanding, participate in the program or stay out of it. And, indeed, some states and localities wanted out. Law enforcement officials in particular began to worry that victims and witnesses to crime would begin to see police as immigration agents rather than protectors.

Since ICE was also requesting that local law enforcement hold people up to 48 hours, excluding weekends, longer than they otherwise would, government officials said the cost of the program was too steep. In Los Angeles County, a 2012 report found that law enforcement was spending more than $26 million per year to hold people at ICE's request, even though they would be released under normal circumstances.

Washington, D.C., was first to attempt to opt of the program in May 2010, not long after Arizona Gov. Jan Brewer (R) signed into law SB 1070, which went in the other direction by increasing local police's participation in immigration enforcement. San Francisco; Arlington, Va. and Santa Clara County, Calif. followed Washington's lead over the next several months. A few governors announced in 2011 they would not participate in the program: first in Illinois, and then New York and Massachusetts. State and local lawmakers thought they could do so, given statements from ICE that it was an optional program. The ICE website even gave instructions as of 2010 for officials to request that the program not be activated in their localities.

But declining to share the fingerprints with ICE wasn't really an option after all, then-DHS Secretary Janet Napolitano said in October 2010. She and other officials explained that because law enforcement shares fingerprints with the FBI already, the FBI could then share them with ICE regardless of objections at the local level.

Lawmakers such as Rep. Zoe Lofgren (D–Calif.) questioned whether ICE had purposefully misled the public.

Meanwhile, state and local officials began rebelling against ICE through a variety of approaches that give law enforcement more leeway on how it interacts with immigration enforcement.

Some officials said costs were a partial reason for pushing back. The Cook County, Ill., Board of Commissioners voted in 2011 to ignore ICE requests to hold people they would otherwise free, based on the estimated price tag of about $15 million per year. When ICE said it would pick up the tab, Cook County rejected the agency's offer.

One of the broadest pushbacks against Secure Communities started in 2011, when California lawmakers and advocates began their effort to put legislation on the books that would keep law enforcement from holding immigrants for ICE except under certain circumstances, such as for convicted felons. Titled the TRUST Act, the bill also instructs law enforcement not to detain people they would otherwise release if the hold request was based solely on a past immigration violation.

After it first passed both state houses, the TRUST Act was vetoed in 2012 by Gov. Jerry Brown (D), who called the bill "fatally flawed." His decision came under pressure from ICE, which was planning behind the scenes to launch a pilot program to address concerns over holds.

Two months after Brown's veto, ICE announced its own changes to how it issued detention requests, or detainers, to put less emphasis on noncriminals and minor offenders. But those reforms weren't enough for advocates of the TRUST Act, who reworked the bill and passed it again in 2013. This time, Brown signed it into law.

The California bill doesn't go as far as many advocates wanted: There are exceptions for which ICE hold requests will be respected beyond just felons, including certain misdemeanor and felony charges. But the TRUST Act has already made a difference in California. The Associated Press reported that in the first two months since the law went into effect, January and February of this year, there was a significant reduction in the number of immigrants being turned over to ICE by local law enforcement in California. The AP looked at data from 15 of the 23 counties responsible for most of the state's deportations, and found that there was a 44 percent drop in people being arrested and held for immigration officials. There was an especially marked change in San Francisco, which has led the fight to limit Secure Communities: The country saw a 93 percent reduction of people held for ICE.

With the early data now in, Angela Chan, an attorney with Asian Law Caucus who has helped lead the movement against Secure Communities, said that the principles behind the TRUST Act should be taken seriously by ICE.

"There was a strong belief from people who were directly impacted that the local police should not be involved in immigration enforcement," she said. "That's the basis of the TRUST Act that needs to be included in the executive action that's being contemplated: leave local law enforcement alone. Let them do their job of public safety and criminal law enforcement."

Connecticut also serves as a case study for what happens when law enforcement limits cooperation with ICE. The state implemented policy changes in 2012 for its Department of Corrections to release certain immigrants on a case-by-case basis, and further changes were formalized in February 2013 after a settlement in the *Brizuela v. Feliciano* case. Under that settlement, the Department of Corrections was instructed to hold people for ICE only if they had been convicted of a felony, had prior removal orders, or met criteria demonstrating they presented a threat to public safety. The settlement also requires law enforcement to notify arrestees that they are being held under an ICE request and provides them with a toll-free number to free legal counsel at Yale Law School if they believe they are being detained wrongly. The Department of Corrections must release information each month on how many people are detained based on ICE requests, and on what grounds.

Connecticut passed its own version of the TRUST Act later in 2013, extending limits on detainers to additional agencies.

In 2011, before the policy changes, Connecticut delivered an average of 33 people to ICE each month. The number of requests per month went down considerably after the new policies on ICE holds were implemented. According to the information released by the Department of Corrections, ICE received an average of 8.5 detainer requests per month from March

2013—after the *Brizuela v. Feliciano* settlement—to February 2014. The state Department of Corrections held people for ICE for about 80 percent of requests, and in about 90 percent of those holds, the individual in question had either a felony conviction or a prior deportation order.

Michael Wishnie, a professor at Yale Law School who has been practicing immigration law for two decades, said ICE could look to Connecticut's example for a more refined approach to enforcement. Fewer detainers are being issued, and a far higher percentage of them are for felony convictions or old deportation orders, more in line with ICE's official priorities, Wishnie said.

"What this suggests to me is that ICE has conformed its issuing practices to meet the enforcement practices of Connecticut," he said.

Not everyone is supportive of changes to ICE policy on releasing people after arrests. Republicans in the House Judiciary Committee sent a letter to Homeland Security Secretary Jeh Johnson earlier this month expressing concern that ICE was allowing criminal immigrants to go free, and asking for more information on what criminal convictions existed for people ICE released.

The Federation for American Immigration Reform, or FAIR, which supports reducing immigration levels, has advocated against state TRUST Acts and other policies meant to combat enforcement programs. By deemphasizing deportation of repeat immigration offenders, FAIR spokesman Bob Dane said, policies like the TRUST Act send the message that immigration law violations aren't important on their own.

"It's corrupting the rule of law, and it's creating this culture of permissiveness for illegal immigration," he said.

Despite these arguments, there are indications that the mindset on deportations is changing within DHS. John Sandweg, who served as the acting director of ICE from August 2013 to February of this year, penned an op-ed for the *Los Angeles Times* in March arguing ICE "should eliminate 'non-criminal re-entrants and immigration fugitives' as a priority category for deportation." He said most ICE officers and agents were supportive of those types of policies so they could "focus their efforts on the most serious offenders and offenses."

The Associated Press reported Monday that DHS is considering limiting deportations of people with repeat immigration violations but no other serious criminal records.

Boogaard, the DHS spokesman, told *HuffPost* that "any report of specific considerations at this time would be premature," adding that Johnson is still seeking opinions from stakeholders and members of Congress.

As for advocates, they said they will believe that a change is in the works when they see it.

"There are lots of reasons to be skeptical that the president and DHS are serious about this," said Wishnie, the Yale law professor. "Recent history suggests that enforcement reviews change very little on the ground. Senior officials make speeches, they issue memos out of headquarters, they sail them out like paper airplanes to the field and very little changes on the ground. I hope this is different."

42. Emerging Challenge for the U.S. Healthcare System

Emmanuel Gorospe

Immigration shapes the diverse character of American society. Through the years, immigrants have richly contributed to the growth of the U.S. population. They comprise a significant workforce with a yearly contribution of $10 Billion to the economy (Mohanty, Woolhandler, Himmelstein et al. 2005). As they get older, immigrants represent a substantial fraction of America's aging population. As of 2000, 9.5 percent of the U.S. population are immigrants age 65 years and older (Rogers and Raymer 2001). Moreover, they continue to grow with the influx of elderly immigrants who are entering the U.S. through lawful immigration programs, sponsored by their family members under the Family Reunification Act (Gelfand 1989). These elderly immigrants will face the problems of adapting to a new environment, culture, and a complex healthcare delivery system. In these terms, they are disadvantaged compared to elderly non-immigrants in accessing and utilizing healthcare services.

Unfortunately, public welfare programs for non–U.S. citizens have been curtailed. The enactment of the Personal Responsibility & Work Opportunity Reconciliation Act (PRWORA), stopped legally admitted immigrants beginning August 22, 1996, from receiving federal cash assistance and food stamps. Furthermore, the Supplemental Security Income (SSI) and Medicaid benefits of poor elderly immigrants have also been abolished (Yoo 2001). These laws have caused and will continue to have significant implications in the provision of healthcare services for legal immigrants.

Original published as E. Gorospe, "Elderly Immigrants: Emerging Challenge for the U.S. Healthcare System," *Internet Journal of Healthcare Administration* 4 Number 1 (2005). Reprinted with permission of the author and publisher.

In this chapter, I intend to present examples of health-related problems that beset the elderly legal immigrants and review possible solutions with respect to the elderly's special circumstances. I shall limit the discussion to legal elderly immigrants, also referred to as, lawful permanent residents. The issue of illegal immigrants is too complicated and political to be dealt adequately in this brief review. This problem, albeit interesting, merits a separate discussion.

Review of Literature

By 2010, the elderly immigrant population is expected to reach 4.5 million. Approximately 60 percent of this increase is attributed to the growing number of elderly immigrants admitted as relatives of U.S. citizens, permanent residents and refugees (Wilmoth, De Jong, and Himes 1997). On average, these immigrants enter the U.S. at 60–79 years of age (Gelfand and Yee 1991). Upon arrival, elderly immigrants settle in neighborhoods established by earlier immigrants. They tend to stay among family members or in ethnically-concentrated communities like Chinatowns. These settlements are mostly found in urban and suburban communities (Rogers and Raymer 2001). These provide a sense of belonging, access to ethnic foods and other cultural paraphernalia.

Elderly immigrants are different from their younger counterparts. Their process of acculturation to U.S. society varies depending on their ethnic background, socioeconomic status, and prior experience with American culture. Limited exposure beyond their ethnically-concentrated communities and strong cultural beliefs can become barriers to successful acculturation (Bowen and Nelson 2002). However, acculturation to the American culture is not entirely ideal (Gelfand and Yee 1991). The shift to high fat, high salt, low fiber diet may even be detrimental (Tong 1991). Acculturation to the fast-paced American way of life is even associated with obesity, smoking, and sedentary lifestyle (Lee, Sobal, Frongill 2000; Aldrich 2000).

Immigration can be a stressful life event for the elderly. It can bring about new financial, medical and psychosocial issues. Newly arrived elderly immigrants can become entirely dependent on their families because of their ineligibility for government healthcare funds and supplementary social benefits. They may not have sufficient savings or insurance coverage from their previous employment from their countries of origin.

In terms of health, they may lack the basic preventive care services such as immunizations, dental care, and cancer screening (Bowen and Nelson 2002). Coming from developing countries, they may have been exposed to harsh working and living conditions detrimental to their aging health. For example, newly immigrated elderly Mexicans have poorer health status compared to their Mexican counterparts who have lived and aged in the U.S. (Angel, Angel, Markides 2000). In terms of mental health, there have been documented cases of migratory grief and depression among elderly immigrant Latinos (Ailinger and Causey 1993), Chinese (Casado and Leung 2001), Indians (Rait and Burns 1997) and other Asian Pacific Islanders (Harada and Lauren 1995). Even if the stringent medical examinations required by U.S. immigration laws have been efficient in screening and barring elderly applicants who may have active diseases of public health significance (LoBue and Moser 2004), newly arrived elderly immigrants still have poorer overall health and well-being compared to their American-born and U.S. naturalized elderly counterparts.

Access and utilization of healthcare services can also be challenging. The complex U.S. healthcare delivery system and its bureaucratic procedures are difficult to understand for new immigrants. In addition to financial issues, language and culture could hinder healthcare utilization. Older immigrants tenaciously hold to their cultural practices and health beliefs (Plawecki 2000). Communication with the elderly immigrant is an important consideration in providing health services. In a Minnesota program that aimed to improve the access of elderly immigrants to health services, limited ability to communicate in English was a significant factor. Latino, Somali and Cambodian elderly who spoke little or no English at all were heavily dependent on family and community members in accessing health services (Bowen and Nelson 2002). In choosing healthcare services, some groups of elderly immigrants still seek their traditional medical practices (Ka 1998). These services are not reimbursed by most insurance plans. Nevertheless, they are generally regarded as cheaper and readily available in their ethnically-concentrated communities such as the herb pharmacies in Chinatowns.

The challenge for healthcare providers is how to render services that are culturally-acceptable to elderly immigrants. Simply providing access to health services does not always guarantee that the elderly will avail themselves to such services. Another challenge is how to finance the healthcare of the uninsured elderly immigrants who are not eligible to Medicare or Medicaid. Free care should not be the only option. Recent data suggest that the incoming aged immigrants are becoming more financially capable due to their supporting families who have successfully established in the U.S. (Trejo 1992). However, there is still a need for insurance coverage. A study among elderly Korean immigrants prove that insurance coverage increases healthcare utilization (Sohn and Harada 2004). The lack of regular health services to the aged could result to catastrophic medical conditions that are more costly to finance. In addition, chronically debilitating diseases in the elderly such as stroke, cardiovascular disease, osteoarthritis, and other chronic degenerative conditions could financially overwhelm families supporting the healthcare of their elderly.

Strategies for Elderly Immigrants

Given the current legal restrictions for public funding of non-citizen residents, the best solution for the elderly immigrants would be to immediately apply for U.S. naturalization after five years of continuous residence in the U.S. Upon attaining U.S. citizenship, elderly immigrants instantly gain eligibility to Medicare and if qualified, including Medicaid, Supplemental Security Income (SSI), food stamps and other state administered programs. Since Medicare and Medicaid provide similar services to all beneficiaries, these government services are instrumental in reducing health disparities and enhancing the quality of lives of elderly Americans regardless of ethnic origin (Eichner and Vladek 2005). However, the process of naturalization requires the ability to read, write and speak English and knowledge of American history which could be difficult for aged immigrants with disadvantaged social and educational background. Fortunately, there are exemptions on certain meritorious cases which waive these requirements.

Aged immigrants who are still capable of working should seek employment opportunities as a means to earn Social Security contributions and possibly even employer-paid health insurance. Employment is also a means to facilitate acculturation, possibly improve language skills, and to broaden social networks. However, because of possible language barriers and physical frailty, elderly immigrants are likely to have limited employment prospects.

Another option is for sponsoring families to procure private health insurance plans for their elderly members. This should not be regarded as unnecessary burden. Besides, federal regulations for immigrant sponsorship require that the sponsoring family member makes at least 125 percent above poverty level as a proof of his financial capability to support the elderly (Yoo 2001). Although enrolling an elderly immigrant in a private insurance plan would significantly have high premium cost, financing the newly immigrated elderly is only temporary while they wait to qualify for U.S. naturalization and to receive Medicare benefits.

Utilizing community and non–governmental resources will be helpful for the aged immigrants and their families. They should learn to organize themselves and create links with institutions, non–governmental organizations and community health centers that specialize in migrant health issues. Their joint mobilization and campaign have been very effective even in the past. After the PROWORA enactment, community organizers and advocates for the elderly successfully lobbied to restore SSI benefits to non-citizen elderly individuals who have resided in the U.S. before the Aug. 22, 1996 cut-off in spite of political resistance and prevailing anti-immigration sentiments during that time (Yoo 2001). Advocates for the elderly minorities must take advantage of the growing influence of naturalized U.S. citizens and minority lobbying groups in both elections and legislative processes to support the cause of disadvantaged elderly.

Strategies for Healthcare Institutions

Healthcare institutions operating in communities with substantial immigrant population should learn to establish links among the different ethnic communities. It is becoming popular among hospitals to provide medical interpreters and clinicians who are bilingual. In this regard, we can appreciate the advantage of diversifying our healthcare professionals. The trend of employing more foreign nurses and physicians might be an unexpected benefit which can answer the growing needs of a culturally-diverse elderly population. Cultural competency training is increasing among healthcare institutions as well as in the educational setting (Cook, Kosoko-Lasaki, and O'Brien 2005).

Providing healthcare to a culturally diverse and elderly population could be very challenging. Not all elderly immigrants are the same. Even among Hispanic immigrants, there are great differences among various South American ethnic groups. Health programs must consider these differences and not be quick to generalize all minorities. Clinicians must understand that older immigrants expect providers to be respectful of their culture, customs and even social status (Plawecki 2000). In terms of services, providers should optimize preventive services such as cancer screening, preventive cardiology and immunizations. The rational use of preventive services could forestall major illnesses that could deplete the limited financial resources of elderly immigrants and their families.

Conclusion

Meeting the challenges of the growing number of elderly legal immigrant requires multisectoral cooperation. Policy makers and the general public should avoid the assumption that immigrants disproportionately consume healthcare resources. On the contrary, healthcare spending for both legal and illegal immigrants is even 55 percent lower than the healthcare expenditures of U.S.-born citizens (Mohanty, Woolhandler, Himmelstein et al. 2005).

Ten years after the enactment of PROWORA, health and social workers realize that elderly legal immigrants are indeed deserving of federal financial aid (Yoo 2001). Unfortunately, there is no upcoming resolution for this issue. The current budgetary constraints, the costly implementation of the Medicare prescription drug plan, and the general mood of the U.S. government to cut spending do not show any signs of possible change on present welfare policies. Like most elderly Americans, aged immigrants and their families should plan ahead. Uncertainties in the future of Medicare and Medicaid suggest increasing reliance for private plans (Lubitz, Greenberg, Gorina et al. 2001) and use of personal resources in the care of the elderly.

REFERENCES

Ailinger, R.L., and Causey, M.R. (1993). "Home health service utilization by Hispanic elderly immigrants: a longitudinal study." *Home Health Care Services Quarterly* 14, 2–3:85–96.
Aldrich, L. (2000). "Acculturation erodes the diet quality of U.S. Hispanics." *Food Review* 23:51–55.
Angel, J., Angel, R., and Markides, K. (2000). "Late life immigration, changes in living arrangements and headship status among older Mexican-origin individuals." *Social Science Quarterly* 81, 1:389–403.
Bowen, J.M., and Nelson, J.M. (2002). "Caring for elderly immigrants. Challenges and opportunities." *Minnesota Medicine* 85, 9:25–7.
Casado, B., and Leung, P. (2001). "Migratory grief and depression among elderly Chinese American immigrants." *Journal of Gerontological Social Work* 36, 1–2:5–26.
Cook, C.T., Kosoko-Lasaki, O., and O'Brien, R. (2005). "Satisfaction with and per-

ceived cultural competency of healthcare providers: the minority experience." *Journal of the National Medical Association* 97, 8:1078–87.

Eichner, J., and Vladek, B. (2005). "Medicare as a catalyst for reducing health disparities." *Health Affairs* 24, 2:365–375.

Gelfand, D. (1989). "Immigration, aging, and intergenerational relationships." *Gerontologist* 29, 3:366–72.

_____, and Yee, B. (1991). "Trends & forces: Influence of immigration, migration, and acculturation on the fabric of aging in America." *Generations* 15, 4:46–58.

Harada, N.D. and Lauren, S. (1995). "Use of mental health services by older Asian and Pacific Islander Americans," In D.K. Padgett (Ed.) *Handbook on Ethnicity Aging and Mental Health*. Westport, CT: Greenwood.

Ka, V. (1998). "Hard choices: the use of Western vs. Chinese traditional medicine by the Chinese homebound elderly, New York City. A community health survey." *Journal of Long Term Home Health Care* 17, 2:2–10.

Lee, S.K., Sobal, J., and Frongillo, E.A., Jr. (2000). "Acculturation and health in Korean Americans." *Social Science Medicine* 51, 2:159–73.

LoBue, P.A., and Moser, K.S. (2004). "Screening of immigrants and refugees for pulmonary tuberculosis in San Diego County, California." *Chest* 126, 6:1777–82.

Lubitz, J., Greenberg, L.G., Gorina, Y., et al. (2001). "Three decades of health care use by the elderly, 1965–1998." *Health Affairs* 20, 2:19–32.

Mohanty, S.A., Woolhandler, S., Himmelstein, D.U., et al. (2005). "Health care expenditures of immigrants in the United States: a nationally representative analysis." *American Journal of Public Health* 95, 8:1431–8.

Plawecki, H.M. (2000). "The elderly immigrant. An isolated experience." *Journal of Gerontology and Nursing* 26, 2:6–7.

Rait, G., and Burns, A. (1997). "Appreciating background and culture: the South Asian elderly and mental health." *International Journal of Geriatric Psychiatry* 12, 10:973–7.

Rogers, A., and Raymer, J. (2001). "Immigration and the regional demographics of the elderly population in the United States." *The Journals of Gerontology Series B: Psychological Sciences and Social Sciences* 56, 1:S44–55.

Sohn, L., and Harada, N.D. (2004). "Time since immigration and health services utilization of Korean-American older adults living in Los Angeles County." *Journal of the American Geriatric Society* 52, 11:1946–50.

Tong, A. (1991). "Eating habits of elderly Vietnamese in the United States." *Journal of Nutrition for the Elderly* 10, 2:35–48.

Trejo, S. (1992). "Immigrant welfare recipiency: Recent trends and future implications." *Contemporary Political Issues* 10, 2:44–53.

Wilmoth, J.M., De Jong, G., and Himes, C. (1997). "Immigrant and non-immigrant living arrangements among America's white, Hispanic and Asian elderly population." *International Journal of Sociology and Social Policy* 17:57–82.

Yoo, G. (2001). "Constructing deservingness: Federal welfare reform, supplemental security income, and elderly immigrants." *Journal of Aging and Social Policy* 13, 4:17–34

43. Illegal Immigrants Most Helped by Emergency Medicaid

Phil Galewitz

During the debate over the 2010 federal health care overhaul, Democrats promised that illegal immigrants wouldn't be among the 27 million people who'd gain coverage. President Barack Obama repeated that pledge last month when he outlined his immigration plan.

But while federal law generally bars illegal immigrants from being covered by Medicaid, a little-known part of the state-federal health insurance program for the poor pays about $2 billion a year for emergency treatment for a group of patients who, according to hospitals, mostly comprise illegal immigrants. Most of it goes to reimburse hospitals for delivering babies for women who show up in their emergency rooms, according to interviews with hospital officials and studies.

The funding—which has been around since the late 1980s and is less than 1 percent of the cost of Medicaid—underscores the political and practical challenges of refusing to cover an entire class of people. Congress approved the program after lawmakers required hospitals to screen and stabilize all emergency patients regardless of their insurance or citizenship status.

Some groups say the services encourage people to cross the border for care, while advocates for immigrants say the funding is inadequate because it doesn't pay for prenatal care and other vital services.

"We can't turn them away," said Joanne Aquilina, the chief financial

Original published as Phil Galewitz, "Illegal Immigrants Most Helped by Emergency Medicaid Program," *Kaiser Health News*, February 13, 2013. Reprinted with permission of the publisher. Kaiser Health News (KHN) is a nonprofit national health policy news service.

officer of Bethesda Healthcare System in Boynton Beach, Fla., which sees many illegal immigrants because of its proximity to farms where they harvest sugarcane and other seasonal crops.

Nearly one-third of Bethesda Hospital East's 2,900 births each year are paid for by Emergency Medicaid, the category that covers mainly illegal immigrants. The category includes a small proportion of homeless people and legal immigrants who've been in the country less than five years.

Hospitals can't ask patients whether they're illegal immigrants, but instead determine that after checking whether they have Social Security numbers, birth certificates or other documents.

"We gather information to qualify patients for something and through that process, if you really hit a dead end, you know they are illegal," said Steve Short, the chief financial officer at Tampa General Hospital.

A 2007 medical article in the *Journal of the American Medical Association* reported that 99 percent of those who used Emergency Medicaid during a four-year period in North Carolina were thought to be illegal immigrants.

The Federation for American Immigration Reform, which seeks to limit immigration, said the funding led more women to give birth in the United States, especially since they knew that children born here would be American citizens. The group believes that tens of thousands of "anchor babies" are born each year to illegal immigrants who hope that giving birth to children recognized as citizens will help the women gain legal status themselves.

Anyone born in the United States is a U.S. citizen. It's unclear how many mothers later get green cards or become citizens.

The Federation for American Immigration Reform doesn't dispute hospitals' right to be reimbursed for care they're required to provide.

"Our focus should be that you could save this money if you prevent the illegal immigration from happening in the first place. You can't do it after the fact," said Jack Martin, the special projects director for the organization.

Groups that advocate for immigrants say it's foolish for Medicaid to pay only for the births and not for the prenatal care that might prevent costly and long-term complications for American children.

"It's a lose, lose, lose," said Sonal Ambegaokar, a health policy lawyer at the National Immigration Law Center, which advocates for low-income immigrants. She said denying broad insurance coverage to legal immigrants hurt doctors and hospitals financially, prevented patients from getting needed care and increased costs for the health system.

"There is no evidence that Emergency Medicaid is the cause of migration," Ambegaokar said. "Immigrants migrate to the U.S. for job opportunities and reunifying with family members."

Data that *Kaiser Health News* collected from seven states that are thought to have the highest numbers of illegal immigrants show that the funding pays for emergency services delivered to more than 100,000 people a year.

California hospitals get about half the $2 billion spent annually on Emergency Medicaid. The rest is spread mainly among a handful of states. In 2011, for example:

- New York spent $528 million on Emergency Medicaid for nearly 30,000 people.
- Texas reported 240,000 claims costing $331 million. (One person could be responsible for multiple claims.)
- Florida spent $214 million on 31,000 patients.
- North Carolina spent $48 million on about 19,000 people.
- Arizona spent $115 million. It couldn't break out the number of people.
- Illinois spent $25 million on the cost of care to nearly 2,000 people.

The federal government doesn't require states to report how many people receive services through Emergency Medicaid payments to hospitals.

Legal immigrants who've been in the United States less than five years aren't eligible for regular Medicaid coverage, though states have the option of extending it to children and pregnant women.

Despite the surge in overall Medicaid spending in the past decade, Emergency Medicaid costs have been remarkably stable. A 2004 study by the Government Accountability Office that looked at data from the 10 states with the highest expected Emergency Medicaid costs, reported $2 billion in spending. State officials say spending varies depending on immigration patterns and that during the economic slowdown, the number of illegal immigrants dropped.

The definition of emergency care and the scope of services available through the Medicaid programs vary by state. For example, in New York, Emergency Medicaid may be used to provide chemotherapy and radiation therapy to illegal immigrants. In New York, California and North Carolina, it may be used to provide outpatient dialysis to undocumented patients.

Other states have tried to narrow the definition of "emergency" to limit what's covered. "Each state has its own interpretation," said Jane Perkins, the legal director of the National Health Law Program, which advocates for the working poor.

Last year, for instance, Florida changed its policy to pay for emergency services for eligible undocumented immigrants only until their conditions had been "stabilized." Previously, its policy was to pay for care that was "medically necessary to relieve or eliminate the emergency medical condition."

Many hospitals—particularly those in the immigrant areas of Miami and Tampa—feared the change would cut millions of dollars in funding. An administrative law judge ruled in December that Florida had enacted the change improperly because it didn't go through a public hearing process; the state is appealing.

Short, the chief financial officer at Tampa General Hospital, said the $10 million the hospital collected each year to treat illegal immigrants was "very important to us." He noted that Medicaid pays the hospital about $1,500 for each day a Medicaid patient is in the hospital.

Jackson Memorial Hospital in Miami collects about $50 million a year in Emergency Medicaid funding, according to the state Agency for Health Care Administration.

Part III

The Future

44. The Rise of the New Baltimoreans

Nancy Scola

Baltimore has steadily lost population since the end of World War II. With 620,000 residents, the city has just two residents for every three it had at its peak in the 1950s. The decline has recently begun to slow, but that isn't enough for the city's sitting mayor, Democrat Stephanie Rawlings-Blake. Since day one, the former city council president has been made it her goal to halt the city's contraction. A city that loses its tax base is unable to secure the funding required to provide services and maintain its infrastructure, she argued in her 2011 inaugural address. "A shrinking city is a place unable to meet even the most basic needs of its people—basic rights that everyone should expect," she said. "A shrinking city simply cannot stand."

Rawlings-Blake ended her speech with a vision of adding some 10,000 families to Baltimore's rolls over the next 10 years. Her strategy: Increase the population in part through attracting more immigrants. These new Baltimoreans will, both with their numbers and high rates of entrepreneurship, strengthen the city's economy, which in turn will drive more growth.

That vision appeared on the national radar this past March when Rawlings-Blake issued an executive order targeted at "new Americans." The directive's intent, according to the mayor's office, was to state loudly and clearly that those Baltimoreans who use city services will not, generally speaking, be asked about their immigration status. Driving the measure

Originally published as Nancy Scola, "The Rise of the New Baltimoreans," www.nlc.org/find-city-solutions/city-solutions-and-applied-research/immigrant-integration/the-rise-of-the-new-baltimoreans. 2013. Reprinted with permission of the publisher, National League of Cities.

was the idea that, for example, victims of or witnesses to crimes should not have to worry about the state of their immigration papers before going to the police.

To Rawlings-Blake, the measure was a continuation of Baltimore's long history as a welcoming city. "Baltimore City has long been a home to immigrants from around the world," her order read, "who come hear seeking peace, stability, and a better life for their families."

What the mayor left unsaid but what many observers heard: That immigrants who chose Baltimore as the place to seek better lives will also help to re-grow and reinvigorate the neighborhoods in which they put down roots.

To critics, Baltimore is ill-prepared to absorb such an influx of new residents. Other observers caution that in focusing on increased immigrant population numbers, the city might be mistaking a sign of urban revival for its cause. But those close to Rawlings-Blake contend that steps taken to make the city more welcoming to new Americans serve, in the end, to make it more attractive to all Americans.

There's reason to believe that immigrants can, indeed, boost the city's challenged economy. "Leaving one's home and immigrating to a new country to start a new life is itself an entrepreneurial act," argued an August 2012 report by the nonpartisan Partnership for a New American Economy. Perhaps not surprising, then, is the fact that immigrants to the United States have been drawn to entrepreneurialism. Immigrants or first-generation Americans, the Kaufmann Foundation has found, have been more than 40 percent of Fortune 500 companies in the U.S. According to research conducted by New York's nonpartisan Fiscal Policy Institute, immigrants own more than 18 percent of the country's incorporated businesses, though they only comprise 13 percent of the population.

There are two trends at work: Native-born Americans have grown increasingly less likely to start businesses, and immigrants are twice as likely as the native-born to begin ones. Immigrant-owned businesses tend to be small, but in the aggregate they have demonstrated considerable economic power. One in 10 workers employed in the private sector works at a business owned by immigrants. Moreover, immigrant-owned businesses contribute some $775 billion to the U.S. gross domestic product each year.

In Baltimore, it's difficult to miss the investments that immigrants are making. Nearly a quarter of the city's small businesses are owned immigrants, a disproportionately high amount considering foreign-born individuals make up only 9 percent of the population and 12 percent of the labor force, according to Fiscal Policy Institute research based on 2010 Census data.

And it's a change felt on the ground. "You could roll a bowling ball down the sidewalk five years ago," says Chris Ryer, president of the Southeast Community Development Corporation, which focuses on the Baltimore's Highlandtown neighborhood. "Now it's busy." As the existing population aged out, young families have moved in. "There's a lot of strollers on the streets," says Ryer.

While many of Highlandtown's new residents are Latino, the freshly vibrant area has attracted immigrant entrepreneurs from diverse backgrounds. The neighborhood's 10-block commercial strip, says Ryer, houses not only a Latino-owned photography studio but an Israeli-owned grocery and a Peruvian chicken joint. Ryer cites statistics on how immigrants open small businesses at higher rates than their native-born neighbors. "We're seeing the fruits of that in Highlandtown," he says.

Rawlings-Blake's targeted appeal to new Americans is the revival of work done in the city years ago. In 2002, the Baltimore's Abell Foundation issued a report, authored by former Connecticut congressman Bruce Morrison, that attempted to understand how 21st-century American cities grow. Morrison found that, the Sun Belt aside, cities of the same size as Baltimore shrink when they don't add newly arrived Americans into their mix. "Immigration is the key to reversing Baltimore's population decline," concluded the Abell report.

The ideas detailed in Morrison's report captured attention in Baltimore. Growing out of that attention was the creation of an Office of International and Immigrant Affairs in the administration of then-mayor Martin O'Malley.

Small Steps to Steady Growth

In the years since, though, institutional support for Baltimore's pro-immigrant push has fluctuated. After O'Malley was elected Maryland governor in 2007 and moved to Annapolis, a large budget deficit put immigration issues to the backburner. The immigration office was cut, its work subsumed by the Office of Neighborhoods and Constituent Services. The effort lost its focus.

Under Rawlings-Blake, the city is reviving the drive to attract new arrivals to Baltimore—within the constraints imposed by its current financial burdens. It's a more modest approach for a more modest time. Says Ian Brennan, spokesperson for the mayor, "it is a lot of little things we're trying to do."

Those efforts include sensitivity training for a police force that has, in the past, faced charges of racial profiling. According to Brennan, the goal of that work is to "make sure the police understand the perspective and needs and specific challenges of New Americans." Brennan points out that this year, Baltimore named as its new police chief Anthony Batts, a veteran of the police departments of Long Beach and Oakland, Calif. The city has also put in a place a liaison to Hispanic communities who is praised for her energy and enthusiasm.

Moreover, local government has held trainings for newly arrived residents to help them understand the legal requirements they face; Brennan points to a session held by the Mexican consulate aimed at helping immigrants with paperwork compliance. The city also works with groups such as Ryer's CDC to help connect fledgling entrepreneurs with façade improvement grants and other tools to help boost small businesses. These small steps are aimed at making Baltimore, bit by bit, more welcoming to immigrants, in large part by equipping them with resources to navigate their new home.

Economists agree that the investment in attracting newcomers will pay off. "Immigration and growth go together," says David Dyssegaard Kallick of the Fiscal Policy Institute. "That much is clear."

But somewhat less clear, says Kallick, is whether the increase in immigrant populations is a cause of a city's population growth or an effect of a city being generally more appealing across the board. Kallick cautions that cities like Baltimore risk overinvesting their hopes and resources in attracting immigrants. Kallick cites New York Mayor Michael Bloomberg's statement earlier this year that the way to re-grow "big hollowed-out cities where industry has left" is to offer city-specific visas. "You would populate Detroit overnight," the mayor has said, "because half the world wants to come here."

To Kallick, there's confusion between what it takes to make a city welcoming in ways that counteract policies in places like Arizona, South Carolina and Alabama that have, in recent years, aimed to discourage undocumented immigrants from settling through aggressive tracking of immigration status. But targeting programs specifically at immigrants can have, argues Kallick, an effect that economists call "pushing on a string." At some point, he says, immigrant-targeted appeals stop making sense, because immigrants are interested in the same things anyone wants: Good jobs, high-quality schools and safe streets.

"You want to create a context that's welcoming to everyone," says Kallick, "and a culture that's welcoming to everyone seems particularly welcoming to immigrants." A lowered likelihood of being aggressively questioned for immigration status, goes the thinking, might appeal to an immigrant in perfect compliance with the law as much as it might to an undocumented new arrival.

Under this approach, a city that is more welcoming sees its population grow. As it grows, its tax base broadens. As its tax base broadens, it helps to support the local economy, better educational resources and more policing. In turn, those effects make Baltimore more appealing not only to new immigrants, but also to native-born or long-tenured Americans living elsewhere in the U.S. Thus begins a spiraling in a positive direction. Immigration, in short, becomes part of a city's population revitalization—but only part of it.

Integrating Talent

Baltimore isn't alone in its embrace of this strategy. Boston, for example, has an Office of New Bostonians that reaches out to the city's immigrant population, in part by identifying official and unofficial liaisons to local communities. A project called Global Detroit has raised more than $4 million earmarked for research into the best strategies for attracting immigrants to the troubled Motor City. A plan called Welcome Dayton hopes to make that southwest Ohio city of 140,000 more receptive to new arrivals and help them along toward citizenship; among the initiative's goals is to develop an international marketplace for immigrant entrepreneurs in an underinvested corner of the city that has demonstrated growth from recent immigrants.

Meanwhile, Pittsburgh is now working to create the social infrastructure to retain incoming talent and recruit more of it. With its thriving tech sector and large universities, it's not hard to see why Pittsburgh already boasts the most highly skilled immigrant group in the country. Over 53 percent (30,542) of the city's immigrants hold a bachelor's degree or higher, according to a recent report from the Brookings Institution. A Welcome Center created by the organization Vibrant Pittsburgh attempts to strengthen the social connections of these new arrivals, pairing them with existing support services from translation to cultural organizations.

Baltimore has particular advantages when it comes to attracting highly skilled immigrants, especially in the fields of science, technology and education. Eight of the top 10 employers in Baltimore are engaged in health, education or both, led by Johns Hopkins University and the University of Maryland (and their medical systems) and the health care organizations MedStar and LifeBridge. That eds-and-meds mix has helped keep the city afloat. The Baltimore region's 7.1 percent unemployment rate puts it in the middle of the pack when it comes to metropolitan areas of a million or more residents.

With Washington, D.C., just 40 miles down the road, Baltimore provides easy access to the region's scores of government contractors and public-sector clients. Immigrants attracted to high-tech fields find support from organizations like the Maryland Business Incubation Association, whose collection of 20 business incubators includes the University of Maryland's Technology Advancement Program, staffed by veterans of start-up firms and the venture capital world, and the Maryland Center for Entrepreneurship in nearby Columbia, which provides affordable workspaces to burgeoning high-tech firms. New businesses in the space find themselves part of a thriving sector, rather than operating in isolation.

And indeed, immigrants are well represented in the innovation realm. A Kaufmann Foundation report found that more than a quarter of technology and engineering companies started in the U.S. in the decade after 1995 had one or more founders who had been born outside the country.

That said, it's worth noting that immigrant entrepreneurs aren't evenly distributed across the United States. In Silicon Valley, for example, some 52 percent of tech companies have at least one foreign-born founder. But the figure for Maryland is less than 20 percent. That gap suggests that the Baltimore region has the capacity to add greater numbers of non-native entrepreneurs to its local high-tech sector.

Becoming a Place Where "People Come and Stay"

Equally important as attracting immigrants is supporting them once they arrive, not to mention fostering their integration into the city's economy. In addition to language classes and job counseling, the city has developed initiatives such as its "Vacants to Value Homebuyer Program" that incentivizes home buying in historically immigrant-heavy sections of the city, like Greektown and the largely–Hispanic Upper Fells Point. The program is open to all newcomers, but the city is doing targeted outreach to immigrant groups. Approved home buyers receive thousands of dollars in deferred loans to be put towards rehabbing vacant properties.

"We're trying to improve the city's economy by any way possible," says Brennan, the mayor's spokesperson. "We can make it a place that people come and stay," no matter where they might be coming from.

In its efforts to connect immigrants with needed resources, Baltimore is finding a major ally in the local Catholic Church. Faced with its own shrinking constituency, the church worked to attract foreign-born Catholics into its fold. Some of those efforts have decades-long pedigrees; the Esperanza Center in Fells Point has been offering English-as-a-Second Language class and job counseling for many years. But much of is of more recent origin. The church is holding more masses in Spanish and Igbo, and inviting in visiting priests from Central America, South America and western Africa. Just last year, Sacred Heart School in Highlandtown changed to a bilingual curriculum, adding *Escuela Sagrado Corazón de Jesús* to its name. Church spaces have been opened to give immigrants a comforting place to meet with police, says Auxiliary Bishop Mitchell Rozanksi of the Baltimore Archdiocese. "We realize that the Catholic Church in America was built by immigrants," says Rozanski. "We are an immigrant church. We have been an immigrant church." He goes on. "We'll always stand with the immigrant.

It has proven to be a controversial position. The Church has actively defended SB-167, or Maryland's so-called DREAM Act. The bill, passed in April and approved by voters in a heavily contested November ballot referendum, gives undocumented immigrants who have attended at least three years of high school in Maryland and whose parents have filed tax returns the opportunity to qualify for in-state college tuition rates. The move made Maryland the first state to implement an immigrant-oriented tuition law by popular vote.

There are signs that all of this will pay off for Charm City. Between 2000 and 2010, reveals census data, Baltimore's population experienced its smallest decrease since the 1950s. The population dropped 4.6 percent, but it comes after a 12 percent plummet in the decade prior. Helping to slow Baltimore's population decrease was an influx of new residents. While the city's black and white populations were falling, the city's Hispanic population doubled over that time, and its Asian population increased by 45 percent. Though the figures include native born residents, there is no denying that immigrants played a role. In 2010, the Census recorded a total of 44,000 foreign-born people living in Baltimore—7 percent of the population and more than double the number living here 20 years ago. Of those new Baltimoreans, some 40 percent came from Latin American and the Caribbean, another 25 percent from Asia and the Middle East, and 15 percent arrived here from Africa.

The numbers give officials hope for Rawlings-Blake's vision. "If we were able to say that we were no longer losing population?" Brennan says. "That's something a mayor [of Baltimore] hasn't been able to say since the '40s."

45. Immigrants Countering Population Losses in Many Metro Areas

Mike Maciag

When Nar Pradhan moved to Cleveland from Nepal in 2008, he had no family connections or other ties to the city. The then 27-year old Bhutanese refugee eventually found work as a dishwasher at a local Indian restaurant before his mother and eight siblings all came over to join him.

In the six short years since, his family established deep roots in the local business community. The Pradhan family bought the Indian restaurant, which now also serves Himalayan cuisine. They later opened up a small grocery store on the city's west side offering a variety of spices, fresh produce and beverages from around the globe.

"We want to spend our lives here in Cleveland now," Pradhan said. "This country is the land of opportunity."

The Pradhans' success story is just the kind of boost Cleveland and other cities desperately need. Some urban areas, particularly in the Rust Belt, continue to record population declines as factories close and residents pack their bags. These same areas, though, are welcoming large numbers of immigrants, a facet that's emerged as a key component of policymakers' strategies to stabilize regions that are struggling both economically and demographically.

Between 2010 and 2013, 73 metro areas registered population losses.

Originally published as Mike Maciag, "Immigrants Countering Population Losses in Many Metro Areas," http://www.governing.com/topics/urban/gov-international-migration-countering-metro-area-population-loss.html. June 2014. Reprinted with permission of the publisher.

244

If not for international migration, 106 would have recorded declines, according to a Governing review of recent Census estimates.

The Cleveland-Elyria metro area countered a net domestic migration loss of 32,000 residents with an international migration gain of 11,600 over the three-year period.

With a steady stream of new residents from 117 different ethnic groups, immigrant communities have flourished throughout the region. Art galleries and restaurants line the streets of Asiatown, just east of downtown. Tourists and locals alike frequent the historic Little Italy neighborhood. Parma, a nearby suburb, is home to the state's largest Ukrainian population.

In pitching themselves to immigrants, Cleveland and other Rust Belt cities enjoy a few notable advantages. For one, housing costs are low, particularly in areas with high vacancy rates. Joy Roller, president of Global Cleveland, also said immigrants feel part of their communities in a way they can't in other larger cities. "Cleveland is changing very rapidly now, and they can be a part of it," she said.

Other Rust Belt cities are experiencing their own steady influx of immigrants. From 2010 to 2013, the Detroit-Warren-Dearborn, Mich., metro area saw its total population dip slightly—by about 1,300 residents—yet it still added 32,500 residents from abroad. The Buffalo metro area lost 1,400 total residents while net international migration climbed 8,000. The total population of the Scranton-Wilkes-Barre-Hazleton, Pa., metro area similarly dropped by 1,600, but still added 3,000 residents via international in-migration.

In each case, slight population declines would have been more severe absent international migration, which includes foreign immigrants, as well as natives moving back home and members of the military. Accordingly, rolling out the red carpet has emerged as a key strategy for propping up a growing number of regional economies.

Global Cleveland, along with state and local leaders, formally launched a talent attraction campaign connecting businesses, higher education institutions and multicultural organizations to potential newcomers in May. The group set a target of luring 60,000 people by 2020. Earlier this year, Cincinnati Mayor John Cranley announced an initiative attracting foreigners to boost redevelopment. Officials previously introduced similar efforts in Dayton, Baltimore and elsewhere.

Research suggests immigrants are more entrepreneurial than other Americans, one reason why the group is so coveted.

Officials frequently express frustration, though, over federal immigration regulations they consider overly restrictive. Some seek alternatives, such as special immigrant visa programs. In April, Michigan announced federal approval of a program allowing wealthier immigrants to secure permanent residency by investing in state businesses.

While the renewed emphasis on immigration has helped better market these regions, far greater numbers still flock to the nation's traditional immigrant hubs. The New York City metro area, for example, welcomed a net total of 400,000 residents from abroad since 2010.

For Rust Belt cities, the biggest challenge is often just getting on the map of where foreigners are looking to move. The typical resident of a village in China hasn't heard of Cleveland, so the region needs to build connections on a global scale to become more of a port city, said Richey Piiparinen of the Center for Population Dynamics at Cleveland State University.

Of course, Rust Belt cities must also offer ample job opportunities, which is a significant hurdle as industries are still reeling from the aftermath of the recession. Certain cultural attitudes held by segments of the population don't help, either. "We really have to fight this cultural insularity so that we don't keep instituting nativist policies," Piiparinen said.

Many of the same reasons why declining cities struggle to hold onto existing residents must be addressed if they're to attract more immigrants. Jeanne Batalova a senior policy analyst at the Washington, D.C.–based Migration Policy Institute, said they'll need to emphasize livability and change how they're perceived.

It's too early, Batalova said, to gauge the effectiveness of some of the newer initiatives aimed at welcoming immigrants. The fact that immigrants are continuing to migrate to these areas, though, is a positive sign.

"As attracting immigrants becomes more of an acceptable policy tool, more local governments are willing to turn to it," she said.

46. Extend Health Insurance to Undocumented Immigrants?

J.B. Wogan

A California state senator plans to introduce legislation that would expand health coverage under the Affordable Care Act to undocumented immigrants.

"Immigration status shouldn't bar individuals from health coverage, especially since their taxes contribute to the growth of our economy," said state Sen. Ricardo Lara in a written statement Jan. 10. Though Lara's announcement caused a stir among some national media outlets, an actual bill doesn't exist yet. About 1 million undocumented immigrants in California would be excluded from health care coverage after the federal law is completely in place, Lara said.

Under the new health care law, undocumented immigrants are ineligible for Medicare, non-emergency Medicaid and the Children's Health Insurance Program (CHIP). Children who are lawfully present under President Barack Obama's 2012 executive order, the Deferred Action for Childhood Arrivals program, are also ineligible. However, undocumented immigrants would still be covered by emergency medical care and emergency Medicaid—if the patients are poor.

At least 15 states and the District of Columbia already cover prenatal care, regardless of the mothers' immigration status, either through the federal CHIP option or state funds, according to a January tally by the National Immigration Law Center. Although CHIP, like Medicaid, is administered

---

Originally published as J.B. Wogan, "California Proposal Would Extend Health Insurance to Undocumented Immigrants," http://www.governing.com/topics/health-human-services/gov-california-proposal-would-extend-health-insurance-to-undocumented-immigrants.html. January 15, 2014. Reprinted with permission of the publisher.

by states, its funding comes from both states and the federal government; when states want to expand coverage for certain populations excluded by federal law, such as undocumented immigrants, they can pay for it themselves. Some states, such as Massachusetts and Illinois, have also decided to provide limited coverage to all children, regardless of immigration status.

A proposal in Vermont would include the state's undocumented immigrants—estimated to be fewer than 4,000—in a future single-payer health care system. Last year the Vermont General Assembly published a report estimating that the cost of including undocumented immigrants would be relatively minor, though the legislature has yet to make a decision on the policy.

Immigrants who lack citizenship status are three times as likely to be uninsured compared with U.S.-born citizens, according to a fact sheet from the Kaiser Family Foundation. They are also less likely to obtain the care they need than U.S.-born citizens. If not for the exclusions in federal law, most non-citizens would meet the income eligibility requirements to qualify for Medicaid or the premium tax credits available for purchasing private insurance on the federal or state-based exchanges.

An estimated 61 percent of the 11 million undocumented immigrants in the United States lacked health insurance coverage in 2012, according to an August 2013 report by the Center for Health Policy Research at the University of California, Los Angeles (UCLA). In California, where almost a quarter of the nation's undocumented immigrants live, about 51 percent were uninsured, the report said. The center's data derived from the Current Population Survey and the Gruber MicroSimulation Model, which forecasts changes in the health care system based on policy interventions.

The UCLA report's lead author, Steven Wallace, said he does not expect the California bill to be a harbinger of other state proposals addressing the health insurance needs of undocumented immigrants—at least not this year. "My guess is for the next couple years there won't be a lot of movement on it because everyone is digesting the current set of reforms," Wallace said. By 2016, however, "more states will look and say we made good progress, but we still have uninsured people left."

47. Selected State Reports on the Impact of Immigrants
Jiashan Cui

This chapter provides select examples of fiscal and economic impacts of immigrants at the state level. The fiscal studies typically examine income and sales tax contributions of foreign-born, compared to costs of education, health care and corrections. A few examine broader economic impacts such as job creation and business development of the foreign born.

Besides presenting the fiscal and economic impacts of immigrants, some studies also provide policy recommendations based on their research results. For example, in the report on immigrants in New England prepared by the Federal Reserve Bank of Boston, the authors provide some policy options on promoting economic growth. The report notes: "To attract skilled immigrants, special initiatives may be needed, such as recruiting foreign students and encouraging them to stay when they graduate from local colleges or universities. In order to attract immigrant entrepreneurs (native entrepreneurs, too), local governments can use tax breaks and other incentives that reduce the cost of doing business. Federal immigration laws can be used to recruit immigrant investors. By creating a Regional Center, authorities can devise community investment projects and attract immigrant investors under a special provision of the immigrant-investor visa program."

This compilation summarizes fiscal impact studies in Arizona, Arkansas, Colorado, Florida, Georgia, Iowa, Maryland, Minnesota, Mississippi, Missouri, New Mexico, New York, North Carolina, Oklahoma, Oregon, Texas, Virginia, and Washington, D.C.; and an article on the New England region.

Original published as Jiashan Cui, "A Summary of Selected State Reports on Fiscal/Economic Impacts of Immigrants," NCSL Immigrant Policy Project, National Conference of State Legislatures, June, 2013. Reprinted with permission of the publisher.

Arizona

Gans, Judith. *Immigrants in Arizona: Fiscal and Economic Impacts.* Udall Center for Studies in Public Policy. 2007.

This study examines the fiscal and economic impacts of immigrants in Arizona. In 2004, the total net state fiscal impact of immigrant was positive: $940 million. The total state tax revenue from immigrant workers was around $2.4 billion, with $1.5 billion coming from unauthorized workers, and $860 million from naturalized citizens. The fiscal cost of education, health care, and law enforcement was $1.4 billion.

Immigrants contributed to the economy through labor participation and consumption. In 2004, about $44 billion, 12 percent of the state's economic output can be attributed to immigrant workers ($15 billion for naturalized citizens and $29 billion for non-citizens). This includes $14.9 billion in labor income and $5.2 billion in other income in the state, resulting in approximately 400,000 full-time equivalent jobs.

In 2004, 14 percent of Arizona's workforce was immigrants. While a large proportion of immigrant workers were low-skilled workers, immigrant workers were over-represented in medicine and science.

Arkansas

Appold, Stephen J., Randy Capps, Michael Fix, Ying Huang, Fafael A. Jimeno S., James H. Johnson, Jr., John D. Kasarda, and Kristen McCabe. *A Profile of Immigrants in Arkansas.* Migrant Policy Institute, University of Arkansas, Kenan Institute of Private Enterprise, University of North Carolina at Chapel Hill. January 2013.

This three-volume report examines the demographic trends of immigrants in Arkansas, their economic and fiscal impacts, and a profile of the Marshallese community in Arkansas.

Arkansas ranked fourth among states in immigrant population growth from 2000–2010. In 2010, approximately 5 percent of Arkansas's residents were foreign-born, 42 percent of whom were unauthorized immigrants. From 2000 to 2010, Arkansas's foreign-born population grew by 82 percent.

Immigrant workers accounted for 7 percent of Arkansas's labor force, clustered in both low-skilled and high-skilled occupations. Between 2008 and 2010, immigrant workers comprised 13 percent of manufacturing workers, 16 percent of construction workers and 9 percent of agriculture workers.

Between 2006 and 2010, approximately 17 percent of physicians and surgeons were foreign-born.

The study shows that immigrants have a slightly negative impact on Arkansas's state budget. In 2010, the tax contributions from immigrants were $524 million, while state expenditures generated by immigrant households (education, health care and corrections) were about $555 million, which implied a net cost of $31 million in total, about $127 per immigrant household member.

The report finds that immigrants have a large economic impact on the Arkansas economy. In 2010, immigrants contributed $3.9 billion to Arkansas's economy through consumer expenditures and tax contributions. Subtracting the state fiscal expenditure ($555 million), the net economic benefit of immigrants to Arkansas was $3.4 billion.

Colorado

Fairley, Elena and Rich Jones. *Colorado's Undocumented Immigrants: What they pay, what they cost in taxes.* The Bell Policy Center. April 2011.

In 2011, Fairley and Jones updated two 2006 studies by the Bell Policy Center. Previous studies argued that costs associated with unauthorized immigrants were approximately $225 million each year, and the revenues generated by those unauthorized immigrants amounted to $159 million, which left a 14 to 30 percent revenue shortfall to state and local government. Fairley and Jones now estimate that the fiscal impact of unauthorized immigrants is slightly positive to Colorado state government. The costs associated with unauthorized immigrants are mainly concentrated in three areas: K-12 education, emergency medical care and incarceration, estimated by the researchers' at approximately $116.6 million per year. On the other hand, those unauthorized immigrants immigrants contribute to Colorado state tax revenues via sales taxes, proper taxes and personal income taxes, about $167.5 million annually, which would fully cover the expenses they impose on the state: a $ 50.1 million net benefit per year.

Florida

Eisenhauer, Emily, Alex Angee, Cynthia Hernandez, Yue Zhang. *Immigrants in Florida: Characteristics and Contributions.* Research Institute on Social and Economic Policy, Florida International University. May 2007.

This report presents statistics about immigrants in Florida and their contributions to the state's economy. Between 2002 and 2004 immigrant workers created greater net benefits than their native-born counterparts. Immigrant workers comprise 25 percent of Florida's labor force. Eisenhauer et al. compared the costs of government services and tax revenues generated between immigrant workers and non-immigrant workers. In 2005, the median wage for immigrant workers was $20,000, compared to $23,400 for non-immigrants. On average, immigrant workers contribute approximately $1,500 per capita annual gains compared to $1,390 by non-immigrant workers. Between 2002 and 2004, on average, immigrant workers paid about $3,258 into tax system, while receiving approximately $3,258 public benefits. Immigrant workers are slightly more likely to be entrepreneurs: approximately 26 percent of immigrant workers are self-employed, compared to 23 percent of self-employed non-immigrant workers.

Georgia

An Analysis of the Economic Impact of Undocumented Workers on Business Activity in the U.S. with Estimated Effects by State and by Industry. The Perryman Group. April 2008.

This study focuses on the economic impact of unauthorized immigrants in the United States and by select states and industries, as well as the estimated costs and benefits analysis of eliminating all unauthorized immigrant workers. The results suggest that unauthorized labor plays a vital role in U.S. business growth.

It cites that without the unauthorized workforce in Georgia (using 2007 dollars for monetary value), in a static scenario, the state would lose $7,120 in expenditures per capita, $2,639 in output losses per capita, and $1,699 in income losses per capita. The static scenario estimates represent the immediate losses resulting from enforcement-only programs. In a dynamic scenario, expenditure losses per capita would be $2,234, $992 for output losses per capita, and $622 for income losses per capita. The dynamic scenario estimates represent losses after market adjustments and new hiring has occurred.

The fiscal impact of unauthorized immigrant workers varies by different levels of governments. The overall taxes unauthorized immigrants pay into the system is greater than the amount of benefits they receive. However, many states and local public entities experience a net deficit because the costs of certain public services (education, health care, law enforcement, etc.) exceed the tax revenues they collect from unauthorized immigrant workers.

Coffey, Sarah Beth. *Undocumented Immigrants in Georgia: Tax Contribution and Fiscal Concerns.* The Georgia Budget and Policy Institute. January 2006.
    The average unauthorized family in Georgia pays from $2,340 to $2,470 in state, local, income, and property taxes combined (based on an estimated unauthorized population of 228,000 to 250,000). State, local, income and sales tax contributions from unauthorized immigrants in Georgia are estimated between $215.6 million and $252.5 million.

Iowa

Pearson, Beth and Michael Sheehan. *Undocumented Immigrants in Iowa: Estimated Tax Contributions and Fiscal Impact.* Iowa Policy Project. October 2007.
    The Iowa Policy Project estimated that each unauthorized immigrant family pays $1,671 a year, amounting to a total of tax payments for unauthorized immigrants in Iowa between $40 and $62 million a year, assuming a 50 percent payment rate. In terms of the cost of K-12 education for unauthorized immigrants, the Iowa Policy Project determined that between 5,445 and 8,415 unauthorized immigrants are between the ages of 5 and 18. Using the per-pupil education cost in Iowa of $6,497, costs to the state for providing K-12 education to unauthorized immigrants is between $35 million and $54 million (2005).
    According to the study, the tax payments made by unauthorized immigrants are 80 percent of the taxes paid by legally documented families with similar incomes; however, unauthorized immigrants do not qualify for as many services.

Maryland

Commission to Study the Impact of Immigrants in Maryland. *The Impact of Immigrants in Maryland.* Final Report, February 8, 2012.
    The Maryland legislature authorized a commission to gain a broader understanding of the economic and fiscal issues surrounding immigration and to provide recommendations to the legislature (HB1602, June 200).
    In 2010, 13.9 percent of Maryland's residents were foreign-born. Between 2000 and 2010, Maryland's work force grew by 15.2 percent and foreign-

born workers accounted for 57.1 percent of its work force growth. From 2000 to 2010, foreign-born workers' share of the labor force increased by 5.9 percentage points (12 percent in 2000 versus 17.9 percent in 2010). Foreign-born workers are overrepresented in some high-skilled occupations. For example, in 2006, foreign-born workers accounted for 27 percent of Maryland's scientists, 21 percent of health care practitioners and 19 percent of mathematicians and computer specialists. Meanwhile, low-skilled immigrant workers also play an important supporting role in the growth of industries such as construction, personal services and tourism in Maryland.

Missouri

Ehresman, Ruth. *Undocumented Workers: Impact on Missouri's Economy.* The Missouri Budget Project. June 2006.

In 2005, the tax contributions from unauthorized immigrant workers including sales, income (from $25 to $50 million) and property tax (from $4 to $7 million), were estimated between $29 million and $57 million (based on a 50 percent compliance rate with employers). This study estimated the cost for educating the children of unauthorized immigrant workers as between $17.5 and $32.6 million in 2005.

Minnesota

Fennelly, Katherine and Anne Huart. *The Economic Impact of Immigrants in Minnesota.* Hubert H. Humphrey Institute of Public Affairs, University of Minnesota. March 2010.

This report includes chapters on Minnesota's demographics, characteristics of immigrants, measuring costs and benefits, and costs attributed to immigrants.

In 2008, there were 386,380 foreign-born residents in Minnesota (about 45 percent of whom were naturalized citizens), comprising 7.45 percent of the region's population. Immigrant workers represented 8.5 percent of Minnesota's labor force. Minnesota has been experiencing an aging population. Between 2000 and 2006 about 49.4 percent of Minnesota's counties experienced population decline, and immigrants have accounted for a majority of the growth in the labor force in Minnesota.

Immigrant workers have been playing an important role in the economy of Minnesota. It is estimated that Minnesota would lose over 24,000 permanent jobs and $1.2 billion in personal income in the absence of immigrant workers. Immigrant-owned businesses generated $331 million in net income to Minnesota in 2000. Immigrants in Minnesota are also active in becoming entrepreneurs: since 1990 the number of Hispanic-owned business has grown about 350 percent.

Mississippi

Bryant, Phil, *The Impact of Illegal Immigration on Mississippi: Costs and Population Trends,* State of Mississippi, Office of the State Auditor, February 21, 2006.

This 2006 study is prepared by the performance audit division of the state of Mississippi. Accordingly, the report first presents the unauthorized immigrant population residing in Mississippi, and then it turns to estimates of costs and tax contributions generated by unauthorized immigrants. The report also summarizes the policies and studies focusing on unauthorized immigrants in other states. Based on the findings, the report provides policy recommendations.

The report asserts that unauthorized immigrants impose a net deficit on Mississippi's budget: a $25 million annual revenue gap generated by unauthorized immigrants (about $510 per unauthorized immigrant). The estimate is based on the assumption that there are 4,900 unauthorized immigrants residing in Mississippi. The revenues mainly come from sales taxes (approximately $41 million) and income taxes (approximately $3 million). The costs associated with unauthorized immigrants total an estimated $69 million annually and include education (including educational costs of unauthorized immigrants' American-born children), health care, incarceration costs and remittance loss.

New England

Orrenius, Pia M. and Madeline Zavodny, *The Role of Immigrants in the New England Economy,* Federal Reserve Bank of Boston, Communities & Banking, Spring 2012, Volume 23, No.2.

This article notes that even though immigrants residing in New England make up a smaller share of labor force than the national level, they have a greater share of the work force growth. This benefits New England's economy since New England, along with Midwestern states, has been experiencing population loss for the past several decades. The article discusses the characteristics of immigrants in New England and their contributions to local economic growth by adding high skills, innovation and entrepreneurship.

The share of foreign-born population differs across New England states. In 2009, three states had a high concentration of foreign-born residents: Connecticut (13.1 percent), Massachusetts (14.3 percent), and Rhode Island (12.7 percent. Other other states had a low proportion of foreign-born population: Maine (3.3 percent), New Hampshire (5.2 percent), and Vermont (3.3 percent).

Foreign-born residents in New England tend to be more educated than the immigrants nationally. Compared to the national immigrant population, immigrants residing in New England are more likely to finish high school (46 percent to 44 percent) and earn a college degree (33 percent to 27 percent).

Immigrant workers in New England are more likely to be employed than their native-born counterparts. Immigrant workers are over represented in STEM fields (science, technology, engineering, and mathematics). Among high-skilled workers, immigrants are more than twice as likely to receive patents as their native counterparts. Immigrants are also active in entrepreneurship in New England: more than one-quarter of biotechnology firms were founded by immigrants.

New Mexico

Undocumented Immigrants in New Mexico: State Tax Contributions and Fiscal Concerns. New Mexico Voices for Children, Fiscal Policy Project. May 2006.

This study estimates that the cost of education for unauthorized students is between $47 million and $69 million, using one study from the Pew Center and one from the INS. Each study found a different estimate of tax payments made by unauthorized immigrants.

For unauthorized immigrants who have been in the U.S. fewer than 10 years, both studies show they generated positive fiscal gains for New Mexico's state government. The Pew Center found $69.26 million were paid in taxes. Using this estimate, the state made $1.814 million from immigrant taxes after the cost of education. The INS estimated $50.371 million were paid in taxes by unauthorized immigrants, so the government gained $1.25 million after the cost of education.

Immigrants and the New Mexico Economy: Working Hard for Low Wages, New Mexico Voice for Children. New Mexico Fiscal Policy Project. June 2008. This study presents the positive economic contribution of the foreign-born population to New Mexico's economy and argues that the impact of the foreign-born population on health care and social security at the national level is relatively small.

Immigrants compose 10 percent of New Mexico's total population: 29 percent of them are naturalized citizens and the rest are non-citizens. Compared to native-born residents in New Mexico, the labor force participation rate of foreign-born population is higher (63.7 percent for foreign-born population versus 62.4 percent for natives). Immigrant workers are more likely to be self-employed and cluster in low-paid sectors such as services and construction industries than their native counterparts. In 2006, 12 percent of native-born families were living under the poverty line, while the number for foreign-born families was 26 percent (15 percent for naturalized citizens' families and 33 percent for non-citizens' families).

New York

Fiscal Policy Institute. *A Profile of Immigrants in the New York State Economy.* November 2007.

This study first provides an overall role of immigrants in the New York State economy, and then looks specifically at immigrants with different characteristics: immigrant residents in New York City, upstate and downstate; authorized and unauthorized immigrants, and different race and ethnic groups within immigrants.

In 2005, approximately 21 percent of residents in New York State were foreign-born, and accounted for 26 percent of labor force. About three quarters of New York State's foreign-born residents are concentrated in New York City. Immigrants were 37 percent of New York's residents. Immigrants residing in New York City tend to have higher labor force participation rate, (64 percent, compared to 60 percent of native-born). Between 2003 and 2004, there were about 635,000 unauthorized immigrants in the New York State, representing 16 percent of immigrants in the state.

In 2006, immigrant workers in New York contributed approximately 22.4 percent ($229 billion) of New York's Gross Domestic Product (GDP). Foreign-born residents are nearly as likely to be home-owners as native-born. In 2005, about 34 percent of foreign-born residents live in owner-occupied homes, compared to 39 percent for native-born New York residents.

Immigrant families contribute to the growth of middle class in New York City: they are most likely to be middle class families. There are no significant differences between the median income of immigrant families and native-born families in New York.

Immigrants are also contributing to entrepreneurship in New York City: between 1992 and 2002, the number of Hispanic-owned firms doubled and the number of Asian-owned firms grew about four-fold. Between 1994 and 2004, neighborhoods with large numbers of immigrants experienced higher growth rate in both employment and in number of business than the average numbers of New York City.

North Carolina

Johnson, James H. and John D. Kasarda. *The Economic Impact of the Hispanic Population on the State of North Carolina*. The University of North Carolina. January 2006.

This study looks beyond comparisons of tax contributions and costs of services for Hispanic populations, and examines the implications of Hispanic workers on the total economic output and competitiveness of the state. It provides breakdowns of Hispanic self-employed workers by industry, average personal wages and salary earnings, taxes paid by Hispanics, etc. (The study includes all Hispanics, whether citizen, legal, or unauthorized.)

The study estimates that Hispanics spent $9 billion in North Carolina in 2004. Total tax contributions from the Hispanic population are estimated at $756 million annually. State costs were estimated at $817 annually (K-12 education–$467 million; health care–$299 million; and corrections–$51 million). This leaves the state with a net cost of $61 million. The report notes that these costs should be put in context of the broader contributions of Hispanics to the state's economic output and cost competitiveness [20]

Oklahoma

A Computable General Equilibrium (CGE) Analysis of the Impact of the Oklahoma Taxpayer and Citizen Protection Act of 2007. The Economic Impact Group, LLC. Edmonton, Oklahoma: March 24, 2008.

In March 2008, the Economic Impact Group analyzed the possible effects of decline in the Oklahoma workforce, from low to high outflow of foreign born workers, after the passage of SB 1804. If 25,000 foreign-born workers leave the state (low impact), in the short run (no offsetting in migration) the outflow would produce a 0.58 percent reduction in the Oklahoma Gross State Product (GSP), or $785.5 million (relative to 2006 production levels). If 50,000 foreign born workers leave the state (medium impact), GSP would decline by 1.32 percent, or $1.8 billion. If 90,000 foreign born workers leave the state (high impact), GSP would decline by 2.27 percent, or $3 billion. According to the study, the 50,000 worker outflow is the most plausible scenario; 50,000 foreign born workers would constitute approximately 3 percent of the Oklahoma labor force.

Oregon

Oregon Center for Public Policy. *Issue Brief: Undocumented Workers Are Taxpayers, Too.* January 25, 2012.

The study calculates the tax contributions by unauthorized workers in Oregon. The 110,000–220,000 unauthorized immigrants residing in Oregon are estimated to earn approximately $2.3 billion to $4.5 billion per year. Their tax contributions are mainly in three areas: state and local income tax, excise and property taxes, social security taxes and Medicare taxes, which total roughly between $154 million and $309 million. In addition to the taxes paid by the unauthorized workers, there are also matching tax contributions from the employers of those unauthorized workers, about $121 million to $243 million per year.

Texas

Combs, Susan. *Undocumented Immigrants in Texas: A Financial Analysis of the Impact to the State Budget and Economy.* Texas Comptroller of Public Accounts. December 2006.

The study looks at the fiscal impact of unauthorized immigrants on Texas state government and the potential impact on the economy in the absence of unauthorized immigrants.

In 2005, approximately 1.4 million residents in Texas were unauthorized immigrants. Unauthorized immigrant workers generated net fiscal benefits to the Texas state government, but net fiscal costs to the local governments. It is estimated that the total revenue contribution, including state revenues and school property tax, from unauthorized immigrants was $1.58 billion. The total estimated cost of unauthorized immigrants, including education, health care, and incarceration, was $1.16 million leaving the net benefit to the state at $424 million in fiscal year 2005. However, localities incurred costs of $1.44 billion in health care and law enforcement costs not reimbursed by the state. In 2000–2001, the total cost of public education for 125,000 unauthorized immigrant students was $806 million. In 2004–2005, the total cost of public education for 135,000 unauthorized immigrant students was $957 million.

The study also estimates that removing those 1.4 million unauthorized immigrants from Texas in 2005 would lead to a 298,000 total employment loss and $17.7 billion of total gross regional product loss.

Virginia

Okos, Sara, Sookyung Oh and Michael Cassidy. *Critical Assets: The State of Immigrants in Virginia's Economy.* The Commonwealth Institute, *October 2012.*

This report highlights the key economic and demographic trends of the foreign-born population in Virginia. In 2010, Virginia ranked as the ninth-largest immigrant state in America, with approximately 900,000 immigrants residing in the state, or about 11.3 percent of the state's total population. In 2010, almost half of foreign-born residents in Virginia were naturalized citizens.

In 2010, foreign-born workers consisted of 15 percent of the labor force. The labor force participation rate among immigrant workers in Virginia is much higher than Virginia natives (74.4 percent versus 65.5 percent), and the ratio is also greater than that of foreign-born workers at the national level (74.7 percent versus 67.7 percent). The poverty rate of immigrants in Virginia is lower than both their native-born counterparts in Virginia and average poverty rate of immigrants at the national level.

Immigrants in Virginia tend to be more educated than native-born counterparts. In 2010, approximately 38 percent of its foreign-born residents received college degree or higher, compared to 34 percent for Virginia natives. The average number of U.S. native-born with college degree is 28.5 percent. Immigrants in Virginia are more likely to be business owners. About 17 percent of Virginia's entrepreneurs are immigrants. Between 2000 and 2010, more than 40 percent growth of entrepreneurship in Virginia can be attributed to immigrants.

The report also points out concerns about foreign-born residents in Virginia: in 2010, about 30 percent of them were not covered by any health insurance, which was three times higher than the native-born. Since 2007, the average earnings remained constant while their native-born counterparts saw a 4 percent increase in wages.

Washington, D.C.

Capps, Randy, Everett Henderson, Jeffrey Passel, Michael Fix. *Civic Contributions: Taxes Paid by Immigrants in the Washington, D.C. Metropolitan Area.* The Community Foundation. May 2006.

This study looks at the tax contributions by immigrant residents in Washington, D.C. Between 1999 and2000, immigrant households earned a total income of $29.5 billion, about 19 percent of the regional aggregate income. About 18 percent ($9.8 billion) of all taxes paid can be attributed immigrant residents in the region.

Immigrant households, on average, have lower income than their native counterparts, but they pay almost the same share of income taxes. The study also examines the income taxes paid by immigrant families and native-born families with different educational attainments. On average, among the most educated and highest earners, immigrant families pay higher taxes than natives. On the other end of education level and lower income groups, immigrants tend to pay less in income taxes than the native-born.

This study finds that better-educated households pay higher taxes whether they are headed by immigrants or natives. In 1999–2000, the average tax payment was three times as high for households headed by immigrants with a four-year college degree as for those headed by immigrants without a high school degree ($36,000 versus $12,000). English-speaking immigrant households also paid more taxes than natives, but native households paid more taxes than non–English speaking immigrant households. The study asserted that by enhancing English language classes for Limited English Proficiency (LEP) immigrants, those immigrants could enhance their income and pay more taxes.

ACKNOWLEDGMENTS

This report was produced for NCSL's Task Force on Immigration and the States through a generous grant from the John D. and Catherine T. MacArthur Foundation.

Appendices

I. United States Conference of Mayors' March 12, 2014, Letter to Congress

March 12, 2014

Dear Representative

Fixing our nation's broken immigration laws is among the most important issues of interest to America's mayors currently before the U.S. House of Representatives. We believe strongly that maintaining the status quo will further damage the economic, political and social structure of our cities and our country. As Mayors, we have a ground-level understanding of the pressing economic and moral imperatives that necessitate changing our national immigration system, and we urge the House to expeditiously bring legislation to the floor.

• Like the constituents we serve, we believe that a meaningful fix to immigration must begin with a strengthening of border security. Further, interior enforcement should be improved to enhance our ability to identify and remove visa overstays, but our state and local law enforcement must be able to remain focused on community policing.

• We believe the nation would benefit from a less bureaucratic and more time-sensitive system that allows workers of all types—seasonal, agricultural, lesser-skilled and high skilled—to lawfully come to America, either temporarily or permanently, and contribute to our economy.

• As we fix immigration, we must also provide a uniform system of employment verification. We recognize that competing technologies and approaches exist and believe they should be tested against one another in determining the best manner for accurately authenticating workers.

• There are equally compelling moral dimensions also related to fixing immigration that underscore the importance of moving forward with the effort. We believe that it is vital for any immigration legislation to enable people to come out of the shadows and fully pursue the American Dream for themselves and their families. This is also essential to our efforts to combat crime and provide effective police protection for our citizens.

Thank you for your consideration of our views. We believe the time is ripe for Congress to pass legislation that fixes immigration and creates a system that builds our economy, meets the nation's future workforce requirements, eliminates the incentives to enter the country illegally, humanely deals with the undocumented persons already here, and works to keep families together.

Sincerely,

U.S. Conference of Mayors

Scott Smith, Mayor of Mesa, AZ, President

Kevin Johnson, Mayor of Sacramento, CA, Vice President

Stephanie Rawlings-Blake, Mayor of Baltimore, MD, Second Vice President

Raul G. Salinas, Mayor of Laredo, TX, Co-Chair, Immigration Reform Task Force

Tom Tait, Mayor of Anaheim, CA, Co-Chair, Immigration Reform Task Force

Mark Stodola, Mayor of Little Rock, AR

Marie Lopez Rogers, Mayor of Avondale, AZ

Georgia Lord, Mayor of Goodyear, AZ

Greg Stanton, Mayor of Phoenix, AZ

Gail Barney, Mayor of Queen Creek, AZ

Mark Mitchell, Mayor of Tempe, AZ

Jonathan Rothschild, Mayor of Tucson, AZ

Kathleen DeRosa, Mayor of Cathedral City, CA

Bruce Barrows, Mayor of Cerritos, CA

Aja Brown, Mayor of Compton, CA

Gilbert Wong, Mayor of Cupertino, CA

Fernando Vasquez, Mayor of Downey, CA

Bill Harrison, Mayor of Fremont, CA

Ashley Swearengin, Mayor of Fresno, CA

Bert Hack, Mayor of Laguna Woods, CA

Bob Foster, Mayor of Long Beach, CA

Eric Garcetti, Mayor of Los Angeles, CA

Aide Castro, Mayor of Lynwood, CA

Jill Techel, Mayor of Napa, CA

Mary Ann Lutz, Mayor of Monrovia, CA

Jean Quan, Mayor of Oakland, CA

Bill Bogaard, Mayor of Pasadena, CA

John Chiang, Mayor of Piedmont, CA

Peter Aguilar, Mayor of Redlands, CA

Alonso Ledezma, Mayor of San Jacinto, CA

Chuck Reed, Mayor of San Jose, CA

Miguel Pulido, Mayor of Santa Ana, CA

Helene Schneider, Mayor of Santa Barbara, CA

Karyl Matsumoto, Mayor of South San Francisco, CA

Abbe Land, Mayor of West Hollywood, CA

Christopher Cabaldon, Mayor of West Sacramento, CA

Steve Hogan, Mayor of Aurora, CO

Michael B. Hancock Mayor of Denver, CO

Phil Cernanec, Mayor of Littleton, CO

Bill Finch, Mayor of Bridgeport, CT
Pedro Segarra, Mayor of Hartford, CT
Manuel Santos, Mayor of Meriden, CT
Toni Harp, Mayor of New Haven, CT
Harry Rilling, Mayor of Norwalk, CT
Vincent Gray, Mayor of Washington, D.C.
Mami Sawicki, Mayor of Cape Coral, FL
Jean Robb, Mayor of Deerfield Beach, FL
Luigi Boria, Mayor of Doral, FL
Joy Cooper, Mayor of Hallandale Beach, FL
Lori Moseley, Mayor of Miramar, FL
Lucie Tondreau, Mayor of North Miami, FL
Buddy Dyer, Mayor of Orlando, FL
William Capote, Mayor of Palm Bay, FL
Frank Ortis, Mayor of Pembroke Pines, FL
John R. Marks III, Mayor of Tallahassee, FL
James Thomas, Jr., Mayor of Hinesville, GA
Bernard Carvalho, Mayor of Kauai, HI

II. National League of Cities' Resolution in Support of Comprehensive Immigration Reform

WHEREAS, historically, the cities and towns of the United States are a melting pot of multiple cultures and nationalities based on our nation's history of welcoming immigrants; and

WHEREAS, when admitted through a well-regulated system, immigrants strengthen the United States by creating economic opportunities, increasing America's scientific and cultural resources, strengthening our ties with other nations, fulfilling humanitarian commitments, and supporting family ties and family values that are necessary to build strong communities; and

WHEREAS, failure on the part of the federal government to secure the borders, track visa recipients in the interior, or enforce worksite laws allows illegal immigration to thrive, with an estimated 11.2 million residents living and working in the United States without legal authorization or proper documentation; and

WHEREAS, despite increases in border security and upgrades in tracking technology, approximately 500,000 people continue to enter the United States illegally each year; and

WHEREAS, 30–40 percent of undocumented workers in the U.S. entered legally and overstayed their student, tourist, or employment visas; and

WHEREAS, the worksite enforcement program does not adequately deter employers who willingly hire unauthorized workers because they face little likelihood that the federal government will investigate, fine, or criminally prosecute them; and it does not help employers who genuinely want to follow the law because their employee verification efforts are hindered by the extensive use of fraudulent documents; and

WHEREAS, the lack of infrastructure and capacity at the federal level makes the federal government unable to adequately track the entry and exit of visitors and temporary workers, and it creates unacceptable application backlogs and long delays, which provide strong disincentives for foreign nationals to abide by the legal means to enter or remain in the country; and

WHEREAS, approximately 268,000 workers in 2011, equal to about half of the undocumented seasonal workers in the United States, used the current temporary, unskilled worker programs (the H2-A and H2-B visas); and

WHEREAS, the current immigration system inadequately addresses the growing numbers of individuals wishing entrance to the United States through a temporary work visa program or as legal permanent residents; and

WHEREAS, roughly two-thirds of undocumented adult immigrants have lived in the United States for ten years or more, 1 million unauthorized immigrants are children, and another 4.5 million U.S.-citizen children have at least one undocumented parent1; and these families are forced to live "underground," unable to get drivers' licenses or car insurance in most states, unlikely to obtain health insurance, and afraid to report crimes to local law enforcement; and

WHEREAS, since immigrants are barred from most federal public assistance, the burden of providing social services, education, and health care falls to the state and local governments, who are increasingly feeling the financial impact of both legal and illegal immigrants living in their communities.

NOW, THEREFORE, BE IT RESOLVED that the National League of Cities (NLC) urges Congress to move quickly to enact comprehensive reform of the current immigration laws with support of the Administration to implement the immigration laws effectively; and

BE IT FURTHER RESOLVED that the federal government enforce its current immigration laws consistently and vigorously to eliminate illegal entry at the borders, visa overstays, working without proper documentation, and employing undocumented workers; and

BE IT FURTHER RESOLVED that the federal government must increase enforcement of visa overstays through the full implementation and staffing of the U.S.-VISIT and SEVIS programs; and

BE IT FURTHER RESOLVED that local personnel, such as police officers, fire inspectors, educators, health personnel and social service personnel, should not be conscripted into federal service because the federal government has not adequately funded and staffed its immigration enforcement agencies; and the federal government must not transfer the responsibility of enforcing U.S. immigration laws to local personnel by making undocumented status in the U.S. a criminal offense; and

BE IT FURTHER RESOLVED that the federal government must strengthen its worksite enforcement capacity and dramatically increase enforcement efforts at places of employment, as well as providing employers with a universal, reliable, effective, secure, non-discriminatory, and non-counterfeitable employee verification system, using the most up-to-date technology that will minimize fraud; and

BE IT FURTHER RESOLVED that the federal government must increase its capacity and infrastructure to enforce the laws and provide efficient means for foreign nationals to obtain legal authorization for temporary visas or legal permanent residency; and

BE IT FURTHER RESOLVED that the federal government must provide an appropriate, legal means of immigration, as is determined to be necessary and effective for the United States, for foreign nationals that want to work here temporarily, become legal permanent residents, or gain citizenship; and

BE IT FURTHER RESOLVED that NLC supports establishment of a process whereby undocumented immigrants currently living in the United States may earn legalized status through payment of appropriate fees and back taxes, background checks, absence of criminal or gang activity, consistent work history, and meeting English and civics requirements; and that the immigrants who have earned such legal status should also be able to apply for citizenship through additional processes, as appropriate and practical, as long as they do not move ahead of applicants with proper documentation waiting to adjust their status or those waiting on lists in their home countries; and

BE IT FURTHER RESOLVED that the federal government should provide local governments with financial and technical assistance to alleviate the local impact of new immigrants, including the costs of providing social services, health care, education, language services, and civic integration; and

BE IT FURTHER RESOLVED that NLC also supports federal legislation like the "Dream Act" that can facilitate state efforts to offer in-state tuition to undocumented students and provide certain students with a path to U.S. citizenship.

III. National Association of Counties' Call to Action

CALL TO ACTION: Urge your members of Congress to enact comprehensive immigration reform in the 113th Congress.

BACKGROUND: There is bipartisan agreement that the U.S. immigration system is broken and needs reform. The U.S. Senate passed the bipartisan Border Security, Economic Opportunity and Immigration Modernization Act (S. 744) on June 27, 2013, by a vote of 68–32. The House Judiciary and Homeland Security committees have passed five incremental bills, and Speaker John Boehner (R–Ohio) recently issued standards for reform that include those five bills and would add a legalization path for undocumented individuals and a citizenship path for individuals who were brought into the country as children. Meanwhile, a bipartisan group of House members have introduced a version of the Senate's comprehensive reform measure in the House (H.R. 15). It remains uncertain when the House will consider immigration reform, and whether the chamber will opt for a comprehensive measure or a series of incremental bills.

While immigration is a federal responsibility, counties are directly affected by immigration. Counties provide health, education and public safety to all residents regardless of immigration status.

Legal immigrants, refugees, undocumented individuals and others enter and remain in this country as a result of federal action or inaction. Our current immigration system is confusing and complicated. There are multiple categories of visas with different requirements for each. There are significant backlogs for visas and individuals often have to wait years to enter the U.S. as permanent residents. There are 4.5 million pending applications for family visas and 4.6 million for employer visas. As employers, county hospitals use employer visas to hire health care professionals and are affected by employer visa backlogs.

Immigration reform impacts counties in numerous other ways. Counties must provide emergency health care to all, including undocumented immigrants, and some counties provide health care to immigrants who are not yet eligible for federal means-tested benefits. Further, immigration reform will likely result in increased demand for English language classes as undocumented immigrants integrate into society. Counties also provide for the public safety of all individuals, and rely on the State Criminal Alien Assistance Program (SCAAP) for reimbursements related to the incarceration of undocumented immigrants.

The comprehensive reform measure (S. 744) passed by the Senate addresses many of these issues and includes the following provisions:

• An earned path to citizenship for nearly 11 million undocumented immigrants wherein they would be required to come forward, apply for Registered Provisional Immigrant (RPI) status, pay fees and fines, demonstrate English language ability, pay back federal taxes and pass several background checks.

• RPI individuals would have to wait until the legal immigration backlog is cleared before they can get Legal Permanent Resident (LPR) status. Most individuals in RPI status would have to wait 10 years before adjusting to LPR status and another three years before applying for citizenship. Youth brought into the country as children (DREAM Act youth) and agricultural workers would be on a faster track.

• Current restrictions against receiving means-tested programs such as Medicaid (except emergency services) would continue for RPI individuals and they would be prohibited from receiving subsidies or tax credits under the Affordable Care Act. The current five-year waiting period for means-tested benefits for most newly arrived legal immigrants would remain in place.

• The measure also amends the current employer and family based visa programs; increases high-skilled visas; allows individuals who obtain a Master's or higher degree in science, technology, engineering and mathematics form an American university to become permanent residents and adds new categories of temporary worker visas for low-skilled and agricultural workers.

A favorable Congressional Budget Office (CBO) score of S. 744 and a compromise amendment on additional border enforcement paved the way for final Senate passage. The CBO score estimated a net deficit reduction of $175 billion from 2014 to 2024 and an additional $700 billion thereafter. CBO also predicted that immigration reform would contribute 3.3 percent to economic growth by 2023 and 5.4 percent by 2034. An amendment offered by Sens. John Hoeven (R-N.D.) and Bob Corker (R–Tenn.) added over $30 billion for border technological improvements and 20,000 more border patrol officers and required completion of the 700 mile southern fence, E-Verify (an employment authorization verification system) and the airport entry and exit verification system before individuals in RPI status would obtain legal permanent residence.

The House incremental bills include the Legal Workforce Act (H.R. 1772), the Strengthen and Fortify Enforcement (SAFE) Act (H.R. 2278), the Agricultural Guestworker Act (H.R. 1773), the SKILLS Visa Act (H.R. 2131) and the Border Security and Results Act (H.R. 1417. The Legal Workforce Act and the SAFE Act are of great concern to NACo and counties. The Legal Workforce Act mandates state and local governments to apply E-Verify to all existing employees. Language was added to the SAFE Act making unlawful presence a criminal violation rather than a civil violation, which will compel all state and local governments to enforce immigration law. NACo will oppose both bills.

Key Issues:
- Counties are required by law to provide emergency health, free elementary and secondary education, and public safety to everyone regardless of immigration status.
- As employers, county hospitals use employer visas to hire health care professionals and are affected by the employer visa backlogs.
- Immigration reform should recognize the inherent federal responsibility to enforce civil immigration law and have no new mandates for state and counties.
- NACo supports comprehensive immigration reform that includes a modernized legal immigration system, establishes a temporary worker program, provides an earned path to citizenship and enhances border security.
- NACo supports a national strategy for consultation and coordination on immigration among federal, state, local and tribal authorities.
- NACo supports a sustainable funding stream to cover the costs of immigrant health care, criminal justice and education, including adult English as a second language and citizenship classes.
- An earned path to citizenship should include requirements to register, learn English and civics, pay back taxes and any fines required by the law, pass criminal and security background checks, and pass English and civics tests

IV. Arlington County Board Resolution Welcoming Arlington's Newcomers

WHEREAS, in Arlington, we believe in a community where people trust their government and each other; a community that welcomes and values all of its residents, treating them with human dignity and respect, regardless of immigration status; and

WHEREAS, Arlington has and will continue to comply with all federal and state laws related to immigration, including those that involve eligibility for state and federal programs; Arlington aggressively prosecutes individuals who commit serious crimes, checks the immigration status of any such person, and forwards this information to appropriate State and federal officials; and

WHEREAS, it is not the role of state or local governments to assume federal responsibilities to enforce complex immigration laws any more than it is a local government responsibility to—enforce federal tax laws, patent laws, interstate commerce regulations, international trade rules, or a host of other federal rules and regulations that can lead to civil or criminal sanctions; and

WHEREAS, there is a political effort to pressure local governments to enact punitive measures that would be counterproductive to the fulfillment of the fundamental missions of local government, such as protecting the health, safety, and welfare of our community; and

WHEREAS, this effort has been attended by increasingly irresponsible rhetoric that implies a lack of respect for a// immigrants and engenders an atmosphere of divisiveness.and mistrust that is unhealthy for our society, and especially harmful for a diverse community like Arlington; and

WHEREAS, creating a culture of fear and distrust of law enforcement makes a community less safe; denying educational opportunities to students who may continue living in this country makes a community less safe; denying basic services such as well baby care, immunizations, and treatment of communicable diseases makes a community less safe; and

WHEREAS, Arlington seeks to have a safe and unified community,

NOW, THEREFORE, BE IT RESOLVED that Arlington County's approach fulfills the fundamental mission of local government, providing for the safety, health, and welfare of our community, and rejecting policies and practices that promote discrimination, exploitation, and fear of government; and

Be it Further Resolved that the Arlington County Board supports the County Manager's implementation of County services in a manner that is inclusive, including the provision of written material in different languages as appropriate, the use of interpreters at public meetings, community policing that provides equal protection to all, and a proactive outreach to and celebration of the many cultures that reside in Arlington; and

Be it Further Resolved that the Arlington County Board calls on the Federal government to pass comprehensive immigration reform that includes strong border security and provides sufficient resources to ensure an effective and timely processing of those eligible for legal permanent residency or naturalization; and

Be it Further Resolved that the Arlington County Board calls upon federal and state officials to enact policies that promote the integration of immigrants into society in a way that provides procedures for employment and access to services for which they are eligible; and

Be it Further Resolved that Arlington County expresses its appreciation to all people from around the country and around the world who have made Arlington their home and in so doing have helped to make Arlington one of the most vibrant, safe, and economically successful communities in the United States.

V. President Barack Obama's 2014 Executive Action on Immigration Speech

My fellow Americans, tonight, I'd like to talk with you about immigration.

For more than 200 years, our tradition of welcoming immigrants from around the world has given us a tremendous advantage over other nations. It's kept us youthful, dynamic, and entrepreneurial. It has shaped our character as a people with limitless possibilities—people not trapped by our past, but able to remake ourselves as we choose.

But today, our immigration system is broken, and everybody knows it.

Families who enter our country the right way and play by the rules watch others flout the rules. Business owners who offer their workers good wages and benefits see the competition exploit undocumented immigrants by paying them far less. All of us take offense to anyone who reaps the rewards of living in America without taking on the responsibilities of living in America. And undocumented immigrants who desperately want to embrace those responsibilities see little option but to remain in the shadows, or risk their families being torn apart.

It's been this way for decades. And for decades, we haven't done much about it.

When I took office, I committed to fixing this broken immigration system. And I began by doing what I could to secure our borders. Today, we have more agents and technology deployed to secure our southern border than at any time in our history. And over the past six years, illegal border crossings have been cut by more than half. Although this summer, there was a brief spike in unaccompanied children being apprehended at our border, the number of such children is now actually lower than it's been in nearly two years. Overall, the number of people trying to cross our border illegally is at its lowest level since the 1970s. Those are the facts.

Meanwhile, I worked with Congress on a comprehensive fix, and last year, 68 Democrats, Republicans, and Independents came together to pass a bipartisan bill in the Senate. It wasn't perfect. It was a compromise, but it reflected common sense. It would have doubled the number of border patrol agents, while giving undocumented immigrants a pathway to citizenship if they paid a fine, started paying their taxes, and went to the back of the line. And independent experts said that it would help grow our economy and shrink our deficits.

Had the House of Representatives allowed that kind of a bill a simple yes-or-no vote, it would have passed with support from both parties, and today it would be the law. But for a year and a half now, Republican leaders in the House have refused to allow that simple vote.

Now, I continue to believe that the best way to solve this problem is by working together to pass that kind of common sense law. But until that happens, there are actions I have the legal authority to take as President—the same kinds of actions taken by Democratic and Republican Presidents before me—that will help make our immigration system more fair and more just.

Tonight, I am announcing those actions.

First, we'll build on our progress at the border with additional resources for our law enforcement personnel so that they can stem the flow of illegal crossings, and speed the return of those who do cross over.

Second, I will make it easier and faster for high-skilled immigrants, graduates, and entrepreneurs to stay and contribute to our economy, as so many business leaders have proposed.

Third, we'll take steps to deal responsibly with the millions of undocumented immigrants who already live in our country.

I want to say more about this third issue, because it generates the most passion and controversy. Even as we are a nation of immigrants, we are also a nation of laws. Undocumented workers broke our immigration laws, and I believe that they must be held accountable—especially those who may be dangerous. That's why, over the past six years, deportations of criminals are up 80 percent. And that's why we're going to keep focusing enforcement resources on actual threats to our security. Felons, not families. Criminals, not children. Gang members, not a mother who's working hard to provide for her kids. We'll prioritize, just like law enforcement does every day.

But even as we focus on deporting criminals, the fact is, millions of immigrants—in every state, of every race and nationality—will still live here illegally. And let's be honest—tracking down, rounding up, and deporting millions of people isn't realistic. Anyone who suggests otherwise isn't being straight with you. It's also not who we are as Americans. After all, most of these immigrants have been here a long time. They work hard, often in tough, low-paying jobs. They support their families. They worship at our churches. Many of their kids are American-born or spent most of their lives here, and their hopes, dreams, and patriotism are just like ours.

As my predecessor, President Bush, once put it: "They are a part of American life."

Now here's the thing: we expect people who live in this country to play by the rules. We expect that those who cut the line will not be unfairly rewarded. So we're going to offer the following deal: If you've been in America for more than five years; if you have children who are American citizens or legal residents; if you register, pass a criminal background check, and you're willing to pay your fair share of taxes—you'll be able to apply to stay in this country temporarily, without fear of deportation. You can come out of the shadows and get right with the law.

That's what this deal is. Now let's be clear about what it isn't. This deal does not apply to anyone who has come to this country recently. It does not apply to anyone who might come to America illegally in the future. It does not grant citizenship, or the right to stay here permanently, or offer the same benefits that citizens receive—only Congress can do that. All we're saying is we're not going to deport you.

I know some of the critics of this action call it amnesty. Well, it's not. Amnesty is the immigration system we have today—millions of people who live here without paying their taxes or playing by the rules, while politicians use the issue to scare people and whip up votes at election time.

That's the real amnesty—leaving this broken system the way it is. Mass amnesty would be unfair. Mass deportation would be both impossible and contrary to our character. What I'm describing is accountability—a commonsense, middle ground approach: If you meet the criteria, you can come out of the shadows and get right with the law. If you're a criminal, you'll be deported. If you plan to enter the U.S. illegally, your chances of getting caught and sent back just went up.

The actions I'm taking are not only lawful, they're the kinds of actions taken by every single Republican President and every single Democratic President for the past half century. And to those Members of Congress who question my authority to make our immigration system work better, or question the wisdom of me acting where Congress has failed, I have one answer: Pass a bill. I want to work with both parties to pass a more permanent legislative solution. And the day I sign that bill into law, the actions I take will no longer be necessary. Meanwhile, don't let a disagreement over a single issue be a dealbreaker on every issue. That's not how our democracy works, and Congress certainly shouldn't shut down our government again just because we disagree on this. Americans are tired of gridlock. What our country needs from us right now is a common purpose—a higher purpose.

Most Americans support the types of reforms I've talked about tonight. But I understand the disagreements held by many of you at home. Millions of us, myself included, go back generations in this country, with ancestors who put in the painstaking work to become citizens. So we don't like the notion that anyone might get a free pass to American citizenship. I know that some worry immigration will change the very fabric of who we are, or take our jobs, or stick it to middle-class families at a time when they already feel like they've gotten the raw end of the deal for over a decade. I hear these concerns. But that's not what these steps would do. Our history and the facts show that immigrants are a net plus for our economy and our society. And I believe it's important that all of us have this debate without impugning each other's character.

Because for all the back-and-forth of Washington, we have to remember that this debate is about something bigger. It's about who we are as a country, and who we want to be for future generations.

Are we a nation that tolerates the hypocrisy of a system where workers who pick our fruit and make our beds never have a chance to get right with the law? Or are we a nation that gives them a chance to make amends, take responsibility, and give their kids a better future?

Are we a nation that accepts the cruelty of ripping children from their parents' arms? Or are we a nation that values families, and works to keep them together?

Are we a nation that educates the world's best and brightest in our universities, only to send them home to create businesses in countries that compete against us? Or are we a nation that encourages them to stay and create jobs, businesses, and industries right here in America?

That's what this debate is all about. We need more than politics as usual when it comes to immigration; we need reasoned, thoughtful, compassionate debate that focuses on our hopes, not our fears.

I know the politics of this issue are tough. But let me tell you why I have come to feel so strongly about it. Over the past few years, I have seen the determination of immigrant fathers who worked two or three jobs, without taking a dime from the government, and at risk at any moment of losing it all, just to build a better life for their kids. I've seen the heartbreak and anxiety of children whose mothers might be taken away from them just because they didn't have the right papers. I've seen the courage of students who, except for the circumstances of their birth, are as American as Malia or Sasha; students who bravely come out as undocumented in hopes they could make a difference in a country they love. These people—our neighbors, our classmates, our friends—they did not come here in search of a free ride or an easy life. They came to work, and study, and serve in our military, and above all, contribute to America's success.

Tomorrow, I'll travel to Las Vegas and meet with some of these students, including a young woman named Astrid Silva. Astrid was brought to America when she was four years old. Her only possessions were a cross, her doll, and the frilly dress she had on. When she started school, she didn't speak any English. She caught up to the other kids by reading newspapers and watching PBS, and became a good student. Her father worked in landscaping. Her mother cleaned other people's homes. They wouldn't let Astrid apply to a technology magnet school for fear the paperwork would out her as an undocumented immigrant—so she applied behind their back and got in. Still, she mostly lived in the shadows—until her grandmother, who visited every year from Mexico, passed away, and she couldn't travel to the funeral without risk of being found out and deported. It was around that time she decided to begin advocating for herself and others like her, and today, Astrid Silva is a college student working on her third degree.

Are we a nation that kicks out a striving, hopeful immigrant like Astrid—or are we a nation that finds a way to welcome her in?

Scripture tells us that we shall not oppress a stranger, for we know the heart of a stranger—we were strangers once, too.

My fellow Americans, we are and always will be a nation of immigrants. We were strangers once, too. And whether our forebears were strangers who crossed the Atlantic, or the Pacific, or the Rio Grande, we are here only because this country welcomed them in, and taught them that to be an American is about something more than what we look like, or what our last names are, or how we worship. What makes us Americans is our shared commitment to an ideal—that all of us are created equal, and all of us have the chance to make of our lives what we will.

That's the country our parents and grandparents and generations before them built for us. That's the tradition we must uphold. That's the legacy we must leave for those who are yet to come.

Thank you, God bless you, and God bless this country we love.

VI. San Francisco Mayor Ed Lee's Executive Directive on Immigration

Executive Directive 14-03

Expansion & Coordination of San Francisco Immigrant Assistance Programs to Align with President Obama's Immigration Accountability Executive Actions

November 21, 2014

San Francisco has long been a leader in welcoming all people, both immigrant and native born. We are a City and nation of immigrants. Immigrants have contributed to the economic backbone and diversity of San Francisco from the start. Today, over a third of our City's residents are immigrants, and 35 percent of San Francisco's small businesses are owned by immigrants.

On November 20, 2014, President Obama announced Immigration Accountability Executive Actions, an important first step to fix our nation's broken immigration system. The President's plan reflects the values of individual responsibility, fairness, hard work and commitment to the United States of America. Current immigration policies and laws are clearly not working and do not benefit the city or nation. Doing nothing to fix a broken system leaves an estimated 11.7 million undocumented immigrants in the United States living in fear and separated from their families and communities.

San Francisco already has the infrastructure, capacity and many of the programs necessary to swiftly implement and support the President's Executive Actions. There are an estimated 102,000 legal permanent residents (LPRs) residing or working in San Francisco and approximately 30,000 to 50,000 undocumented immigrants who live in fear and isolation. As a City of Refuge, we have myriad laws, programs, and services that support the wellbeing, integration and full participation of all people in our City, regardless of their immigration status.

San Francisco has been a leader on immigrant integration and comprehensive immigration reforn1 for decades. From the City and County of Refuge Ordinance ("Sanctuary Ordinance") passed in 1989, establishment of the Immigrant Rights Commission in 1997 and the Office of Civic Engagement & Immigrant Affairs (OCEIA) in 2009 to coordinate policies, programs and services for immigrants, limited-English speaking persons and low-income, vulnerable communities, the City has continued to support the integration, inclusion and safety of immigrant communities.

In July 2013, my Administration launched the San Francisco Pathways to Citizenship Initiative, a long-tenn public-private-nonprofit partnership between the City, local foundations and seven community-based organizations, to promote citizenship and civic participation. The initiative provides free, multilingual application and legal assistance for Legal Permanent Residents through large citizenship workshops and one-on-one counseling to help immigrants on their path to full participation as American citizens.

Providing a pathway to legal status for millions of undocumented immigrants nationwide and an estimated 12,000 in San Francisco alone will allow our undocumented immigrants to work, participate in civic life, and contribute to the community and City without fear. The President's Executive Actions are a first and necessary step to providing these immigrants the opportunity to take responsibility for themselves as taxpayers and community members.

My Administration is ready to fully and quickly implement President Obama's Executive Actions and help thousands of our fellow San Franciscans begin their journey towards legal status, while the nation awaits congressional action on comprehensive immigration reform.

Therefore, by virtue of the power and authority vested in me by Section 3.100 of the San Francisco Charter to provide administration and oversight of all departments and governmental units in the executive branch of the City and County of San Francisco, I do hereby issue this Executive Directive to become effective immediately:

1. Planning, Coordination and Implementation: The Office of Civic Engagement and Immigrant Affairs (OCEIA) is charged with overseeing San Francisco's efforts to assist immigrants and implement programs and services consistent with the President's Executive Actions, including developing a Citywide strategic plan within 30 days, working with City departments, community-based service providers, philanthropic and regional partners, and Federal Agencies such as the USCIS to coordinate efforts. Leveraging its current programs for Citizenship, Deferred Action, Day Laborers, Anti-Fraud Education and Language Access, OCEIA will work with cross-sector partners to identify and execute effective outreach strategies and messages, identify health and social service needs, coordinate resources and grants, develop strategies to streamline city document processes, and organize multilingual, multicultural outreach, education and awareness activities.

2. Anti-Fraud and Consumer Education: OCEIA will immediately coordinate with appropriate local, state and federal agencies and community organizations on multilingual, culturally appropriate strategies to prevent immigration services scams and fraud.

3. Departmental Representation and Involvement: OCEIA will work closely with the Mayor's Office to identify City Departments that are currently supporting services and programs to assist or that affect immigrants in San Francisco. OCEIA will convene and brief core departments as well as

other departments that provide information or services to the public. Each core department identified by OCEIA will designate a senior-level staff representative to serve as a primary point of contact for this effort. Departments will partner closely with OCEIA on the following:

• Identifying Resources: Identifying resources, including staff, printing and materials, that can be redirected to support the City's outreach efforts, and specifically OCEIA's work related to immigrant integration and services;

• Modifying Existing Grant Agreements: Whenever allowable, workplans for community-based organizations holding agreements or contracts with city agencies and departments may be modified to include appropriate and related outreach, education and assistance activities associated with the President's Executive Action;

• Publishing Timely and Accurate Information in Multiple Languages: Disseminating general and/or translated information on services and programs in a timely and complete manner.

4. Ensuring Confidentiality and Safety: All Departments and Agencies will work with OCETA to ensure that relevant city personnel are trained on and understand the Sanctuary City Ordinance and confidentiality of information. No data provided or gathered by city employees in connection with this directive may be used for enforcement actions of any kind related to immigration status offenses. Potential applicants for Administrative Relief programs outlined in the President's Executive Actions will be reassured of their safety in seeking application assistance and documentation in San Francisco.

For questions concerning this Executive Directive and its implementation, please contact Adrienne Pon, Executive Director, Office of Civic Engagement & Immigrant Affairs at adrienne.pon@sfuov.org, telephone (415) 581.2317. More information is available to the general public at www. sfgov.org/oceia.

This Executive Directive will take effect immediately and will remain in place until rescinded by future written communication.

Edwin M. Lee
Mayor
City and County of San Francisco

VII. List of Sanctuary Cities
Congressional Research Service

Arizona
Chandler
Mesa
Phoenix
Tucson

California
Bell Gardens
City of Commerce
City of Industry
Coachella
Cypress
Davis
Downey
Fresno
Greenfield
Lakewood
Long Beach
Los Angeles
Lynwood
Maywood
Montebello
National City
Norwalk
Oakland
Paramount
Pico Rivera
Richmond
San Bernardino
San Diego
San Francisco
San Jose
Santa Clara County

Santa Cruz
Santa Maria
Sonoma County
South Gate
Vernon
Watsonville
Wilmington

Colorado
Aurora
Commerce City
Denver
Durango
Federal Heights
Fort Collins
Lafayette
Thornton
Westminster

Connecticut
Hartford
New Haven

Florida
DeLeon Springs
Deltona
Jupiter
Lake Worth
Miami

Georgia
Dalton

Illinois
Chicago

Cicero
Evanston

Kansas
Wichita

Louisiana
New Orleans

Maine
Portland

Maryland
Baltimore
Gaithersburg
Montgomery County
Mount Rainier
Takoma Park

Massachusetts
Cambridge
Chelsea
Northampton
Orleans
Sommerville
Springfield

Michigan
Ann Arbor
Detroit

Minnesota
Austin
Minneapolis
St. Paul
Worthington

Nevada
Reno

New Jersey
Camden
Fort Lee
Hightstown
Jersey City
Newark
North Bergen
Trenton
Union City
West New York

New Mexico
Albuquerque
Aztec
Rio Ariba County
Santa Fe

New York
Albany
Bay Shore
Brentwood
Central Islip
Farmingville
New York City
Riverhead
Shirley/Mastic
Spring Valley Village
Uniondale
Westbury

North Carolina
Carrboro

Chapel Hill
Charlotte
Chatham County
Durham
Raleigh
Winston-Salem

Ohio
Columbus
Dayton
Lima
Lorain
Oberlin
Painesville

Oklahoma
Oklahoma City
Tulsa

Oregon
Ashland
Gaston
Marion County
Multnomah County
Portland

Pennsylvania
Philadelphia
Pittsburg

Rhode Island
Providence

Texas
Austin
Baytown

Brownsville
Channelview
Dallas
Denton
El Cenizo
Ft. Worth
Houston
Katy
Laredo
McAllen
Port Arthur

Utah
Salt Lake City

Vermont
Burlington
Middlebury

Virginia
Alexandria
Fairfax County
Virginia Beach

Washington
King County
Seattle

Washington, D.C.

Wisconsin
Madison
Milwaukee County

Wyoming
Jackson Hole

VIII. Guidelines for Developing a Language Access Plan
lep.gov

Guidelines

If your organization receives federal funds, either directly or through the state, your agency is required to develop a language access plan (this does not mean hiring staff for every conceivable language spoken by your clients).

1. Learn the requirements of Title VI, Executive Order 13166, and your state laws.
2. Determine language needs using DOJ's four-factor assessment:
   a. Number or proportion of persons with Limited English proficiency (LEP) in the eligible service population.
   b. Frequency with which these LEP persons come into contact with your program. c. Importance of the benefit or service.
   d. The resources available.
3. Based on the assessment's results, identify the languages that will be included in the agency's language access plan and how the agency will provide interpretation services to LEP clients.
4. Develop an outreach plan to notify LEP persons that services are available.
5. Integrate your agency's language access policies and procedures into the agency's regular policies and procedures manual for use by *all*, not only bilingual, staff.
6. Train all staff and volunteers on language access laws:
   a. Federal laws: Title VI and Executive Order 13166.
   b. State laws on court interpretation to determine:
   • clients' rights to interpreters in civil courts,
   • who provides the interpreters,
   • who pays for interpretation.
   c. Protocols for filing a Title VI complaint with the Department of Justice should a client's language access rights be denied by a federal grant recipient.

7. Implement and train staff about language access advocacy and agency protocols on:

a. Responding to LEP callers and in-person contacts.

b. Advocating for and asserting LEP clients' rights to qualified interpreters in courts and other systems.

c. Providing LEP clients with tools (such as "I speak..." cards) that assist them in asserting their right to language access in the courts and other public agencies.

d. Responding to court requests that bilingual advocates interpret by attempting to decline and disclosing their conflict of interest on record.

e. Working with interpreters, including basic knowledge about interpretation: types, modes, code of ethics, qualifications and roles.

f. Identifying and responding to poor, incorrect or biased interpretation.

8. Evaluate plan's effectiveness regularly to ensure it meets the needs of LEP persons.

9. Monitor demographic changes and immigration/refugee resettlement patterns to identify new LEP populations your agency will need to serve.

10. Engaging courts and public agencies in a dialogue on language access and Title VI.

IX. Federal Benefits Available to Unauthorized Immigrants

In general, unauthorized immigrants within the United States **are not eligible for any federal public benefits, except:**

1. Emergency medical treatment under Medicaid, if the individual otherwise meets the eligibility requirements and the medical condition is not related to an organ transplant procedure
2. Immunizations for immunizable diseases and testing for and treatment of symptoms of communicable diseases (does not include assistance from Medicaid)
3. Short-term, non-cash, in-kind emergency disaster relief
4. Programs, services, or assistance that deliver in-kind services at the community level, do not have conditions for assistance on the recipients' income or resources, and are necessary for the protection of life and safety
   - Includes access to soup kitchens, crisis counseling and intervention, short-term shelter, mental health services, and child and adult protective services
5. To the extent that an immigrant was receiving assistance on 8/22/08, programs for housing, community development, or financial assistance administered by the HUD Secretary, which include:
   - Financial assistance in rural areas to farmers, owners, developers, and the elderly for loan insurance, the purchase of property, housing for trainees, and low rent housing for farm workers under title V of the Housing Act of 1949
   - Loans and grants for water access and waste treatment to

alleviate health risks under Section 306C of the Consolidated Farm and Rural Development Act

6. Free public education for grades K–12
7. Federally subsidized school lunch and school breakfast programs for individuals eligible for free public education under state or local law
8. At state option, medical coverage under SCHIP, including prenatal care and delivery services, for unborn children who meet other program eligibility criteria

Note: Exceptions 2 and 3 above only grant access to disaster relief and emergency assistance for the protection of life and safety, and do not extend to non-emergency aid based on each recipient's need.

Unauthorized immigrants are eligible for the following nutrition assistance programs:

- Special Supplemental Nutrition Program for Women, Infants, and Children (WIC)
- Child and Adult Care Food Program (CACFP)
- Summer Food Service program
- Special Milk program
- Commodity Supplemental Food Program (CSFP)
- The Emergency Food Assistance Program (TEFAP)
- Food Distribution Program on Indian Reservations (FDPIR)

Note: States may, at their discretion, deny unauthorized immigrants' access to the above programs.

Unauthorized immigrants also appear to be able to receive services provided by federally funded community health centers regardless of immigration status; however, migrant health center services are statutorily prohibited to unauthorized immigrants by Title IV of PRWORA.

Affordable Care Act: Unauthorized immigrants and Deferred Action for Childhood Arrivals (DACA) grantees are not eligible to purchase insurance on the exchanges or receive premium tax credits or lower copayments; they are exempt from the individual mandate.

X. National Immigration Resource Directory

African Immigrant and Refugee Foundation, airfound.org
African Immigrant Service, www.aisfotl.org
American Civil Liberties Union, www.aclu.org
American Immigration Council, www.americanimmigrationcouncil.org
American Immigration Lawyers Association, www.aila.org
American Planning Association, www.planning.org
Arab American Family Services, arabamericanfamilyservices.org
Arab Resource and Organizing Center, araborganizing.org
Asian American Justice Center, www.advancingequality.org
Asian and Pacific Islander American Health Forum, www.apiahf
Asian Law Caucus, www.advancingjustice-alc.org
Center for Immigration Studies, www.cis.org
Center for Law and Social Policy, www.clasp.org
Center for Popular Democracy, populardemocracy.org
Center on Budget and Policy Priorities, www.cbpp.org
Children's Defense Fund, www.childrensdefense.org
Executive Office for Immigration Review, www.justice.gov/eoir
Food and Nutrition Service (USDA), www.fns.usda.gov/fns
Food Research Action Center, www.frac.org
Immigration Advocates Network, www.immigrationadvocates.org
Immigration Law Help, www.immigrationlawhelp.org
Immigration Policy Center, www.immigrationpolicy.org
Institute on Taxation and Economic Policy, www.itep.org
Interfaith Worker Justice, www.iwj.org
International Association of Chiefs of Police, www.theiacp.org
International City/County Management Association, icma.org
Migration Policy Institute, www.migrationpolicy.org
National Association of Counties, www.naco.org
National Center for Law and Economic Justice, www.nclej.org
National Center for Youth Law, www.youthlaw.org

ᴄe of State Legislatures, www.ncsl.org

ᴧ of La Raza, www.nclr.org

ᴩloyment Law Project, www.nelp.org

ᴧealth Law Program, www.healthlaw.org

ᴧ Immigration Forum, www.immigrationforum.org

ᴧnal Immigration Law Center, www.nilc.org

ᴧational Lawyers Guild, National Immigration Project, www.nationalimmigrationproject.org

National League of Cities, www.nlc.org

National Legal Aid and Defender Association, www.nlada.org

National Network for Arab American Communities, www.nnaac.org

National Network for Immigrant and Refugee Rights, www.nnirr.org

National Senior Citizens Law Center, www.nsclc.org

Office of Special Counsel for Immigration-Related Unfair Employment Practices, www.usdoj.gov/crt/osc

Population Reference Bureau, www.prb.org

Priority Africa Network, www.priorityafrica.org

REFORMA (National Association to Promote Library and Information Services to Latinos and the Spanish-Speaking), www.reforma.org

Sargent Shriver National Center on Poverty Law, www.povertylaw.org

Social Security Administration, www.ssa.gov

Urban Institute, www.urban.org

Urban Land Institute, urbanland.uli.org

U.S. Citizenship and Immigration Services (USCIS), www.uscis.gov

U.S. Committee for Refugees and Immigrants, www.refugees.org

U.S. Conference of Mayors, www.usmayors.org

U.S. Customs and Border Protection (CBP), www.cbp.gov

U.S. Department of Health and Human Services, www.hhs.gov

U.S. Department of Labor, www.dol.gov

U.S. Equal Employment Opportunity Commission, www.eeoc.gov

U.S. Immigration and Customs Enforcement (ICE), www.ice.gov

About the Editors
and Contributors

Contributors' positions are as of the time of their authorship.

Julie **Bell** is the education program director for the National Conference of State Legislatures.

John C. **Brown** is city administrator of Woodburn, Oregon.

Cindy **Chang** covers the L.A. County Sheriff's Department for the *Los Angeles Times*.

Kevin **Clark** is the senior consultant and founder of Clark Consulting and Training, Inc.

Jiashan **Cui** is with the Immigrant Policy Project of the National Conference of State Legislatures.

Yu Ren **Dong** is professor and director of the Bilingual Education Program, Queen's College, City University of New York.

Jamie **Durana** is program associate with the Municipal Action for Immigrant Integration Program of the National League of Cities.

Anthony **Faiola** is a veteran journalist and the *Washington Post*'s Berlin bureau chief.

Peter **Fimrite** is a former firefighter and now reporter with the *San Francisco Chronicle* who serves as the newspaper's regional news and weekend editor.

Elise **Foley** is an immigration and politics reporter for the *Huffington Post*.

Phil **Galewitz** is a senior correspondent at *Kaiser Health News*.

Joaquin Jay **Gonzalez** III is the Mayor George Christopher Professor of Government and the Russell T. Sharpe Professor of Business at Golden Gate University.

Emmanuel **Gorospe** is a practicing physician with the Prevea Center for Digestive Health, Medical College of Wisconsin–Green Bay Campus.

Steven **Greenhouse** is a journalist and labor and workplace correspondent for the *New York Times*.

Anuj **Gupta** is executive director of Mt. Airy USA, a comprehensive community development corporation based in Philadelphia, Pennsylvania.

Rob **Gurwitt** is a *Governing* contributor and freelance writer who covers state and local issues, public education and how communities deal with change.

Cheryl **Harrison** is a contributor to ERIC Clearinghouse on Adult, Career, and Vocational Education, United States Office of Educational Research and Improvement.

Julie **Hernandez** is local government consultant with Management Partners and former president of the International Hispanic Network.

Ryan **Holeywell** covers energy for the *Houston Chronicle* and previously wrote about transportation and municipal finance for *Governing* magazine.

Alex **Hutchinson** contributes to *Urban Land* magazine and is an urban planning/real estate development practitioner and freelance writer.

Robin **Imperial** is a REFORMA member and the librarian's toolkit task force leader.

Elizabeth **Kellar** is president and CEO of the Center for State and Local Government Excellence and serves as deputy executive director for the International City/County Management Association.

Roger L. **Kemp** is distinguished adjunct professor at Golden Gate University and was city manager in New Jersey, Connecticut and California for more than 25 years.

Samuel **Kleiner** is a fellow at the Yale Law Information Society Project and has written on international and legal affairs in the *New Republic* and the *Los Angeles Times*.

Kate **Linthicum** covers immigration and city hall for the *Los Angeles Times* and has reported from Africa, South America and across the United States.

Mike **Maciag** is *Governing's* data editor and writes on a variety of topics and manages the Governing Data portal for Governing.com.

Diana **Miranda-Murillo** is a REFORMA member and librarian with the Austin Public Library in Texas.

Ann **Morse** is program director of the Immigrant Policy Project at the National Conference of State Legislatures.

Tod **Newcombe** is senior editor of *Governing* magazine and has more than 20 years of experience covering state and local government.

Paul **Overberg** is an investigative reporter who finds news in data and helps shape *USA Today's* demographic coverage.

Paul **Pontieri** is mayor, Village of Patchogue, New York.

Jeremy **Redmon** covers immigration and politics for the *Atlanta Journal-Constitution.*

Jason **Reed** is the Limited English Proficiency program manager for the Economic Services Administration within the Washington State Department of Social and Health Services.

Thomas **Reynolds** is director of Education Services of the Maryland Municipal League.

Cristina **Rodriguez** is Leighton Homer Surbeck Professor of Law, Yale Law School

Nancy **Scola** is a reporter and writer whose work focuses on the intersections of technology and politics, policy, and civic life.

Paola **Scommegna** is senior writer and editor at the Population Reference Bureau in Washington, DC.

Dylan **Scott** is staff writer with *Governing.*

Anthony **Strianese** is police chief of the City of Delray Beach, Florida.

Charles **Taylor** is senior staff writer, NACo County News—The Voice of America's Counties.

Christine **Tien** is deputy city manager of Stockton, California.

Greg **Toppo** is *USA Today's* national K-12 education writer.

David **Torres** is administrative services director, City of Philadelphia, Pennsylvania.

Rebecca **Trounson** writes for the *Los Angeles Times.*

Susan **Urahn** is executive vice president of the Pew Charitable Trusts.

Jonathan **Walters** is senior editor of *Governing* and has been covering state and local public policy and administration for more than 30 years.

J.B. **Wogan** is staff writer with *Governing* covering public programs aimed at addressing poverty and writes the monthly human services newsletter.

Michele **Wucker** is vice president of studies at The Chicago Council on Global Affairs and was past President of the World Policy Institute.

Index